Sexuality

According to the popular imagination, psychoanalysis is about men wanting to sleep with their mothers and women wanting penises. *Sexuality: Psychoanalytic Perspectives* tells a different story about what has happened to sex in psychoanalysis over the past century.

In the book, a range of distinguished contributors challenge the view that sexuality is nothing other than historically and culturally determined. Introducing the ideas of sexuality from the viewpoint of a number of theoretical schools, they then go on to offer contemporary psychoanalytic views of

- Sexuality in childhood
- Female and male sexuality (heterosexual and homosexual)
- Sexual perversions.

Sexuality: Psychoanalytic Perspectives is a comprehensive introduction to the subject, covering its development over the last 100 years, and bringing it up to date for the twenty-first century. The book will make enlightening and essential reading for both professionals and students involved in psychoanalysis, psychotherapy and counselling.

Celia Harding is a psychodynamic counsellor and psychoanalytic psychotherapist in private practice in East London. She trained with the Westminster Pastoral Foundation. She is a Member of the Foundation for Psychotherapy and Counselling. She has organised and run courses for professional counsellors and psychotherapists belonging to FPC for the past eight years. She is a Founder Member and Secretary of the Association for Psychotherapy in East London (APEL).

5 191 800 7

Sexuality

Psychoanalytic perspectives

Edited by Celia Harding

Brunner-Routledge
Taylor & Francis Group

HOVE AND NEW YORK

First published 2001
by Brunner-Routledge
27 Church Road, Hove, East Sussex BN3 2FA

Simultaneously published in the USA and Canada
by Taylor & Francis Inc.
325 Chestnut Street, Philadelphia PA 19106

Reprinted 2002 by Brunner-Routledge
27 Church Road, Hove, East Sussex BN3 2FA
29 West 35th Street, New York NY 10001

Brunner-Routledge is an imprint of the Taylor & Francis Group

Typeset in Times by
J&L Composition Ltd, Filey, North Yorkshire
Printed and bound in Great Britain by TJ International Ltd,
Padstow, Cornwall
Cover design by Jim Wilkie

British Library Cataloguing in Publication Data
A catalogue record for this book is available
from the British Library

Library of Congress Cataloging in Publication Data
A catalogue record for this book has been requested

ISBN 0–415–22097–1 (pbk)
ISBN 0–415–22096–3 (hbk)

Contents

The contributors

Susan Budd is a psychoanalyst, a full Member of the British Psycho-analytical Society. She belongs to the Independent Group. She was formerly Editor of Books for the Society. She is the author of various books and articles, most recently, 'Ask me no questions and I'll tell you no lies: the social organisation of secrets', in *The Presentation of Case Material in Clinical Discourse* (Freud Museum, 1997) and 'The shark behind the sofa: the psychoanalytic theory of dreams', *History Workshop Journal* (1999): 48. She is in private practice in London and Oxford.

Warren Colman is a Professional Member of the Society of Analytical Psychology and a Full Member of the Society of Psychoanalytic Marital Psychotherapists. He was a Senior Marital Psychotherapist at the Tavistock Marital Studies Institute until 1997 and is now in full-time private practice in St Albans. He has published numerous papers on sexuality, gender and couple relationships and, more recently, on the self.

Celia Harding is a psychoanalytic psychotherapist in private practice. She trained with the Westminster Pastoral Foundation. She is a Member of the Foundation for Psychotherapy and Counselling. She is a Training Therapist for the FPC (WPF). She organises FPC's post-qualification courses and has facilitated seminars on the sexuality series. She is a Founder Member and Secretary of the Association for Psychotherapy in East London.

Ann Horne. After varied careers as a secondary school teacher, lecturer, researcher and social worker, Ann Horne trained as a Child and Adolescent Psychotherapist at the British Association of Psychotherapists, where she recently headed the training. She

works at the Portman Clinic, London, and is particularly interested in problems of gender confusion, delinquency and sexual
abusing – indeed, how and why acting out with the body occurs
in children and young people.

Marie Maguire is a psychoanalytic psychotherapist practising in
South London. She is author of *Men, Women, Passion and Power:
Gender Issues in Psychotherapy* (Routledge, 1995) and Co-Editor
of *Psychotherapy with Women: Feminist Perspectives* (Macmillan,
1996).

Steven Mendoza is a member, supervisor and training psychotherapist of the London Centre for Psychotherapy. He has been
a teacher for trainings in art therapy, analytical psychotherapy and
counselling since 1984. He has a first degree in Psychology and
an M.Phil. in Human Learning. He worked as a generic social
worker while training as a psychotherapist.

David Morgan is a psychoanalyst, Associate Member of the British
Psychoanalytical Society and Full Member of the British
Association of Psychotherapists (BAP). He is a training therapist
and supervisor for the BAP, Lincoln Centre and London Centre
for Psychotherapy. He is also Consultant Clinical Psychologist/
Psychotherapist at the Portman Clinic, London, where he runs the
difficult patient workshop.

Robert Royston is a psychoanalytic psychotherapist in private practice. He is a member of, and training therapist and lecturer for,
the London Centre for Psychotherapy. His papers on narcissism
and intellectual dysfunction have appeared in the *British Journal
for Psychotherapy*.

Jean Thomson is a member of the Society of Analytical Psychology
(SAP). Previously a psychiatric social worker, she is now a Jungian
analyst in private practice. While employed in the NHS she became
interested in working with groups and families from a psychoanalytic perspective. She worked in the Adolescent Department
at the Tavistock Clinic. There and later as a tutor in Student
Counselling at Birkbeck, she gained and tested ideas about adolescent breakdown. She has contributed to *Contemporary Jungian
Analysis*, ed. Alister and Hauke, and to *Erotic Transference and
Counter-transference*, ed. D. Mann. She is Editor of the SAP magazine, SAPLINK.

Robert M. Young is Professor Emeritus of Psychotherapy and Psychoanalytic Studies at the Centre for Psychotherapeutic Studies, University of Sheffield, and a psychotherapist in private practice in London. He is also Co-Director of the Bulgarian Institute of Human Relations. He founded Free Association Books and is Editor of *Free Associations* and Associate Editor of *Psychoanalytic Studies*. His books include *Mind, Brain and Adaptation*; *Darwin's Metaphor*; *Mental Space and the Culture of British Psychoanalysis*. He moderates various email forums and edits the human-nature.com website, where most of his writings are available.

Acknowledgements

This publication began as a series of lectures and seminars on sexuality (theoretical and clinical perspectives) for Professional Members of the Foundation for Psychotherapy and Counselling (WPF). Every speaker contributed something from their lectures and their recommended reading to the introduction and, indeed, to my chapter. In addition thanks are due to Sirha Dermen, Francis Grier, Anne Hurry, Dorothy Lloyd-Owen, David Mann, Jenny McDonnell, Phil Mollon, Eilish Quinn, Joanna Ryan, Jane Temperly, Estela Welldon. Also I want to thank my friend and colleague Gill Bannister and all those FPC members who participated in these courses and contributed their interesting ideas and rich case material to our discussions.

I am indebted to Josephine Klein for her tremendous support throughout this project: she helped me to plan the two lecture series, supported and encouraged my writing and has given me invaluable editorial guidance.

David Mann's book *Psychotherapy: An Erotic Relationship* was an essential guide through the hundred-year-old maze of psychoanalytical theories of sexuality. I have appreciated and benefited from his clarity as a writer and contributions as a seminar leader on the second course and for his generous support with this project.

My thanks to my brother David, and sister Joy, for their encouragement and their helpful ideas. I am grateful to Michael Lamprell for all his support during this project, especially for helping me to steer through the rocky patches. Finally, I am indebted to Jeremy Shaw for his considerable part in this achievement, which means so much to me.

Introduction
Making sense of sexuality

Celia Harding

There is more to life than sex. Even so, life begins with sex and sexuality is integral to a person's identity. Sex comes to mind unbidden even when sex or babies are not – apparently – on the agenda. Sex is such a natural human preoccupation that it is most conspicuous in its absence. Whenever two people find themselves together they have to negotiate the hetero-erotic or the homo-erotic potential of their relationship in some way (Mann 1997: 55). One of the mysteries of human sexuality is its pivotal and pervasive influence in human psychology.

Another mystery is why many people feel sexually inhibited, when sex is a biological function that we might reasonably expect to come as naturally as any other. Since sex is something we all share and know about (even chaste minds recognise sexual puns), the anxieties that proverbially surround it beg explanation.

Freud addressed these questions. He believed that sexuality is ubiquitous because we are born with a sexual drive which, along with its counterpart the aggressive drive, is subject to formidable social restraints. Our basic drives are destined for relegation to the unconscious except in their most socially acceptable forms. Human sexuality is often concealed or indirectly expressed because unrestrained sexual and destructive inclinations threaten our social relationships, indeed civilisation as we know it. Understanding how sexual and destructive drives become integrated into conscious life and relationships (or disrupters from their sojourn in the unconscious) became Freud's work, developed by his psychoanalytic successors. In this introduction I place the ideas developed by the contributors to this book into theoretical and historical context. I go on to examine some of the recurring debates in the literature: What are the limits to sexuality? Is the concept of sexual drive relevant today? Whatever happened to erotic transference? Why is sex so difficult?

Background

In his paper *Three essays on the theory of sexuality* (1905), Freud drew together ideas about the nature of human sexuality that he had been gathering over many years, laying for himself and others the groundwork for further understanding. He suggested that infants are born with sexual drives seeking gratifying objects until impulses and objects become firmly coupled. Children's sexual development passes through stages organised around erotogenic areas of the body. But the outcome is not a foregone conclusion: firstly because the sexual drive is extraordinarily versatile in its chosen aims and targets, and secondly because the sexual drive conflicts with other psychic demands. Gratifying and frustrating experiences intervene as the sexual drive develops. The components of the sexual drive follow their own pleasure trail in infancy and childhood: these components may become fixated on certain objects, so pleasurable that they are pursued as ends in themselves rather than means towards the ultimate goal of genital satisfaction. Genital sexuality is only one possible outcome of libidinal development.

The Oedipus complex (1923, 1924) became the cornerstone of Freud's theories of sexuality. Freud came to see the conflict between the life instincts (sex and self-preservation) and death instincts (destructiveness and aggression) as the prime mover in the human mind (1920). He also came to recognise that children's minds incorporate aspects of their relationships with their caretakers: the earliest notion of 'internal objects' (1917, 1923). The positive Oedipus complex shows boys directing their amorous genital desires towards mother and their murderous impulses towards father. They renounce mother as their object of desire in deference to father, and identify with his incest prohibition and castration threat which, in turn, forms the nucleus of the superego, or conscience. Freud (1933) suggested that girls follow the same route as boys, only acquiring a feminine sexuality when they renounce their desire for a male genital and settle for a baby from father (see Horne, Chapter 5; Maguire, Chapter 6; Morgan, Chapter 8).

Some of Freud's ideas have been validated by clinical experience. For example Horne (Chapter 5) offers a contemporary view of children's sexual development. The concept of developmental stages has been modified, but child therapists have confirmed many of Freud's speculations about how children make sense of sexuality. Other ideas have been developed or modified, or have prompted new theoretical departures. His theories about female sexuality were particularly contentious: Colman argues (Chapter 7) that Freud mistook the phallocentric nature of male sexuality as characteristic of all sexuality. Maguire (Chapter 6) describes the heated theoretical debate of the 1920s and 1930s, and the subsequent attempts to conceptualise the distinctive qualities of women's sexual experience. The shift in attention onto female sexuality was followed, particularly in Britain, by challenges to the drive model and a reorientation towards object-related models. Young (Chapter 1) and Royston (Chapter 2) give their interpretations of the 'relocation' of sexuality in object relations. Budd (Chapter 3) argues that the distinctively British attitude to sexuality contributed to 'domesticating Freudian sexuality for Anglo-Saxon consumption'. Melanie Klein was a leading architect of these shifts. Viewed retrospectively and schematically, Klein complemented Freud's ideas by emphasising the centrality of object relationships in psychic structure; installing mother alongside father; and giving more weight to the role of aggression and destructiveness in sexual development.

Although Klein initially used the vocabulary of instinct, she revolutionised Freud's theories about the contribution of object relations to psychic structure (Greenberg and Mitchell 1983). She believed infants were born oriented towards their objects, ready to love and possess (in phantasy) the good feeding object and to hate and destroy (in phantasy) the bad feeding object. Young argues (Chapter 1) that Klein translated instincts into feelings and maintained that infants connect emotionally with internal and external objects from the outset. Klein installed mother at the centre of development. As the mother is the infant's primary caretaker and the provider of the 'breast', the infant's first intense relationship is with mother, particularly mother's body.

Klein's contention that infants relate passionately to their objects with love and hate convinced her that aggression was more problematic than eroticism. Initially infants deal with their aggression by splitting their objects into good and bad. They keep these apart, protecting their loving feelings towards good objects from their hostile feelings towards bad objects. This is the basis for the paranoid-schizoid position towards objects, maintained through phantasies[1] of

---

1 The authors of the papers in this publication are writing from different theoretical positions and use the terms fantasy and phantasy differently. Some contributors use 'fantasy' to denote conscious fantasy and 'phantasy' to denote unconscious fantasy. Others refer to conscious fantasy and unconscious fantasy. Where I refer to both conscious and unconscious fantasies above and in chapter 10 I have indicated this by ph/fantasy.

omnipotent control. As infants gradually recognise that their good and bad object are one and the same, they become consumed with anxiety for the safety of their good object, imperilled by their hatred and destructiveness towards their bad object. When they are overly anxious about their aggression, children lose faith in their loving and reparative capacities and become stuck in paranoid-schizoid relating. But when they feel sure of the strength of their loving feelings and intentions towards their objects, they can relate in the depressive position and relinquish (phantasied) control of their internal and external objects. In her papers about the Oedipus complex, Klein (1928, 1945) shows how children, anxious about their aggression, are unable to draw on their potentially creative and reparative genital feelings towards their parents: in the paranoid-schizoid position, genital feelings are experienced as threatening and damaging. This perspective maintains that experiences at the breast influence the outcome of all subsequent development, and weights the influence of aggression more heavily than sexuality in the progress of development. Green (1995, 1997) regards these shifts in focus as ousting sexuality from the heart of psychoanalytic thinking:

> By regarding the infant as relating to objects from the beginning, Klein established the relationship with the breast as the primary organising experience for future development including genital development. Sexual development understood in terms of feeding and nurture rather than 'ecstasy in mutual enjoyment'.
>
> (Green 1995: 877)

Nevertheless, as Morgan (Chapter 8) and Mendoza (Chapter 9) show, Klein's ideas about the vicissitudes of aggression have contributed substantially to psychoanalytic understanding of sexuality. Freudians and Kleinians regard the Oedipus complex as the cornerstone of sexuality. Whereas Freud emphasised children's coming to terms with the implications of their incestuous desires and castration anxieties, Klein concentrated on children's hostility towards their parents for having a relationship from which they are excluded (Breen 1993). Young (Chapter 1), Morgan (Chapter 8) and Mendoza (Chapter 9) explore how this perception, and acceptance, of parents as a couple in a sexual relationship is central to the achievement of the depressive position, that is, to the capacity for intimate relationships (Britton 1989, 1992).

French analysts, closely following Freud's ideas, have contributed significantly to psychoanalytic understanding of sexuality (Budd, Chapter

3). Lacan regards the castration complex and the genital differences between men and women as the point of divergence in sexual development for males and females. For Lacan the symbol of the phallus represents the differences between the sexes. The phallus represents a lack for men and women: it is an ideal that men strive to become and that women desire to possess (Mitchell and Rose 1982). Other analysts from the French school, particularly Chasseguet-Smirgel (1985), and McDougall (1972, 1995), emphasise the importance of coming to terms with the differences between the generations and the sexes for healthy sexual development. Recently Green (1995, 1997) has drawn on French and British traditions and proposed a theory of sexuality integrating drive and object relations (see below).

Klein's emphasis on mother–baby relationships, and translation of drives into feelings, demoted sexuality in psychoanalysis, but proponents of british object relations marginalised its relevance still further (Maguire, Chapter 6). Rather than counterbalancing Freud's emphasis on drives, fathers and male sexuality with Klein's emphasis on object relations, mothers and female sexuality, object relationists *replaced* father with mother and drive with object. Budd (Chapter 3) argues that sexuality disappeared when attention focused on the mother–infant relationship. The paradigm of the therapist–patient relationship became the mother and child (Mann 1997). Infant observation informed the therapeutic relationship. Regression to infantile states was commended to reach the patient's problems conceptualised as developmental arrests or deficits sustained in infancy, rather than drive conflicts. Patients were regarded as sexually neutral infants. Their sexual problems were seen as defences against more elemental and primary sources of difficulty such as dependency and separation anxieties (Green 1995). Now sexuality was viewed simply as one unremarkable form of relating in an intimate relationship. If sex was a problem it was because damage sustained in the early infant–mother relationship had impaired the person's capacity for intimacy (Royston, Chapter 2; Budd, Chapter 3).

Current psychoanalytic debates about sexuality

The limits of sexuality: perversity or variety

Freud (1905) maintained that infants are born with polymorphous sexual impulses that requisition biological functions (such as eating and excretion) in the service of erotic pleasure. He claimed that human beings are psychologically bisexual. Sexual drives may attach to any object and pursue a variety of aims. Children develop sexually through a series of stages and may get stuck or regress at any point. Given these vicissitudes, each individual's sexuality is an achievement with its own personal shape and history. In short, human sexuality is infinitely variable and its developmental outcome cannot be assumed.

Even so, Freud frequently concluded that 'anatomy is destiny': although human beings are constitutionally bisexual, they tend to align their male or female anatomy with a masculine or feminine sexuality. This view was consistent with the prevailing view of sexuality at the turn of the twentieth century: normal sexual relations are between a man and woman whilst sexual relations between members of the same sex violate the natural, biological order (McLaren 1999). Young (Chapter 1) describes the social constructionist critique that argued that sexuality is not determined by biology but is socially and historically constructed and therefore part of the symbolic universe. Between these extremes Colman (Chapter 7) explores the interrelationship between anatomy and psychological meanings. He argues that both contribute to shaping a person's sexuality, describing our biological equipment as the genetic hardware to our symbolic, cultural software.

Views about what has shaped people's sexuality tend to evolve into assessments of its health and/or perversity. By proposing a notion of sexual development through specific stages Freud implied normal and perverse types of sexuality. Sexuality is fully developed and organised when each stage has been negotiated, in particular, the phallic phase and the Oedipus complex (Young, Chapter 1). By this standard, people who become stuck at earlier stages develop an immature sexuality (Freud 1940: 155). Freud (1905) understood sexual perversion as essentially the persistence into adult sexuality of polymorphous infantile aims and objects. Later (1919) he recognised that perversion may serve as a defence, especially against oedipal anxieties (Gillespie 1956).

During the latter half of the twentieth century social attitudes to sexuality changed (McLaren 1999). The range of acceptable sexual practices gradually extended from the narrow parameters of genital sex between men and women to a broad spectrum formerly considered perverse (Young, Chapter 1). In psychoanalysis, Meltzer (1973) reconsidered the meaning of polymorphous sexuality (Mendoza,

Chapter 9). Kernberg illustrates this re-theorising in his account of the potential for couples to deepen their intimacy, giving and receiving pleasure to one another through full expression of their polymorphous sexuality (1995: 23, quoted in Chapter 10).

Since Freud identified destructive and sexual instincts as the primary protagonists in the psyche, aggression and sexuality have been understood as integrally related. Some theorists see aggression as innate, prone to (enviously) attack whatever is good and loving. Meltzer (1973) distinguishes between polymorphous sex (variety) and polymorphous perverse sex, based not on sexual practices but on the underlying, loving or hostile, unconscious phantasies. In particular he understands perverse sexuality as motivated by hostile attacks on the oedipal parents. Mendoza (Chapter 9) draws on Meltzer's theories and considers the relative health and pathology of homosexuality in terms of the phantasies that drive it: aggressive hostility and control in the paranoid-schizoid position or loving concern and mutual pleasure in the depressive position.

For Glasser (1979) people react aggressively when their psychic survival feels jeopardised. Sexuality poses this threat to people who long for fusion and merging but fear that by getting close to someone they will become absorbed by them, and lose their separate identity. In self-defence they react aggressively towards the longed-for/threatening person only to find themselves alone, feeling abandoned and isolated, which in turn threatens their fragile sense of self. One solution to such 'core complex anxieties' may be to eroticise their aggression as a sort of damage limitation measure, and maintain a relationship at a safe distance by relating to each other sadomasochistically. When intimacy is threatening but also craved, solutions have to be found to make survival possible. Royston (Chapter 2) describes how people may use sexuality to defend themselves against intolerable anxieties. In Chapter 10 I consider what happens when intimacy is experienced as an opportunity to assume a dominant position in the relationship: when the powerful nature of sexual experience reinforces this perception, sexual relationships may turn into (frightening and/or exciting) power struggles.

Stoller termed perversion 'an erotic form of hatred'. He maintains that all sexuality contains a degree of hostility and therefore perversity. He distinguishes between perversity and variety in these terms:

> The non-perverse person does not powerfully fear intimacy, because he or she is not afraid that it will lead to a merging

that swallows up identity. To be practical, we might best say 'perversion' when one uses an erotic act for the purpose of avoiding intimacy – intimacy of personhood, not just anatomy – with another.

(Stoller 1985:43)

Chasseguet-Smirgel (1985), McDougall (1972, 1995) and Kaplan (1993) regard avoidance of the realities represented by oedipal dilemmas as the basis of immature sexualities. People with a perverse sexuality are attempting to deceive themselves and others: that their sexuality is superior to heterosexual genital sex, is the secret of sexual pleasure and/or aims for pleasure and personal fulfilment (rather than aggression and revenge). In phantasy they have reinvented the primal scene because the realities it represents – in particular that the difference between the sexes is a condition of sexual desire – were too painful to bear (McDougall 1972; Kaplan 1991).

When the polymorphous nature of human sexuality is accepted (Meltzer 1973; McDougall 1995), people have a vast repertoire of sexual pleasures available. Human sexuality is as varied as, to use Stoller's expression, the 'erotic imagination'. But *human sexuality serves multiple purposes*. In health, sex gives mutual pleasure and enriches the intimacy of couples in stable, loving relationships. But sex can equally be used defensively to serve other needs: psychic survival (McDougall 1995), a pseudo-substitute intimacy when real intimacy is fraught with anxiety and traumatic potential (Stoller 1985; Kaplan 1991), a disguise for hostile intentions and revenge for pains and offences sustained in the past (Stoller 1985; Meltzer 1973; Kaplan 1991) or to eroticise aggression when intimacy is liable to unleash it (Glasser 1979). When used for psychic survival, sexual phantasies and activities are compulsive, enacted in the context of restrictive relationships, driven to obtain relief from anxiety rather than pleasure and intimacy (Gillespie 1956; Glasser 1979; McDougall 1995). The question then shifts from whether human sexuality is normal or perverse, to thinking about the extent to which people are protecting themselves or others through their sexuality, from what and how.

Of lust and love: sexuality in the drive model and in the object relations model

In Freud's view, people are motivated by their drives arising from their bodies and demanding satisfaction. Our sexual and aggressive drives are subject to internal and external constraints. Unrestrained sexual and aggressive impulses are incompatible with social life: our needs for instinctual gratification *and* social relationships coexist uneasily (Freud 1930).

Young (Chapter 1) and Royston (Chapter 2) pronounce Freud's drive model outdated, superseded by object relations. Our psychic lives are organised around our needs for others, not around biologically rooted drives. Sexual feeling is one form of attachment in negative and positive variations. Young understands our emotional attachments to external objects as reflections of internal object relations. For Royston, the inner world of objects reflects the child's early relationships with external objects in their environment.

Royston (Chapter 2) argues that sexuality has been replaced in psychoanalysis by infantile vulnerability and dependence. He suggests that this development has escaped public attention because, unlike exciting sexuality, infantile vulnerability is painful and unwelcome. However, in Chapter 10 I argue that it is precisely the prospect of becoming vulnerable and exposed in sexual relationships that may render intimacy disturbing: sexual partners put themselves in each other's hands. From this angle, sexuality is as disturbing in its own way as the helpless infantile condition, and sexualising that vulnerability is one defence against these anxieties.

In Freud's theory drives connect body with mind (Freud 1915a: 121f). If we jettison drive theory we may lose our grasp on the integral relationship between mind and body (Budd, Chapter 3; Mendoza, Chapter 9). Infants relate initially through their bodies and build up a psychic life from their mental representations of their physical experiences. In adulthood, sexual partners also relate to one another through their bodies. Erotic ph/fantasies have irresistible and immediate impacts on the body which in turn generate intense physical and emotional responses. Mind and body are intimately connected especially in sex. In Chapter 10 I suggest that physical arousal, demanding satisfaction, contributes to the power of sex.

Analytic relationships mobilise erotic feelings and ph/fantasies (see below). Sexuality has been problematic for psychoanalysis, especially before transference and counter-transference processes were understood and translated into ethical and clinical principles (Thomson, Chapter 4). Budd (Chapter 3) argues that the shift of the centre of analytic gravity from sexual drive to infantile relationships encouraged therapists to see their patients as de-eroticised infants and themselves as de-eroticised mother-figures. Therapists who regard their patient's sexual problems as primarily defences against primitive infantile anxieties may overlook the difficulties they might be experiencing in their adult sexual relationships. When sexuality is too hot to handle, therapists may resort to mentally de-sexualising their own and their patient's bodies, thereby compounding problematic body–mind splits and heightening the danger of acting out erotic desires (Mann 1997). Disposing of the drive model, and with it, the significance of the body–mind connection, may have (unwittingly) encouraged this eventuality by appearing to marginalise the significance of tricky erotic transferences. But it is feasible that this reinforced anxieties about the possibility of containing and thinking about physical as well as emotional needs, since erotic ph/fantasy often converts into compelling physical urges that are forbidden expression in therapy (Thomson, Chapter 4).

The disappearance of sexuality from analytic discussion provoked Green's question: 'Has sexuality anything to do with psychoanalysis?' (1995). Stein (1998b) reviews the 40th Congress of the International Association (1997) which addressed this issue. She observes that contributors continued to speak of sexuality in the context of drives. Although none offered an object relations theory of sexuality, she detected a consensus that sexual drives only make sense within the context of object relationships: sexuality is no longer treated as an expression of an impersonal drive. Green, for example, argues that human sexuality only becomes meaningful when drives are understood in the context of relationship needs. Since a drive cannot 'love' (or 'hate'), it will be directed to a part object purely for satisfaction unless it is transformed and expressed within a relationship to a whole object: at this point instinctual gratification becomes a part of loving (Green 1995, 1997). Mendoza (Chapter 9) takes a similar position: he argues that sexual relationships involve both sexual drives seeking satisfaction and needs for intimacy with another person, indeed, what he calls 'sexy sex' is inconceivable without the interaction of both aspects. Mendoza designates as 'phallic' the sex that is exclusively directed at satisfaction, regardless of the object, and designates as 'genital' the sex that also involves love and concern for the partner. He suggests that phallic sexuality corresponds to sex in the paranoid-schizoid position, relating to a part-object, and genital sex corresponds to sex in the depressive position.

The erotic transference: infantile and oedipal sexuality

The phenomenon of transference came to light when Breuer's patient fell in love with him and the therapeutic relationship collapsed. Freud was consulted and came to regard the transference as the essence of psychoanalytic therapy. He traced the origin of erotic transferences to the Oedipus complex. Young children repress their erotic longings towards their parents when they renounce them as objects of their genital desires. The superego is established to reinforce and safeguard that renunciation and repression. However, those sexual longings towards parents survive unconsciously and seek expression. When people enter therapy their repressed erotic feelings are resurrected and attach to their therapist. 'Falling in love with the doctor' is a case of mistaken identity: the patient has unwittingly muddled the doctor with the desired parent. Under the intense and compelling force of their amorous desires they try to turn therapist into lover. Falling in love is, after all, much more exciting and pleasurable than therapy. Freud (1915b) realised that the blossoming of the erotic transference created a crossroads: either the patient will eschew therapy in order to preserve their passionate attachment or they will accept that they have mistaken their therapist for their parent and work through their forbidden incestuous feelings. If they can resist action and *think about* their passionate longings, their sexuality can be released from their primary objects, for fulfilment in appropriate relationships. The erotic transference Freud discovered originated in childhood genital sexuality and the Oedipus complex.

When the therapist–patient relationship became modelled on the mother–infant relationship, therapists re-conceptualised the transference as regression to early infantile relationships (Mann 1997). Infants cannot distinguish between themselves and mother, between inside and outside, where they stop and their environment starts. When these primitive confusions arise in the transference, patients cannot tell whether their feelings and phantasies originate from inside them or their therapist. Therapy concentrates on working towards unravelling these confusions to enable patients to establish a more accurate sense of their own identity and a more realistic relationship with external reality, especially the reality of other people. However, when the therapist–patient relationship (and the mother–infant relationship on which it was modelled) becomes de-eroticised, the erotic, instinctual roots of the infant's intense and confusing feelings and phantasies tend to be overlooked. For example, wishes and anxieties about passively merging with mother or sadistically intruding into her, of devouring her or being devoured by her, of controlling or being controlled by her, may be infused with intense erotic feeling. Mann (1997) understands the de-eroticisation of the transference and counter-transference as indicating a compelling need to unhinge the tremendous power and influence of mothering from erotic feelings towards her baby. The mother, if gripped by her erotic desires, may abuse her powerful position by using her child to meet her own primitive needs and discouraging them from becoming independent of her (Welldon 1992). The very idea incurs 'erotic horror' too dreadful to contemplate. Similarly, a therapist is seen as abusing their powerful position if they lose control of their erotic desires for their patient and become embroiled in a sexual relationship with them. As Mann suggests, pre-oedipal and oedipal eroticism has felt too dangerous to think about and sanctuary has been found in regarding the mother–infant relationship as unerotic.

Thomson (Chapter 4) addresses the problems that arise when thinking about transgressions of the therapeutic relationship when therapists become sexually involved with their patients. The Jung/Spielrein affair occurred in the early days of psychoanalysis, before the dynamics of the transference and counter-transference had been understood and clear analytic boundaries established to preserve the analytic relationship. Thomson shows how difficult it can be to establish a space for thought and understanding without resorting to punitive condemnation, on one hand, or condoning the unacceptable, on the other.

Sexual inhibition and dissatisfaction in everyday life

Freud believed that much psychological illness originated in sexual problems. He cited civilisation as one of the culprits. Civilisation requires us to restrict our desires and 'inhibit' our sexual aims in the interests of maintaining relationships, interests and activities in the family, at work and in society. Unrestrained sexual expression is incompatible with social life. Sex was socially permissible, but hardly free, in marriage before artificial contraception. Couples concerned about how many children they procreated, and about the toll on health and purse, had to restrain the expression of their sexual desires, consequently suffering frustration and neurosis (Freud 1908).

Freud maintained that the 'demands' of civilisation, as well as the vicissitudes of libidinal development, predispose us to problematic sex lives. We all have to face this dilemma at the Oedipus complex when our incestuous desires for our first loves – parents and siblings – are met by the incest taboo of 'civilisation' (Marucco 1997). The incest prohibition and love for our oedipal rival encourage us to renounce these first passionate objects of desire. But when sexual desires remain closely tied to their original incestuous object in the unconscious, adult sexual relationships are bound to be inhibited (Freud 1910, 1912: 208). Even people who are able to enjoy loving sexual relationships uninhibited by incestuous anxieties, will sometimes feel dissatisfied with their sexual partners who, according to this theory, are substitutes for their first loves (Freud 1912: 187f). Freud concluded that 'something in the nature of the sexual instinct itself is unfavourable to the realisation of complete satisfaction' (1912: 188f). At various times he offered some speculative explanations. He suggested that we have transcended our animal origins at the cost of feeling uncomfortable with, even repulsed by, some of our most basic forms of sexual attraction and excitement, such as smell. He also suggested that when people restrict themselves to monogamous sex with the opposite sex, their natural bisexual desires remain unsatisfied (1930: 106). (In Chapter 9 Mendoza outlines a contemporary understanding of bisexuality.)

Since Freud's time, people's sex lives have been freed by artificial contraception and a marked relaxation of social censorship on various forms of sexual expression which are now more accepted as matters of personal choice (McLaren 1999). Even so, sexual liberation is not guaranteed.

Horne (Chapter 5) traces childhood sexual development: when this goes awry adult sexual problems may result. Sources of difficulty from pre-oedipal experiences originate in the intense physical intimacy of the earliest relationship between mothers and babies. Their mother's body, also a medium through which they explore and discover their own body, tremendously fascinates growing children. Mother–infant physical intimacy recedes as the child increasingly relates, emotionally and cognitively, to other people in the expanding world. When the child renounces the parents as erotic objects, physical intimacy between child and parents is inhibited. In adolescence, with the advent of adult sexuality, the intense quality of physical intimacy from infancy is recaptured (Harding, Chapter 10). The pleasures of merging with, penetrating into, possessing the beloved sexual partner, and the temporary loss of self in mutual sexual ecstasy, are rejuvenating. Problems arise when merging with another is experienced concretely and permanently, as possessing and being possessed and dissolving as a separate person. Penetrating and penetration may be experienced as aggressive intrusion. These are 'core complex anxieties' (Glasser 1979). Maguire and Colman (Chapters 6 and 7) give examples of how men and women experience these fears of loss of self differently in the light of their gendered, anatomical differences. Harding (Chapter 10) explores the way such 'core complex' anxieties become experienced, expressed and defended against in the power dynamics between lovers.

Phantasies from the oedipal situation also contribute to the sexual inhibitions and excitements structuring adult sexuality, in particular primal scene phantasies (Kernberg 1995). The parent's sexual relationship was a source of sexual curiosity and excitement in childhood. It was also a source of painful feelings of exclusion, rage and jealousy, guilt and anxiety (McDougall 1972; Kaplan 1991). Some people experience exclusion from the oedipal couple as an unbearable narcissistic injury. One perverse solution to their pain is to convert it into erotic excitement obtained by expelling their pain and helplessness and inflicting it on someone else. Morgan (Chapter 8) gives examples of perverse scenarios sustaining denial of the parental relationship. These cases show how subsequent relationships are organised around avoiding the mental links that represent the presence of the parental couple.

Even when inhibition and anxiety do not overly impede sexual fulfilment, sex may feel essentially unsatisfactory. One source of sexual dissatisfaction may emanate from conflicts between our needs as individuals and our needs for object relationships. Just as children sacrifice their oedipal desires to preserve their relationships with their parents, so, throughout life, people must find a balance between their own needs, the needs of their partners, and their relationship needs. Marucco argues that children renounce their incestuous desires to preserve their relationships with their parents but, in the process, they may renounce their sexual drives wholesale and consequently grow up to be 'normopathic individuals increasingly remote from their drives' (1997: 354). Royston (Chapter 2) suggests that sometimes it may be necessary to temporarily depersonalise their sexual partner in order to find greater satisfaction in sexual activity which might otherwise be inhibited by awareness of the partner.

Budd (Chapter 3) identifies another source of sexual dissatisfaction and disappointment in the differences between the sexes. Men and women may come together expecting to find in each other what they lack in themselves. But two people do not fit together neatly. She argues, through reference to Lacanian concepts, that men and women have different desires which are not fully complementary and symmetrical, leaving lovers feeling dissatisfied and cheated: it is as if they come from different planets. Maguire and Colman (Chapters 6 and 7) elaborate some of the differences between masculine and feminine desires originating in the different anatomies of men and women, in different early experiences, and from different cultural and social expectations: these translate into different desires.

Pursuit of sexual gratification without concern for the object, purely for heightening sexual excitement, is likely to unhinge people from their humanity. Bataille, in the *Story of the Eye*, creates a fantasy of unrestrained pursuit of sexual excitement, and shows how both subject and object are dehumanised in the process. Stein (1998a) however suggests that Bataille captures the transcendence of the sexual experience through crossing boundaries into the prohibited and excessive. Green (1995, 1997) argues that human sexual fulfilment requires the context of a secure intimate relationship and a caution born of wishing to preserve the integrity both of the self and of the relationship. When sexual excitement is sought regardless of these containing principles, destructive aggression supersedes loving sexuality: sexual arousal is pursued to excess, to the limits of physical and psychic survival, and generates dangerous confusional states, and even death (Green 1997: 346). The practice of heightening sexual arousal by restricting oxygen to the brain is an example of this phenomenon. Royston (Chapter 2) gives examples of such perverse rituals aimed at mastering traumatic experiences.

On the face of it, this catalogue of sexual inhibitions and dissatisfactions makes it surprising that people go on wanting sexual relationships. Yet, despite the obstacles, sex seems to offer the most direct and pleasurable route to satisfying a multiplicity of (constructive and destructive) needs and purposes. Alternative routes to meeting these needs involve frustration, pain and mental effort (sublimation) and pressing needs demand the most direct route. But sexual pleasure and excitement (or relief) is short-lived, and holds the seeds of its own dissatisfaction, unless it strengthens a relationship, that is, fulfils purposes beyond itself as well as fulfilment of itself.

References

Bataille, G. (1928) *Story of the Eye*, trans. Joachim Neugroschal. London: Penguin, 1982.

Breen, D. (ed.) (1993) *The Gender Conundrum: Contemporary Psychoanalytic Perspectives on Femininity and Masculinity*. London: Routledge.

Britton, R. (1989) 'The missing link: parental sexuality in the Oedipus complex', in J. Steiner (ed.), *The Oedipus Complex Today*. London: Karnac.

—— (1992) 'The oedipus situation and the depressive position', in R. Anderson (ed.), *Clinical Lectures on Klein and Bion*. London: Tavistock/ Routledge.

Chasseguet-Smirgel, J. (1985) *Creativity and Perversion*. London: Free Association Books.

Freud, S. (1905) 'Three essays on the theory of sexuality', *Standard Edition: 7*. London: Hogarth Press.

—— (1908) 'Civilized sexual morality and modern nervous illness', *Standard Edition*: 9. London: Hogarth Press.

—— (1910) 'A special type of choice of object made by men', *Standard Edition*: 11. London: Hogarth Press.

—— (1912) 'On the universal tendency to debasement in the sphere of love', *Standard Edition*: 11. London: Hogarth Press.

—— (1915a) 'Instincts and their vicissitudes', *Standard Edition*: 14. London: Hogarth Press.

—— (1915b) 'Observations on transference: love', *Standard Edition*: 12. London: Hogarth Press.

—— (1917) 'Mourning and melancholia', *Standard Edition*: 14. London: Hogarth Press.

—— (1919) 'A child is being beaten: a contribution to the study of the origin of sexual perversions', *Standard Edition*: 17. London: Hogarth Press.

—— (1920) 'Beyond the pleasure principle', *Standard Edition*: 18. London: Hogarth Press.

—— (1923) 'The ego and the id', *Standard Edition*: 19. London: Hogarth Press.

—— (1924) 'The dissolution of the Oedipus complex', *Standard Edition*: 19. London: Hogarth Press.

—— (1930) 'Civilisation and its discontents', *Standard Edition*: 21. London: Hogarth Press.

—— (1933) 'New introductory lecture on psychoanalysis XXXIII: Femininity', *Standard Edition*: 22. London: Hogarth Press.

—— (1940) 'An outline of psychoanalysis', *Standard Edition*: 23. London: Hogarth Press.

Gillespie, W. H. (1956) 'The general theory of sexual perversion', *International Journal of Psychoanalysis* 37: 396–403.

Glasser, M. (1979) 'Some aspects of the role of aggression in the perversions', in I. Rosen (ed.), *Sexual Deviation*, 2nd edn. Oxford: Oxford University Press.

Green, A. (1995) 'Has sexuality anything to do with psychoanalysis?', *International Journal of Psychoanalysis* 76(5): 871–84.

—— (1997) 'Opening remarks to a discussion of sexuality in contemporary psychoanalysis', *International Journal of Psychoanalysis* 78(2): 345–50.

Greenberg, J. and Mitchell, S. (1983) *Object Relations in Psychoanalytic Theory*. Cambridge, MA, and London: Harvard University Press.

Kaplan, L. J. (1991) *Female Perversions*. London: Penguin, 1993.

Kernberg, O. F. (1995) *Love Relations: Normality and Pathology*. Newhaven and London: Yale University Press.

Klein, M. (1928) 'Early stages of the Oedipus complex', in M. Klein, *Love, Guilt and Reparation and Other Works*. London: Routledge.

—— (1945) 'The Oedipus complex in the light of early anxieties', in M. Klein, *Love, Guilt and Reparation and Other Works*. London: Routledge.

Mann, D. (1997) *Psychotherapy: An Erotic Relationship. Transference and Countertransference Passions*. London: Routledge.

Marucco, N. C. (1997) 'The Oedipus complex, castration and the fetish: a revision of the psychoanalytic theory of sexuality', *International Journal of Psychoanalysis* 78(2): 351–61.

McDougall, J. (1972) 'Primal scene and sexual perversion', *International Journal of Psychoanalysis* 53(2): 371–84.

— (1995) *The Many Faces of Eros*. London: Free Association Books.

McLaren, A. (1999) *Twentieth Century Sexuality: A History*. Oxford: Blackwell.

Meltzer, D. (1973) *Sexual States of Mind*. Perthshire: Clunie.

Mitchell, J. and Rose, J. (eds) (1982) *Feminine Sexuality*. London: Macmillan.

Stein, R. (1998a) 'The poignant, the excessive and the enigmatic in sexuality', *International Journal of Psychoanalysis* 79(2): 253–68.

—— (1998b) 'Review of the psychoanalytic theory of sexuality', *International Journal of Psychoanalysis* 79(5): 995–8.

Stoller, R. J. (1985) *Observing the Erotic Imagination*. New Haven and London: Yale University Press.

Welldon, E. V. (1992) *Mother, Madonna, Whore: The Idealization and Denigration of Motherhood*. London: Guilford Press.

Chapter I

Locating and relocating psychoanalytic ideas of sexuality

Robert M. Young

In recent decades Freud has had a bad press from practically every direction. He was thought a biological determinist and reductionist both by the upholders of traditional morality and then by feminists who wanted to contest the idea that biology is destiny and that not having a penis was an irreparable disadvantage. My initial encounter with psychoanalysis as a first-year undergraduate in 1953 certainly supported this view. My new room-mate, a New Yorker, had been to a grand private school in New England (the equivalent of an English public school – called a prep school in America), while I had been to a state school in Texas. He hooted when he learned that I had not heard of Freud or psychoanalysis: 'He's the guy who says everything is sex; all neckties are dicks, and all doorways are cunts.' I confess that it made a kind of instant sense to me. When I began to read Freud for myself a couple of years later I had little reason to think again about this characterisation of sex as basic to all human relations and its symbolism as ubiquitous.

Now, nearly half a century later, I cannot imagine myself thinking that way or characterising psychoanalysis in those terms. The concept of libido, which meant sex drive to me then, means something as wide as negative entropy to me now. (Entropy is a concept in thermodynamics indicating the tendency of systems to disorganise, for their energy to run down to equilibrium; negative entropy characterises energised, complex, relatively organised systems.) The libido theory, which I will sketch anon, is out of fashion in most quarters and has been replaced by object relations theory. In the great Freudian triad of instinct, aim and object, the emphasis has shifted decisively from aim to object, and the mental representations of instincts are to the fore rather than their biological roots. Indeed, one of the founders of object relations theory, Ronald Fairbairn, went so far to say that libidinal attitudes do not determine object relations. On the contrary, object relations determine libidinal attitudes (Greenberg and Mitchell 1983: 137). One way to characterise the change is that what was once rooted in biology has come to be grounded in relationships; what was focused on sexual areas – erogenous zones – is now focused on the unconscious phantasies in the inner world. In some circles the privileging of certain body parts in Freudian theory has been replaced by a claim that any part of the body, any function, *anything at all* can be the legitimate focus of sexual preoccupation, excitement and gratification. Still others (e.g. O'Connor and Ryan 1993: 246) seek to root out all naturalism from sexual identity, orientation and behaviour.

Don't get me wrong. Sexuality, sexual parts, erogenous zones and phases of psychosexual development have not been purged from psychoanalytic theory. The most helpful thing that can be said is that they have moved from the foreground to the background. My approach to sketching the history of psychoanalytic ideas of psychosexual development is to try to 'locate' Freud's thinking and then to show how other psychoanalytic ideas have stretched his ideas, while still others have broken with them – with the consequence that sexuality has been progressively relocated.

One feature of the libido theory has, in certain quarters, been placed under critical scrutiny: the centrality of the Oedipus complex in psychosexual and moral development. There are those – I am not among them – who seek to discard any notion that there is a privileged path of development which we must all pass through if we are to attain maturity. They also reject the claim that failure successfully to negotiate the Oedipus complex is certain to land one in psychological trouble. On this matter there can be no compromise as far as Freudians are concerned. Freud called the Oedipus complex, the painful working out (from about three and a half to five years in childhood) of psychosexual relations between the child and the parents, 'the core complex' or the nuclear complex of every neurosis. In a footnote added to the 1920 edition of *Three Essays on the Theory of Sexuality,* he made it clear that the Oedipus complex is the immovable foundation stone on which the whole edifice of psychoanalysis is based:

> It has justly been said that the Oedipus complex is the nuclear complex of the neuroses, and constitutes the essential part of their content. It represents the peak of infantile sexuality, which,

through its after-effects, exercises a decisive influence on the sexuality of adults. Every new arrival on this planet is faced with the task of mastering the Oedipus complex; anyone who fails to do so falls a victim to neurosis. With the progress of psychoanalytic studies the importance of the Oedipus complex has become more and more clearly evident; its recognition has become the shibboleth that distinguishes the adherents of psychoanalysis from its opponents.

(Freud 1905: 226n)

No compromise is possible with respect to the significance of the Oedipus complex, then. However, if you read the *Three Essays on the Theory of Sexuality* with an open mind, Freud's ideas about sexuality come across as rather more liberal and tolerant of aberration than many of his critics represent them as being. For example, the first essay is not about normality but about sexual aberrations. The second essay is about infantile sexuality, and the third is about puberty. You could say that normal adult sex comes last. Indeed, 'The Finding of an Object' of one's affections turns up in the very last section of the third and last essay. You could say that normal love is something reached by a circuitous path from polymorphous perversity through a series of fixations and incestuous wishes, eventually renounced, although the girl does not finally sort out hers until she has a child, i.e., a symbolic substitute penis. (Nagera 1981: 67–72; Klein 1928, 1945: 50ff and 72–4).

In the first essay Freud stresses just how wide the range of human sexual behaviour is. His is not a rigid position. He says quite straightforwardly that everyone is to some extent a deviant. Freud wrote,

No healthy person, it appears, can fail to make some addition that might be called perverse to the normal sexual aim; and the universality of this finding is in itself enough to show how inappropriate it is to use the word perversion as a term of reproach. In the sphere of sexual life we are brought up against peculiar, and, indeed, insoluble difficulties as soon as we try to draw a sharp line to distinguish mere variations within the range of what is physiological from pathological symptoms.

(Freud 1905: 160–1)

This allows for quite a lot of latitude, but there is still a definite limit. His model is one of norm and deviation – deviation up to a point, but you are supposed to get back onto the appropriate path in the end. There were definite taboos, as well. According to Freud, it was a perversion if the lips or tongue of one person came into contact with the genitals of another or if one lingered over aspects of foreplay which, as he quaintly put it, 'should normally be traversed rapidly on the path towards the final sexual aim' (Freud 1905: 151, 150; cf. 211). He regarded 'any established aberration from normal sexuality as an instance of developmental inhibition and infantilism' (Freud 1905: 231). On the other hand, contrary to what many Freudians believe, Freud did not himself regard homosexuality or perversion as illnesses (Abelove 1986: 59, 60).

So, although Freud was adamant about the Oedipus complex, he was somewhat flexible about sexual behaviour and allowed for a degree of deviance. What, then, is Freudian orthodoxy with respect to sexual development? You can read straightforward accounts of this in Humberto Nagera's *Basic Psychoanalytic Concepts on the Libido Theory* (1981), which claims to include every reference Freud made to this matter, and in Phyllis and Robert Tyson's *Psychoanalytic Theories of Development: An Integration* (1990). If we want to locate Freud in a wide spectrum of theories, we would have to say that he is toward the fixed or biologically determinist end of the spectrum. At this end of the spectrum we encounter the findings of ethologists and the claims of the sociobiologists (Wilson 1975, 1978). Among the most startling discoveries of the science of animal behaviour are the highly ritualised mating patterns of practically all subhuman species, replete with innately determined releasers, fixed patterns, displays. Biology is veritably destiny, whether one is observing fighting fish, spiders, greylag geese, peacocks, walruses, elk or chimpanzees. Students of human behaviour from an ethological point of view claim to detect similar patterns and rituals, biologically determined at base but varied and flexible in expression – so much so that much of our money gets spent on artificial adornments, cosmetics, ways of altering the odours we give off, means of affecting our shape and appearance so as to continue to appear youthful and sexually alluring. Human ethologists and sociobiologists claim that there is no discontinuity between animal sexual determinism and human.

Here is a summary of Freudian orthodoxy on human psychosexual development. It starts with a definite developmental scheme, as modified and enriched by Karl Abraham and, some would say, Erik Erikson. We begin with primary narcissism and pass through psychosexual phases, in which the child is preoccupied with successive erogenous zones – oral, anal, phallic and genital (oral for the first year and a half, anal for the next year and a half and phallic beginning toward the close of the third year. See Brenner 1973: 26; Meltzer 1973: 21–7). As I have said, the classical Oedipal period is ages three and a half to six (some say five). This leads on to the formation of the superego and a period of relative latency, during which boys are quintessentially boyish and horrid, with their bikes, hobbies and play, and girls are sugar and spice and everything nice, playing nurse and mommy (or so it is said; cf. Chodorow 1978). There are zones of variation and various subdivisions within this framework, but its basis is as determined as any analogous developmental scheme in any other part of the animal kingdom. At the earlier end of the scheme Abraham offers some quite detailed subdivisions of the basic phases, e.g., anal retentive and anal expulsive (Abraham 1924). Things get fraught again in adolescence when biological changes coincide with agonising problems about gender identity (Waddell 1992: 9–10), sexual exploration and maturation, conflict with parents, competitiveness and achievement. Erik Erikson spells out a further set of stages, beginning with a psychosocial moratorium in late adolescence, followed by young adulthood, adulthood and mature age, the last of which he characterises as a period in which the central conflict is between integrity, on the one hand, and disgust and despair, on the other (Erikson 1959: 120).

The classical Freudian scheme defines 'normal' as remaining within this chronological developmental framework. If you miss out a phase or fail to move on from one or try to skip one and miss out a developmental task, you are liable to fixation and perversion or even to psychosis. A common definition of perversion is pseudo-maturity, gaining sexual gratification from a substitute object because one is afraid of the appropriate, mature one. According to Robert Stoller (1986), all perversions involve immaturity and all are aggressive. He calls perversion 'the erotic form of hatred' but claims that every perversion, like every neurosis, is a compromise involving holding onto some connection with a mature object. Chasseguet-Smirgel (1985) dwells on the putative pervert's attempt to substitute an immature sexual organ for a grown-up one, and describes the dishonesty of trying to pass a little penis off for a daddy one, without bearing the pain of passing through the Oedipus complex and coming to terms with one's limitations and ambivalence. Limentani (1989a, cf. 1989b) breaks homosexuality into three categories – a situational behaviour which goes away after one leaves, for example, school, the navy or prison; a pseudo-homosexual one which is focused on fear of women and of castration; and true homosexuality, which is a defence against psychotic breakdown and which one approaches psychotherapeutically at one's peril. This completes my exposition of Freudian orthodoxy.

I want now to turn to developments in psychoanalysis and in broader debates about sexuality which have challenged this orthodoxy and which have led many to relocate sexuality in psychoanalytic theory. The key claim is that the relevant framework for considering these issues is that *sexuality is inside the symbolic order*, not purely an expression of instinctual needs. Biological determinants are not wholly cast aside, but the rigidity of their determining role is greatly reduced. More space is claimed for a range of sexual needs, feelings and practices – a range which is as broad as symbolism, rather than as narrow as instinctual determinism. At one level, all but the most conservative and fundamentalist moralists and religious zealots concede something to this way of thinking. It is now a commonplace that *sexuality has a history*, that is, it is inside the contingency of culture, not merely fixed and innate in a stereotyped way. To place it inside history is to grant a lot to the dissidents. In my own lifetime and my own sexual history there have been important changes in all sorts of areas. Things which were taboo when I was a boy are now commonplace, starting with public discussion of sex, including programmes on the radio and television and sex books prominently displayed in all book shops. In the writings of Alex Comfort (1950, 1972, 1974) and others, foreplay has been extended indefinitely, and the boundary between exploration and abnormality has been blurred.

As I write about these things I am moving into the domain of 'plastic sexuality', a phrase drawn from the writings of Anthony Giddens, whose book *The Transformation of Intimacy* (1992) provides a useful perspective on the changes which we are in the midst of. I do not feel altogether comfortable with the degree of relativism involved in this way of thinking, but I have no doubt that this is a useful way of summarising the current debate in culture and in psychoanalysis. Defenders of plastic sexuality attack the boundary between the normal and the abnormal or perverse. They argue that the statistically normal should no longer be confused with medical and moral categories. Indeed, new statistics are put forward by the advocates of greater latitude. For example, it is claimed that 40 per cent or more of married men in the United States have regular sex with other men at some point in their married lives (Giddens 1992: 146). As Giddens puts it, 'Plastic sexuality might become a sphere which no longer contains the detritus of external compulsions, but instead takes its place as one among other forms of self-exploration and moral constitution' (1992: 144). Sex is no longer confined to certain sorts of relationship; the rule of the phallus and power relations are subverted (1992: 140, 147).

> The 'biological justification' for heterosexuality as 'normal', it might be argued, has fallen apart. What used to be called perversions are merely ways in which sexuality can legitimately be expressed and self-identity defined. Recognition of diverse sexual proclivities corresponds to acceptance of a plurality of possible life-styles . . . 'normal sexuality' is simply one type of life-style among others.
>
> (Giddens 1992: 179)

Giddens calls this a 'radical pluralism'(ibid.). Looking at the cultural and philosophical dimensions of the debate, he concludes that

> [this] incipient replacement of perversion by pluralism is part of a broad-based set of changes integral to the expansion of modernity. Modernity is associated with the socialisation of the natural world – the progressive replacement of structures and events that were external parameters of human activity by socially organised processes. Not only social life itself, but what used to be 'nature' becomes dominated by socially organised systems. Reproduction was once a part of nature, and heterosexual activity was inevitably its focal point. Once sexuality has become an 'integral' component of social relations . . . heterosexuality is no longer a standard by which everything else is judged. We have not yet reached a stage in which heterosexuality is accepted as only one taste among others, but such is the implication of the socialisation of reproduction.
>
> (1992: 34)

He is right about the changes in social and philosophical theory, and one point at issue – a profound one – is whether being right about what is happening in *history* is more or less fundamental than what is claimed about *nature*. The tradition he is describing asserts that nature is a societal category, that truth is made, not found, and that our ideas of nature, including those about human nature, are social constructs. People who think this way are called 'social constructivists' if you agree with them and 'relativists' if you don't (Young 1992).

Certain broad – and other particular – developments in psychoanalysis can be seen as compatible with this approach to sexuality. The broad movement is the decline in adherence to biologism and the classical libido theory and the rise of object relations theory. Object relations theory developed in the work of Melanie Klein, Ronald Fairbairn and Donald Winnicott (Greenberg and Mitchell 1983). There are important differences between their formulations. For example, Fairbairn was explicitly turning his back on biology in a way which Klein did not. But the effect on psychoanalytic thinking was to point to relations with the good and bad aspects of the mother and other important figures and part-objects and to treat relations with objects in the inner world, rather than the expression of instincts, as the basic preoccupation of psychoanalytic thinking and clinical work. The focus is on relations rather than drives, on 'the object of my affection [who] can change my complexion from white to rosy red' (as the song says), rather than the aim of the instinct as specified in a biologistic metapsychology (Greenberg and Mitchell 1983: 126). Once you do this, sex, sexuality and sexual energy no longer provide either the rhetoric or the conceptual framework for how we think about the inner world. Love, hatred, unconscious phantasy, anxiety and defences have come to the foreground (1983: 137). As I mentioned above, for Freud, 'sexual' was all-embracing and meant any attribute of living tissue expressing negative entropy. This is what he meant by 'libido' (Stoller 1986: 12). Object relations theorists approach the matter the other way round: libido is not seen as pleasure-seeking but object-seeking (Greenberg and Mitchell 1983: 154). It has been my recent experience that sex in its narrow sense plays a surprisingly small role in psychotherapy training and supervision and the literature. Indeed, some years ago I went to a public lecture by a psychoanalyst, Dr Dennis Duncan, with the title 'Whatever happened to sex in psychoanalysis?'

Along with the turn away from the libido theory has come less attention devoted to the psychosexual developmental scheme and fairly strict chronology which it specified. If you read Klein and her followers, you find phrases like 'oral, anal and phallic elements' jumbled up and part of a pot-pourri. What emerged later in the orthodox Freudian scheme, at specified developmental and chronological points in the libido theory, somehow gets mixed in at an earlier stage in Klein's approach.

I now want to say something about alternative developmental paths. Some of the most interesting writers in this debate make this their most important point: 'What's so wonderful about the developmental path specified by the libido theory?' In asking this question they are attacking the centrality of the Oedipus complex in orthodox Freudianism. They write in explicit opposition to the Freudian Law of the Father on which the importance of the Oedipus complex is based (Fletcher 1989: 113) As the gay theorist John Fletcher puts it, 'What is refused here is not masculinity or the phallus in itself, but the polarity at the heart of the Oedipal injunction: "You cannot *be* what you desire, you cannot *desire* what you wish to be"' (1989: 114). What the Freudians claim as natural is what the sexual dissidents attack as a cultural norm to be struggled against. They argue for a re-symbolisation and re-investment in a new kind of sexuality.

Support for this approach is found in the writings of the eminent French psychoanalyst, Jean Laplanche, co-author of the standard work defining psychoanalytic concepts, *The Language of Psychoanalysis* (Laplanche and Pontalis 1973). The list of erogenous zones specified by the libido theory is accepted: mouth, anus, urethra, genitals. However, they are described less biologistically as places of exchange between inside and outside (Fletcher 1989: 96). However, *any* bodily zone can take on a sexual level of excitement, as can ideas. The traditional understanding of perversion is an alteration or deviation from the fixed, biologically determined order of privileged zones, culminating in genital intercourse to orgasm. But if we refuse to accept this spontaneous unfolding of a unitary instinctual programme, sexuality itself can be seen as polymorphous and therefore, to put it ironically, perverse. Laplanche expresses this starkly by saying that

> the *exception* – i.e., the perversion – ends up by *taking the rule along with it*. The exception, which should presuppose the existence of a definite instinct, a pre-existent sexual function, with its well-defined norms of accomplishment: that exception ends up by undermining and destroying the very notion of a biological norm. The whole of sexuality, or at least the whole of infantile sexuality, ends up becoming perversion.
>
> (Laplanche 1970: 23)

Fletcher puts this in symbolic terms, terms which increase the range, scope and flexibility of sexuality: 'The whole of sexuality as a mobile field of displaceable and substitutable signs and mental representations is a *perversion* of the order of biological needs and fixed objects' (Fletcher 1989: 98–9). If perversion is ubiquitous, it cannot be called exceptional; it is commonplace, the rule, normal: hence ' "perversion" as "normal" ', and the pejorative connotations of the term become obsolete.

Writing about bisexuality and lesbianism, Beverly Burch takes a similar line in opposition to biologism and in favour of social constructivism. She says that 'Lesbianism *and* heterosexual identities are social constructs that incorporate psychological elements' (Burch 1993: 84–5). These differ from one woman to another and have manifestations and sources as varied as individual biographies. 'The unity of heterosexual theory does not live up to the diversity of sexual orientations' (1993: 85). She places sexual orientations on a continuum and argues that any point on it might be defensive; 'no position is necessarily or inevitably pathological' (1993: 91). She surveys the literature and finds a relativism of theory to match her relativism of developmental pathways: 'The point is that no one view is complete, and there are divergent routes on the way to final object choice. The road is not a straight one toward heterosexuality, and we cannot regard other destinations as a wrong turn' (1993: 97).

Writers on these issues draw different lines between what they consider pathological and what they treat as merely human diversity. As I said, Robert Stoller defines perversion as 'the erotic form of hatred' and offers critical analyses of fetishism, rape, sex murder, sadism, masochism, voyeurism, paedophilia. He sees in each of these 'hostility, revenge, triumph and a dehumanised object' (Stoller 1986: 9). On the subject of homosexuality, however, he is a champion of pluralism:

> What evidence is there that heterosexuality is less complicated than homosexuality, less a product of infantile-childhood struggles to master trauma, conflict, frustration, and the like? As a result of innumerable analyses, the burden of proof . . . has shifted to those who use the heterosexual as the standard of health, normality, mature genital characterhood, or whatever other ambiguous criterion serves one's philosophy these days . . . Thus far, the counting, if it is done from published reports puts the heterosexual and the homosexual in a tie: 100 percent abnormals.
>
> (Stoller 1985, quoted in Burch 1993: 97)

Another gem from Stoller:

> Beware the concept 'normal'. It is beyond the reach of objec-
> tivity. It tries to connote statistical validity but hides brute judge-
> ments on social and private goodness that, if admitted, would
> promote honesty and modesty we do not yet have in patriots,
> lawmakers, psychoanalysts and philosophers.
>
> (Stoller 1985: 41, quoted in Burch 1993: 98)

The extreme point in this debate in psychoanalytic theory is that of
certain lesbian theoreticians on gender identity who have reached the
point, as we have seen, where they can claim that the exceptions overwhelm the rule and can put forward the long-term goal of 'eschewing all forms of naturalism in psychoanalytic thinking' (O'Connor
and Ryan 1993: 246).

Wouldn't that be a lovely note on which to end? Unfortunately,
my own sense of reality is not that optimistic, ringing and tidy. It
would be convenient to argue that abandoning the bad old libido
theory and embracing object relations and social constructivism
combine to hold out hope of a new pluralistic consensus in psychoanalytic theory and in cultural and moral norms. Alas, I don't think
it does, and the fly in the ointment is recent Kleinian ideas about the
Oedipus complex. This may not trouble those convinced by the line
of argument I have just been spelling out, but it troubles me, because
I cannot square what I have written so far with what I write below.
I wish I could, but I can't.

Kleinians, as we have seen, go along with the tendency to abandon strict adherence to the chronology of the libido theory. Indeed,
Klein's assertion that she had found the superego operating years
earlier in the development of the child than Freudians thought it
existed was the most obvious bone of contention in the heated controversies which culminated in the famous or infamous (depending
on how you feel about such rows) 'controversial discussions' between
Kleinians and Freudians at the British Psycho-analytical Society
from 1941 to 1945 (King and Steiner, 1991). I am not trying to draw
you into an esoteric spat. I think they were right to be so exercised.
I think this, because I think two importantly different views of
human nature and the basis of morality were in play and that how
we think about sexuality and, indeed, civility and civilisation may
very well hang on what we decide about these matters.

Put very simply, as we have seen, the Freudians claimed that development consisted of a set of preordained tasks which one came upon at biologically predetermined stages on life's way. There is a sense that one can complete a developmental task and have its fruits under one's belt, as it were. The advocates of plastic sexuality reject this idea of human nature and development and argue for a plurality of paths and destinations or objects, and the Freudians deny them this postmodernist supermarket of satisfactions.

At first glance there is a similarity between the advocates of plastic sexuality and Kleinian ideas. Kleinians slide all round the chronology. It has been cogently argued by Ruth Stein that they don't even *have* a theory of psychic structures but rely fundamentally on a set of 'core feelings and nuclear affective structures' (Stein 1990: 504), in particular, the paranoid-schizoid and depressive positions. But what Kleinians appear to give with one hand – slipping all over the chronology and eschewing a basic set of mental structures – they take back with the other. That is, the Oedipus complex may not be the centrepiece of development at say, three and a half to six, reprised at adolescence. Instead, under the name 'Oedipal constellation', this hurdle reappears at every important point in life when one is faced with crises and moral dilemmas. According to Kleinian psychoanalysis, the struggle between love and hate is unresolvable and recurrently centres on the Oedipal triangle. Indeed, far from being something one can refuse *à la* Fletcher's rhetoric about the normality of polymorphousness, it becomes a precondition for being a responsible person who can love and make moral and intellectual judgements of a profound kind and be capable of integrated insights and deep concern for others.

As the Kleinian analyst David Bell puts it,

> The primitive Oedipal conflict described by Klein takes place in the paranoid-schizoid position when the infant's world is widely split and relations are mainly to part objects. This means that any object which threatens the exclusive possession of the idealised breast/mother is felt as a persecutor and has projected into it all the hostile feelings deriving from pregenital impulses.
>
> (Bell 1992: 172)

If development proceeds satisfactorily, secure relations with good internal objects leads to integration, healing of splits and taking back projections.

The mother is then, so to speak, free to be involved with a third object in a loving intercourse which, instead of being a threat, becomes the foundation of a secure relation to internal and external reality. The capacity to represent internally the loving intercourse between the parents as whole objects results, through the ensuing identifications, in the capacity for full genital maturity. For Klein, the resolution of the Oedipus complex and the achievement of the depressive position refer to the same phenomena viewed from different perspectives.

(ibid.)

Another Kleinian, Ronald Britton, puts it very elegantly:

the two situations are inextricably intertwined in such a way that one cannot be resolved without the other: we resolve the Oedipus complex by working through the depressive position and the depressive position by working through the Oedipus complex.

(Britton 1992: 35)

Hence, the ability to tolerate the mixture which is life, to be concerned with whole objects and to integrate experience and make reparation are the fruits of negotiating the Oedipal triangle.

That provides a key to translating between the Freudian and Kleinian conceptual schemes. In the work of post-Kleinians this way of thinking has been applied to broader issues, in particular, the ability to symbolise and learn from experience. Integration of the depressive position, which we can now see as resolution of the Oedipus complex is the *sine qua non* of the development of 'a capacity for symbol formation and rational thought' (Britton 1992: 37). Greater knowledge of the object

includes awareness of its continuity of existence in time and space and also therefore of the other relationships of the object implied by that realisation. The Oedipus situation exemplifies that knowledge. Hence the depressive position cannot be worked through without working through the Oedipus complex and vice versa.

(1992: 39)

Once again, Britton also sees 'the depressive position and the Oedipus situation as never finished but as having to be re-worked in each new life situation, at each stage of development, and with each major addition to experience or knowledge' (1992: 38).

This way of looking at the Oedipal situation offers a very attractive, even profound, way of thinking of self-knowledge or insight:

> The primal family triangle provides the child with two links connecting him separately with each parent and confronts him with the link between them which excludes him. Initially this parental link is conceived in primitive part-object terms and in the modes of his own oral, anal and genital desires, and in terms of his hatred expressed in oral, anal and genital terms. If the link between the parents perceived in love and hate can be tolerated in the child's mind, it provides him with a prototype for an object relationship of a third kind in which he is a witness and not a participant. A third position then comes into existence from which object relationships can be observed. Given this, we can also envisage *being* observed. This provides us with a capacity for seeing ourselves in interaction with others and for entertaining another point of view whilst retaining our own, for reflecting on ourselves whilst being ourselves.
>
> (Britton 1989: 87)

I am going to leave it here. If it were not for Klein and recent developments of the Kleinian way of thinking, I believe plastic sexuality might have an easy path to general acceptance. But the point of view I have just outlined says as starkly as any orthodox Freudian ever did that the problem posed by the Oedipal triangle cannot be evaded if one is to become a person capable of profound thoughts and concern for others. This recalls the intolerance of Chasseguet-Smirgel's Freudian orthodoxy, whereby the creations of perverts (a term she insists on using) could only be pseudo-creations.

This dilemma between the developing credibility of pluralism, on the one hand, and Kleinian thinking, on the other, is a stark one. Freud said in 1903,

> I advocate the standpoint that the homosexual does not belong before the tribunal of a court of law. I am even of the firm conviction that homosexuals must not be treated as sick people, for a perverse orientation is far from being a sickness. Wouldn't that oblige us to characterise as *sick* many great thinkers and scholars whom we admire precisely because of their mental health?
>
> (quoted in Abelove 1986: 60)

Freud is making a very basic point. Are we to so pathologise the character and creations of many of our most admired cultural icons, e.g., Ludwig Wittgenstein, E. M. Forster, Michelangelo, Marcel Proust, Simone de Beauvoir, Michel Foucault, Alan Turing, Socrates? In closing, I can only pose the dilemma and offer it as food for thought. Psychoanalysis has come a long way from the classical Freudian concept of sexuality by way of the object relations tradition and developments in cultural norms. On the other hand, plastic sexuality and the Kleinian concept of maturity, as defined in the depressive position, don't mix, though I dare say that enlightened Kleinians may one day rethink their position, one which currently leads to an illiberal clash. Something called 'perversion' may be normal for gays, lesbians, Laplanchians and some *avant garde* sociologists, but it's still neurotic for orthodox Kleinians. It is clear that concepts of sexuality and gender are no longer moored to the biological reductionism of the libido theory of the original Freudian concept of sexuality. However, it remains unclear where, if at all, these debates will settle. It appears that they are permanently on the move, that is, that they are historical – both in theory and in practice – rather than purely biological.

References

Abelove, H. (1986) 'Freud, homosexuality and the Americans', *Dissent* (Winter): 59–69.
Abraham, K. (1917) 'Ejaculatio praecox', in Abraham (1979), pp. 280–98.
—— (1924) 'A short study of the development of the libido, viewed in the light of mental disorders', in Abraham (1979), pp. 418–501.
—— (1979) *Selected Papers on Psycho-Analysis*. London: Maresfield.
Bell, D. (1992) 'Hysteria: a contemporary Kleinian perspective', *British Journal of Psychotherapy* 9: 169–80.
Brenner, C. (1973) *An Elementary Textbook of Psychoanalysis*, rev. edn. New York: International Universities.
Britton, R. (1989) 'The missing link: parental sexuality in the Oedipus complex', in R. Britton, M. Feldman and E. O'Shaughnessy (1989), *The Oedipus Complex Today*, ed. John Steiner. London: Karnac, pp. 83–102.
—— (1992) 'The Oedipus situation and the depressive position', in R. Anderson (ed.), *Clinical Lectures on Klein and Bion*. London: Routledge, pp. 34–45.
Britton, R., Feldman, M. and O'Shaughnessy, E. (1989) *The Oedipus Complex Today: Clinical Implications*. London: Karnac.
Burch, B. (1993) 'Heterosexuality, bisexuality, and lesbianism: psycho-

analytic views of women's sexual object choice', *Psychoanalytic Review* 80: 83–100.

Chasseguet-Smirgel, J. (1985) *Creativity and Perversion*. London: Free Association Books.

Chodorow, N. (1978) *The Reproduction of Mothering: Psychoanalysis and the Sociology of Gender*. London: University of California Press.

Comfort, Alex (1950) *Sex in Society*, rev. edn. London: Duckworth.

—— (1974) *More Joy: A Lovemaking Companion to 'The Joy of Sex'*. New York: Crown.

—— (ed.) (1975) *The Joy of Sex: A Gourmet Guide to Lovemaking*. London: Quartet pbk.

Erikson, E. (1959) *Identity and the Life Cycle: Selected Papers, Psychological Issues,* vol. 1, no. 1, monograph 1. New York: International Universities Press.

Fletcher, J. (1989) 'Freud and his uses: psychoanalysis and gay theory', in Shepiero and Wallis (eds), *Coming on Strong*. London: Unwin Hyman, pp. 90–118.

Freud, S. (1953–73) *The Standard Edition of the Complete Psychological Works of Sigmund Freud*. London: Hogarth. (*Standard Edition*).

—— (1905) 'Three essays on the theory of sexuality', *Standard Edition* 7, pp. 125–245. See esp. appendix – 'List of writings by Freud dealing predominantly or largely with sexuality', pp. 244–5.

Giddens, A. (1992) *The Transformation of Intimacy: Sexuality, Love and Eroticism in Modern Societies*. Cambridge: Polity; pbk., 1993.

Greenberg, J. R. and Mitchell, S. A. (1983) *Object Relations in Psychoanalytic Theory*. Cambridge, MA: Harvard University Press.

King, P. and Steiner, R. (eds) (1991) *The Freud–Klein Controversies 1941–45*. London: Tavistock/Routledge.

Klein, M. (1928) 'Early stages of the Oedipus conflict', *International Journal of Psycho-analysis* 9: 167–80; reprinted in Klein (1975), vol. 1, pp. 186–98.

—— (1945) 'The Oedipus complex in the light of early anxieties', *International Journal of Psycho-analysis* 26: 11–33; reprinted in Klein (1975), vol. 1, pp. 370–419 and in Britton *et al.* (1989), pp. 11–82, esp. summary, pp. 63–82.

—— (1975) *The Writings of Melanie Klein*, 5 vols. London: Hogarth.

Laplanche, J. (1970) *Life and Death in Psychoanalysis*. Baltimore, MD: Johns Hopkins University Press, 1976; pbk., 1985.

Laplanche, J. and Pontalis, J.-B. (1973) *The Language of Psycho-Analysis*, ET. London: Hogarth; first publ. 1967.

Limentani, Adam (1989a) 'Clinical types of homosexuality', in Limentani (1989c), pp. 102–14.

—— (1989b) 'Perversions: treatable and untreatable', in Limentani (1989c), pp. 230–49.

—— (1989c) *Between Freud and Klein: The Psychoanalytic Quest for*

Knowledge and Truth. London: Free Association Books.

Meltzer, D. (1973) *Sexual States of Mind.* Strath Tay: Clunie Press.

Nagera, H. (ed.) (1981) *Basic Psychoanalytic Concepts on the Libido Theory.* London: Karnac.

O'Connor, N. and Ryan, J. (1993) *Wild Desires and Mistaken Identities: Lesbianism and Psychoanalysis.* London: Virago.

Rudnytsky, P. L. (1987) *Freud and Oedipus.* New York: Columbia University Press.

Sophocles (1947) *The Theban Plays.* Harmondsworth: Penguin.

Stein, R. (1990) 'A new look at the theory of Melanie Klein', *International Journal of Psycho-analysis.* 71: 499–511.

Stoller, R. J. (1985) *Observing the Erotic Imagination.* New Haven: Yale University Press.

—— (1986) *Perversion: The Erotic Form of Hatred,* pbk. (1975). London: Maresfield; first publ. 1975.

Tyson, P. and Tyson, R. L. (1990) *Psychoanalytic Theories of Development: An Integration.* New Haven: Yale University Press.

Waddell, M. (1992) 'From resemblance to identity: a psychoanalytic perspective on gender identity', typescript.

Wilson, E. O. (1975) *Sociobiology: The New Synthesis.* Cambridge, MA: Harvard University Press.

—— (1978) *On Human Nature.* Cambridge, MA: Harvard University Press.

Young, R. M. (1992) 'Science, ideology and Donna Haraway', *Science as Culture* 3(15): 165–207.

—— (1994) 'New ideas about the Oedipus complex', *Melanie Klein and Object Relations* 12 (2): 1–20.

—— (1996) 'Is "Perversion" obsolete?', *Psychology in Society* 21: 5–26.

Chapter 2

Sexuality and object relations

Robert Royston

The British object relations school inherited from Freud a bold and vividly articulated sexual theory. It aspired to the status of a science but was also a compelling vision of the human struggle to ascend from the chaotic and primitive to the ordered and civilised. Sex was pre-eminent in this vision in its manifold forms as behaviour, motivational energy, life force and gender.

This emphasis on sex as ubiquitous rapidly achieved fame. The Oedipus complex, seduction theory, symptoms as the product of repressed sexual drives, constitutional bisexuality, castration anxiety, penis envy – these were outrageous concepts, disgusting, exciting, ridiculous, insulting to the species and strangely flattering, too.

Even today the public mind remains fixated on psychoanalysis as a system in which sex explains everything, and rejects psychoanalysis on the very same grounds. The irony is that the rejected concept is out of date by many decades. Everything is now different, altered by a sea change in analytic theory that began more than sixty years ago. Sex both as behaviour and motivating force remains an important preoccupation, but classical drive theory's vision of a galvanising sexual force with tension release as its primary aim has been profoundly questioned by the British object relations school (Fairbairn 1943) and by the later formulations of American Self Psychology (Kohut 1977). Mitchell writes:

> Infantile sexuality, like adult sexuality, surely exists; the question is – what is it? Is the child driven toward certain predetermined experiences and fantasies, or do the exquisite sensations provided through bodily experiences with others take on passionate significance and meaning from the relational context in which they occur? ... Ironically, the linking of sexuality with drives can

serve to conceal the meanings and true appeal of experiencing sexuality as an atavistic holdover from our bestial ancestry.

(1988: 92)

The image of mankind in Freud and the object relations school

That the radical change in psychoanalytic thinking and practice bypassed public attention should surprise no one. In Freud people are sexually interesting, even heroic. The object relations picture, on the other hand, is different and strenuously undramatic: humans are poignant, no shadowy sexual beast lurks inside, but instead a starved or a motherless baby, or with luck a contented baby. This idea is not headline material.

Again, Freud's famous cases were put forward empirically as science, but are absorbing simply on the level of literature. They create a picture of a social world and of Viennese culture. The Wolf Man, Frau Emmy von N, the Rat Man, Anna O, these were not only cases, but characters. Object relations theory, by contrast, is infinitely ignorable outside psychoanalytic circles. Where are the epic cases, the characters who linger in the imagination? If there is a world at all it is hermetic, internal, peopled by interacting subselves, called by Fairbairn (1943), for example, the Anti-Libidinal Object, the Internal Saboteur, or the Rejecting Ego. The whole changing culture of psychoanalysis focused less on the Oedipal triangle, more on the relationship between mothers and babies, and the internal world inside the patient, and particularly on the idea of the internal object. In a sense the internal object is the world in which the self lives.

The origins of re-evaluation

The re-evaluation which led to this situation had its earliest post-Freudian beginnings in the papers of Melanie Klein (1921). Since that time analytical focus in Britain shifted from sex to dependency, from the Oedipal years to early infancy, from the phallus to the breast, from the sexually charged trio of mother, father and child to the tender but undramatic mother–baby unit. Logically, this did not mean that sexuality in the ordinary sense of the word was off the agenda. Sexual drive theory, the idea that an essentially sexual galvanising energy animates the species, was abandoned or marginalised. But was the British object relations school interested in sex in the sense of behaviour, arousal, fantasy, the erotic?

At first the answer to this question appears to be negative. There was no grand sexual challenge to Freud's infamous formulations. There were revisions and rejections, but little more. Instead, during the formulation of new theory all eyes were riveted on the primitive, on early phenomena and early sources of patients' problems. People became intensely focused on the suckling child, her phantasies, on maternal deprivation, on the most primitive self-expression of the infant, on the internal world of conflicting selves and objects generated in the first weeks and months of life.

Could there be a place here for sexuality? It is a world of women, of mothers where fathers are curtly given two undetailed roles: to support mother and to be a bridge for the child from mother to outside world. It is a pre-childhood picture which ante-dates forms of memory available to the adult patient. The child as toddler is relatively elderly in this zone and walks unsteadily out of the theoretical frame at a remarkably early age (Fairbairn 1943;Winnicott 1958; Balint 1968).

Nevertheless object relations theory did not ignore sex. There is a clear, persuasive and consistent idea about sexuality, which has been hugely influential. Simply stated, it is that the psychodynamics of the earlier era, the oral stage, are gathered up by the toddler and transported to the later phases where they are stamped onto all aspects of the older child's emerging sexuality. Sexuality, then, is infancy in a new erotic form, babyhood in a different jacket.

Here the early order has been turned on its head. In Freud the mind was formed around sexuality and conflict. Sex was protean and sought to bend things to its will. In the new body of theory sex is plastic, merely a follower, dominated by the needs of the hungry baby within the adult, or is formed around more primitive asexual needs.

The man endlessly seeking sexual adventure, for example, may be driven by early longings not for the sexual mother of the Oedipus complex, but mother as feeder, nurturer, protector and platonic love object; or, instead, may be motivated by revenge fantasies against a depriving mother. The woman who cannot have pleasurable vaginal sex may well be seen as denying entry, not to an abusive father, but to an intrusive metaphorically (or physically) force-feeding mother. Hypersexuality is seen as having nothing to do with physiological sex drive but with a need for stimulus to compensate for underlying emptiness. And the empty self? It is the product of a schizoid withdrawal from objects, from parents who were at first sought out for emotional nutrition but then discarded as depriving or dangerous.

In this theoretical shift away from classical ideas, then, sexuality lost its pre-eminent position. The human struggle as conceived by Freud (1905, 1926) – which was to tame the wild horses of the id – came to be seen as the struggle, in the stage of infantile dependency, to form and maintain a nutritive relationship with a good object. Sex was part of some larger, more tender but equally epic psychic move-ment – the transition from the total dependency of infancy to matu-rity, conceived of as the ability to form close relationships with other people, to love, to take in good contributions from others, but to simultaneously remain separate and a free-functioning creative self.

The outline of this new psychological continent developed rapidly through various phases.

Melanie Klein

Melanie Klein extended the work of psychoanalysis to children and evolved the technique of play therapy, delivering in 1925 her first of a number of papers eventually collected in *The Psycho-analysis of Children* (1932). This, she believed, offered a new psychological per-spective and extended Freud's ideas. However, her theoretical papers were not initially seen as at all helpful to the Freudian cause and became highly controversial, but also influential.

While the term 'object relations' was first applied to her work, this usage was later dropped and the phrase applied only to the work of people influenced by her, particularly Fairbairn and Winnicott. Klein, then, is important to but not a member of what came to be termed the British object relations school.

The history of the 'object' from Freud to Klein

The 'object' in psychoanalysis is a minor character in the core of Freud's scheme. This is because the child was thought of as polymorphous perverse. Anything would do as long as drive was satisfied. Object was what libido or drive – say the sucking drive – happened to light upon. The object, originally mother, did not exist as an intuition in the mind of the child. There was no ghostly internal programme in libido which directed the baby to look for the nipple. The object was haphazard. But once this highly fortunate though entirely gratuitous bumping together of drive and object has occurred the object takes on increasing importance.

Klein, an ardent Freudian, nevertheless rejected this formulation. Her objection had a philosophical ring: logically there can be no desire unless it is a desire for something. Need knows its object *a priori*: there can be no formless undirected want. Therefore drive and the object of that drive exist inside the psyche of the child simultaneously as a continuum, as a dim precognition of the breast. This seemed to Klein an important insight but not at all revisionist. In fact it was a defining moment in the development of psychoanalytic thinking and practice.

Years previously Freud had abandoned seduction theory. This was the idea that neurosis was caused by childhood sexual abuse. Freud rejected this concept and substituted a different explanation: that the vague but insistent 'memories' of obscure abuses which patients brought to analysis were not memories at all. They were fantasies forged by the Oedipus complex. The child fantasises seduction out of a wish for Oedipal gratification. With this new idea, which was persuasively argued, psychoanalysis took on its more recognisable, more finished shape, and walked away from the outside world as a generator of mental disturbance. Neurosis was generated from within.

Klein's revision of drive theory can be read as a deeper step towards inner space. The object exists before the real breast is encountered. The internal breast is independent of the external and lives in inner space entirely vulnerable to the child's phantasy life. The baby, filled with destructiveness, attacks this internal breast which then becomes corrupted and is experienced as a destructive and hateful entity.

Destructiveness is not a reaction to the real breast out there. Freud's death instinct theory stated that aggressive libido was present at birth in the form of masochistic or self-destructive energy. This energy had to be focused outward to protect the organism. Clearly, then, the entire world-within-a-world described by Klein was auto-generated by the baby: the internal object, or breast, existed before the real one and the destructive drive existed before any real provocation.

Freud's concept of internalisation was also influential here. This is the idea that the child takes into itself images of significant others in the outside world. These then become independent of their source and function as parts of the child's personality. A parent punishes a child. The child then has a silent voice inside which inhibits the proscribed action or punishes it with guilt, depression or self-destructive behaviour. The punishing parent has become an internal object, set up in the superego.

This idea makes the internal object contingent upon the outer. In Klein's work the failing or damaging mother was not elaborated. The emphasis was not on the external world. Klein's urgent focus, instead, was on the baby's struggle to master the infantile internal world, which she conceived of as an inferno of mental sexuality and violence, occurring in a realm called unconscious phantasy. The role of the mother was to ameliorate this world by her benign presence.

A sense of the teeming character of the internal world is offered by a passage in Klein's *Criminal Tendencies in Normal Children* (1927). Here Klein states that children's sexual theories are the basis of a variety of sadistic and primitive fixations, and writes:

> According to the oral- and anal-sadistic stage which he is going through himself, intercourse comes to mean to the child a performance in which eating, cooking, exchange of faeces and sadistic acts of every kind (beating, cutting, and so on) play the principal part. I wish to emphasize how important the connection between these phantasies and sexuality is bound to become in later life . . . their unconscious effect will be of far reaching importance in frigidity, in impotence and in other sexual disturbances.
>
> (1927: 170)

This is not a theory of sexuality as such. For Klein and her followers adult sexuality is a given. It is a fact of life. There is little to say about it as thing-in-itself. Of later object relations theorists, the same is true. Sexual theory may be described in this way: *sex is good between loving adults who have resolved infantile conflicts; it is a bridge between loving people; it is something emotionally profound which one both gives and receives in the act of intercourse; it may also, however, embody the destructiveness that derives from the psychic world of infancy.*

The theory might continue by stating that every person has an internal history. For Kleinian theory this history is primarily one of aggression. Destructiveness, rage, envy of the breast, mental attacks on the phantasy of the parental couple in intercourse – these are commonplace elements in the early paranoid-schizoid history of the infantile psyche, and derive from the death instinct, from constitutional destructiveness present at birth. In Klein sexuality, a basic drive, is fused with another more important basic drive, destructiveness. Because the organism must be defended against this destructiveness, infantile psychic history is also the history of evolving mental mechanisms, such as projection and splitting. Hypothetically pristine adult sexuality therefore must, if infantile conflict has not been resolved, take on board a cargo of destructive impulses and distorting mental mechanisms. These profoundly affect sexual desire, experience and performance.

For psychoanalysis an important theme is the relative importance, or lack of it, of the causal outside world. Some might argue that an adult's sexuality is formatively influenced by external excitations. Or further that painful and disturbing experiences may be sexualised in an attempt to master what was originally frightening or humiliating. In other words a child's – later an adult's – sexuality may be excited, formed or distorted by the behaviour of adults. If one closely followed a line suggested by Kleinian theory, however, one would emphasise instead the exigencies of the internal world, mental mechanisms and imperative drives in the shaping of both infantile and adult sexuality.

These internal influences are demonstrated in a case history of one of Klein's followers, Ruth Reisenberg Malcolm (1970). Malcolm explains that the case demonstrates the use of a perversion as a defence against psychosis; this covert psychosis is the product of attacks on internal objects, particularly on mother as a sexual being and the parental couple in intercourse. The patient is a woman of 42 years of age who has been through a period of compulsive but cold-hearted and contemptuous promiscuity. This period culminated in a breakdown during which she was hospitalised. Subsequently for twenty years her sex life consisted exclusively of masturbation with perverse fantasies. Her central fantasy involved a mirror in which sadistic and often violent sexual activities took place between grotesque and bizarre couples who are controlled by the patient and barred from experiencing pleasure.

The fantasy is interpreted as expressing the patient's extreme feeling of exclusion from the parents' sexual relationship. It is an attack on the parental couple in intercourse, the mother and the good breast. Malcolm writes during the description of a session:

> I summarised the interpretations for her and how this excitement was in my view an attempt to bypass the 'awfulness' she felt

about what she does to me in her mind, as she did to her parents when she was little.

(1970: 132)

Later she writes:

> To be able to make real progress . . . she would have to face intense pain and frustration in experiencing love for her objects and the consequence of the attacks to which she had submitted them. But the horror that this situation produces in the patient makes her resort to further fragmentation.

(1970: 133)

The mirror fantasy, Malcolm explains, is a type of psychic capsule by means of which the patient managed to keep her destructiveness within certain limits and prevent it from affecting the whole of her personality.

Details are given, but play no explanatory role in the case. The patient's parlous psychic state as a consequence of sexual envy and attacks on the good, is a refrain. These attacks come from a place unaffected by the historical details of the patient's life as a child. The real parents are ignored. This represents a particular clinical and theoretical approach within the broad Kleinian position.

In the case above historical details, though sparse and clinically sidelined, are nevertheless interesting. The patient's father was tyrannical, ill-tempered, rigid and dominated the mother. In his youth he had had a mental breakdown. Life at home for the patient was gloomy, restricted and isolated. At the age of about ten, Malcolm tells us, the patient and her younger sister spied on a couple in a neighbouring house having sexual intercourse and a few days later the sisters started a homosexual relationship which lasted for five years.

One may protest that Malcolm's prescription for this patient – that she comes to love her objects – is a tall order given these circumstances. Her childhood was a gloomy and distressing ordeal. She suffered paternal tyranny and maternal abandonment. Yet her illness is described as all her own work and exists because she cannot love her objects and is full of destructiveness. And this destructiveness and envy and sense of enraged exclusion from the parental sex act has devastated her own sexuality, which has become hopelessly interwoven with her pathology.

However, Malcolm represents only one position within the Kleinian school, and views range from hers to others considerably closer to the object relations model and the relational model (Mitchell 1988) which see the child formed in the context of relationships.[1]

Fairbairn

W. R. D. Fairbairn lived in Edinburgh, far from the centre of psychoanalytical debate. Perhaps for this reason he was the most independent of thinkers and the most challenging of the post-Freudian revisionists. While Winnicott diplomatically proclaimed himself a man intent simply on mining the Freudian reef, Fairbairn simply came out with it and said the gold should be approached through a separate shaft.

His major work, *Psychoanalytic Studies of the Personality* (1943), a collection of closely linked papers, is an attack on the Freudian concept of life energy as quintessentially sexual.

Fairbairn's central act of redefinition was to de-eroticise libido. Life energy, he said, was in a sense drive and need but there was no evidence for its erotic character. Libido was an impulse towards loving objects in the real world. Libido's aim was to form psychologically strengthening relationships. There was instinctive knowledge that relationships with loving others is necessary for psychic growth. With that stroke Fairbairn reintroduced the real-world-as-causal into psychoanalysis for the first time since the abandonment of seduction theory and reinvented psychoanalysis as a type of social psychology.

Freud (1905) saw the human organism as quintessentially pleasure-seeking. Pleasure of a covertly sexual type could derive from any of the excitable bodily zones and each of these zones had its age-appropriate onset and its own psychology. The psychology of anal-stage sexuality, for example, may involve excitement through mess, or in the later anal stage, through control, through hoarding or through playing on the boundaries between retention and expulsion. What was behind all this was simply sex itself, mankind's hunger for erotic sensation, and its psychic ramifications, which include the socially imposed necessity to control the lust for the pleasurable discharge of tension.

1 See David Morgan, Chapter 8 in this volume, for a Kleinian position closer to the object relations model [*editor*].

This picture was incomplete, proclaimed Fairbairn. We are not pleasure-seeking hedonists, but object-seeking social creatures whose aim is to grow in psychic health and strength. The child's psychic work involves maintaining good contact with, and eliminating bad aspects of, important caretakers. The immediate world of the child must be reliably benign. Through internalisation the child cleanses the world of disturbing images, setting them up in the self instead. This is like vacuum-cleaning the outer world and using the self as the rubbish bin.

The external world having been cleansed of bad objects, the crisis moves to the internal realm and bad internal objects. How to get rid of them becomes the central problem, and the means employed by the developing mind of the child takes its character from the famous Freudian libidinal stages. Yes, there is an anal stage: it is a phase whose behavioural character was well described by Freud, asserts Fairbairn. But anal retention, for example, is tied up with the control of a bad internal object. And anal expulsivity involves an attempt to purge the mind of bad objects. Neither activity involves the pursuit of pleasure and relief for pleasure's sake.

It is similar in the matter of repression. Whereas in Freud the unconscious was filled with repressed sexual drives, many of them Oedipal in character, in Fairbairn the unconscious consists of relationships. These are of an active and dynamic kind between internalised objects and selves, and replicate aspects of the infant's relationships with caretakers. In the realm of the repressed, for example, one may find a depriving object in relationship with a deprived self. Or a superegoic object endlessly imposing self-denial on a type of anorexic but horribly starved self. These 'selves' and 'objects' become part of the person's character, as they silently deny or scold themselves over issues of appetite and need. Whole complexes of such internalised relationships occupy a major area of the infant's mind, removed first from the interactional real world, then set up in the conscious mind, then repressed.

Pleasure, said Fairbairn, is a signpost to good objects. So while Freud's libido was unruly, and Klein's an anarchic hell, Fairbairn's is tender, humane and constructive. Gone is the romantic conflict with society, its place occupied now by an urgent but easily damaged impulse whose ultimate end is the transition from total dependency to adult strength and independence through interaction with caring parents. Healthy independence is not truculent or isolationist but includes an ability to form a loving attachment, to support and nurture and be supported and nurtured in turn.

Sex in Fairbairn, therefore, is de-emphasised and an important victim of this is Freud's Oedipus complex, the core of classical analytic theory, the defining moment in the child's developmental struggle. Fairbairn claimed the child's sexual attraction to a parent was not natural and by no means inevitable. It occurred when normal efforts on the part of the child to make loving contact with a caretaker failed. The desperate child may then eroticise the relationship in order to have more to offer the negligent parent. Incestuous impulses in the child emerge only if the parent rejects loving interaction.

To demonstrate this, Fairbairn offered a vignette of a woman who as a girl had despaired of ever making emotional contact with her father. Finally, the girl registered the thought, 'Surely it would appeal to him if I offered to go to bed with him!' (1943: 23) The Oedipus complex then was a lifeline to an unresponsive loved object.

Guntrip

Fairbairn's ideas were initiated by his concern with a mental state termed the schizoid condition. This is said to occur when relationships with others are too painful and depriving to endure. The child defends by withdrawing. In adulthood the schizoid character cannot form vital relationships and has lost contact with subjective emotional states.

Harry Guntrip, a patient of Fairbairn's and later his follower, elaborated the concepts of his mentor (1968). He described different facets of the schizoid experience, the peculiar alienation, the sense of life and the physical world operating behind a thick window, the haunting emptiness, a sense of physical fragmentation, fears of total loss of contact, an intellectual acuteness that was the outcome of a person's role as non-participating observer on the fringes of the social world. In this state the need for relationships, the full range of dependency needs, are repressed.

Emotion, a sense of history and significance, is leached out of human relationships. What is left is a hollow outward form. The outcome of all of this is a place of mental safety which is barren and imprisoning. Taken to an extreme this defence is registered by the subject as not at all reassuring but terrifying, sometimes accompanied by fearful dreams of incarceration, as all feeling is lost and the continued existence of the self is threatened by the emergence of a powerful regressive need.

In this internal crisis sex may come to the rescue of the alienated self, operating in two ways: it is a form of hyper-stimulation which brings a dead emotional world to life; and it is an emergency bridge to objects. The intensity of the sexual experience makes sex particularly useful for these purposes. If one is numb, then heightened experience is demanded. Perversion is a field in which sex can roam in search of ever more extreme forms of heightened intensity. Pain can combine with sexual excitement in flagellation or sado-masochistic torture scenarios. Many perversions involve risk. An exhibitionist risks arrest. A man who wears a mask in a bondage enactment places his life in the hands of his partner, who has control over a breathing tube which is his only oxygen supply. Danger, risk, pain, physical constriction and helplessness cooperate in inventive if bizarre sexual playacting. The aim of these is to re-establish lost contact with object and restore the self, whose continued existence is threatened, and to whip aliveness out of the failing body of the emotions.

This, however, is an account of pathological sexuality. Sexual life in Guntrip is explored in its role as a defence, almost as pseudo-sexuality.

To find just a hint of an account of the psychology of healthy sexuality one has to look to the contribution of a man whose clinical interest in sex was minimal, and whose attention instead was closely focused on mothers and babies, with fathers present only as shadows on a wall.

Winnicott

D.W. Winnicott was a paediatrician who trained as a psychoanalyst and worked analytically with both children and adults. He developed a body of theory highly characteristic of his own intellectual and clinical style – good-natured, intuitive, confiding, though occasionally vague.

In Winnicott's contribution the self is a natural entity. It is the quintessential person. It is our liveliness and spontaneity, as well as our sense of personal agency. This self unfolds naturally according to its own unique agenda, but requires an attentive and uninvasive mother to facilitate the process. There can be no infant, psychologically speaking, without a mother, wrote Winnicott.

However, an impinging mother allows her own agendas and difficulties to interrupt the fragile but energetic unfolding of the real self. The infant, instead of a healthy total involvement with the experience of the emerging self, will adapt to the needs of the mother. The child's own developmental programme will be shelved and a compliant false self emerge, incapable of spontaneity, of contact with others or with the real, emotional self, but capable of managing the world.

These ideas share common ground with the exploration into the schizoid condition undertaken by Fairbairn and Guntrip. False-self sexuality is schizoid sexuality. It is defensive. Its project is not creative contact with a loved partner but is, in a sense, an imitation or a distortion of real sex.

However, it is with Winnicott's concept of transitional space that a glimpse is afforded into a possible new concept of sexuality. Winnicott wrote that the developing infant must be allowed the subjective experience of the invention of the world. Omnipotently, the infant feels that the discovery and exploration of objects is part of personal creativity. There is a sense of power in this, despite the evident fact that a baby is the most vulnerable and inexperienced of creatures. The objects discovered or 'invented' by the infant come to occupy a mental zone called transitional space. Here they pass from their identity as creations of the self to their more mature status as denizens of a pre-existing outside world.

Poised between omnipotent self and potentially overpowering outside world, transitional space is an omnipotent zone of invention, make-believe and play. This concept, whose most pure application is situated in the nursery, is nevertheless widely applicable. Winnicott himself speculated that transitional space may be the matrix of culture.

Although his was a pre-sexual world and he formulated few theories directly relevant to sexual matters, the idea of transitional space is not irrelevant to the theme. In perverse sexuality one may speculate that the real self of the protagonist has been crushed or driven into hiding by an invasive mother. This mother, the idea continues, did not allow transitional space. Here the child might have played, been infused with a sense of power and might have only gradually discovered the hard-edged reality of the world. The fantasies and role-playing that are characteristic of perversion, then, may be attempts to create a belated transitional world of omnipotence and play and indulgence of the real self.

In perverse enactments the sexual partner is dehumanised and used as a plaything. This, however, is a familiar aspect of playing in transitional space. A commonly reported experience is one of elation and airy freedom following the perverse act. Is this because the real self has been contacted and the invasive object expelled, appeased or negated, albeit temporarily? Unsupportive of the idea of traditional space as a sexual realm is the fact that repetition and strictly scripted acts, rather than creative spontaneity, are characteristic of the perversions, as well as the fact that in the perversions the subject does not develop, but is bound to endless re-enactments aimed at mastering a core of trauma.

This, like so many object relations formulations of sexuality, is a description of pathological, or at best damaged, sexuality. But perhaps there is another side to the matter. In Klein perversion is destructive, linked to destructive narcissism. But in the view suggested above, perversion has a deeply buried intention which is at least partly positive – to forge a space where at least in some form the embattled self may find a zone of freedom from a crushing or perverse object.

There is a further point. Freud suggested that a degree of perversion is universal, although this is normally woven into the fabric of mature sexuality. It is possible to argue that each person has an agenda of sexual themes which, if expressed in a sound relationship, may animate sexuality. If they involve a degree of depersonalisation, this may enhance the experience of both partners, and may heighten not only excitement but emotional contact. After all, the erotic as a genre in literature and art – an area of sexually charged make-believe – often relies for impact both on a level of dehumanisation as well as the depiction of asymmetrical relationships. Fantasies and games, one might argue, could have their roots in the person's natural or real self. Mitchell makes this point:

> the use of the other as a transitional object, to be arranged and controlled for one's own pleasure, may be an essential ingredient not just in perverse sexuality but in the most mature sexual relationships as well, where the partners shift back and forth between the roles of subject and object, actor and acted upon.
>
> (1988: 98)

Clearly there is a distinction between full-blown perversion in which the other person is simply a thing, and relational sexuality.

Clinical study

What of object relations theory in clinical practice? Some brief material may illustrate. A male patient in his thirties, stably married and with children, presented sexual inhibition as a mild problem, though as the treatment progressed it loomed larger and was identified as an aspect of a central theme. Sex took place at very irregular intervals and was marred by a sense that the fiery, and also tender, core of the sexual experience was teasingly absent. Asexual thoughts came unbidden during the act and his assessment afterwards was that it had been blandly pleasant, a relief and a disappointment.

This man, something of a workaholic, was occasionally haunted by memories of a relationship in his early twenties with a passionate and unstable older woman, whose moods and rages, carnivorous appetite for him one moment and dismissive self-preoccupation the next, tormented him. A vivid excitement, however, was discernible within the torment, and a romantic fantasy of being on the edge, at the core of life.

The sexual problem was complex. One aspect involved the inhibition of a sector of the self. In this sector lived the patient's starvation, his emotional hunger, a taste for masochistic hyper-stimulation, and anarchic rage. These were products of his relationships with his emotionally absent parents. His father was quick-tempered and would cuff the boy on occasions. Both parents demanded more than respect from their son, a type of awed appreciation of their wit and general excellence.

The boy had become disruptive at junior school. After sessions with an educational psychologist, this settled down, but resurrected itself in the domestic environment. After a dangerous row with father, with intimations of serious paternal violence, the boy became withdrawn and distracted.

Another sector of the personality was involved in the suppression of the turbulent libidinal part of the self. This part was powerful, dry, proscriptive and punitive. It may be theorised as an object introjected from the real world. It was the parent as depriver, the parent who counsels the importunate child to control need in the service of self-sufficiency, and the parent who menaces and strikes. This depriving object was not ego-alien. There was a way in which the patient liked it, because, fearing his own tempestuous nature, he valued a quiet life, and did not connect it with his lack of fulfilment.

The patient's sado-masochistic involvement with the former lover, then, was a re-enactment of childhood rows. These generated excitement, but not because of the presence of free-floating masochistic libido. Instead, the fights were a form of intense emotional contact, even if negative in nature. The boy had reached his father. Father had concentrated on him an energetic involvement.

The tempestuous hungry self also harboured the patient's creativity. To reconnect with it, the patient had to express his need and anger in the therapeutic relationship, after the analysis of resistance to emotional hunger and the need-denying self.

Object relations and the erotic

Object relations sexual theory has transformed analytical thinking and practice. Sexual impulses now are seldom seen as *sui generis*, but as assuming their character in an interpersonal context. That said, the erotic is often underplayed or pathologised. Stein, commenting on this, writes that getting behind sexualisation to deep-rooted distress, may bring the patient relief. She continues:

> However to my mind such unfolding may often be misused as a general strategy, namely employing object-related thinking as the total explanatory bedrock for the diversity and intensity of sexual manifestations, mostly to explain their pathological expressions, thereby leaving very little room for explaining sexual phenomena in terms of sexuality proper.
>
> (1998: 253)

Clinical practice, in fact, shows that people have their own wide-ranging erotic scenarios which emerge in fantasy. These are the product of excitations (not all of them originally sexual) and impressions gathered in childhood. Polymorphous-perverse in early childhood, humans have the capacity to be excited by a range of situations, objects, people or stories. Past experience and present imagination weave elaborate narratives. This process, within limits, is benign, a source of sexual creativity. Enacting these scenarios in a relationship may bring partners into deeper contact, even though this may require the temporary and playful depersonalisation of one or other protagonist.

There is, however, a clear point where sexual enactments become a cause for genuine concern. A hard-core perversion, like addiction, has its own labyrinthine *modus vivendi*. It does not merely colonise sex, but leeches the self, binding its creative energy into obsessions so private they are often unreadable to outsiders. Sexual intercourse is demoted, and often considered trivial, and the intense secret excitement that is central to perversion takes over and becomes a lifelong pursuit, whose real aim is not sexual at all, but is rather the mastery of severe trauma and the rejection of dependency.

So, while popular culture has neither forgiven nor forgotten Freud for his contribution to sexual theory, and for his suggestion that all people have perverse traits, it has neither blamed nor heard of object relations theory. The question is: Did Freud's emphasis on the subject accurately reflect the central role of sexuality in people's lives and in human psychology? Or, could one argue that Freud's view, though scandalous, is less threatening than that of object relations theory – that vulnerability, dependency and need are the states against which the strongest defences are erected?

References

Balint, M. (1968) *The Basic Fault*. London and New York: Tavistock.

Fairbairn, W. R. D. (1943) *Psychoanalytic Studies of the Personality*. London: Routledge & Kegan Paul, 1984.

Freud, S. (1905) *Three Essays on the Theory of Sexuality*. London: Hogarth Press and Institute of Psycho-Analysis.

—— (1914) 'On the history of the psychoanalytic movement', *Standard Edition*: 14. London: Hogarth Press, pp. 17–18.

—— (1926) 'Inhibitions symptoms and anxiety', *Standard Edition*: 20. London: Hogarth Press, p. 163.

Guntrip, H. (1968) *Schizoid Phenomena, Object Relations and the Self*. London: The Hogarth Press, 1977.

Klein, M. (1921) 'The development of a child', in *Love, Guilt and Reparation and Other Works, 1921–1945*. London: Hogarth Press and the Institute of Psycho-analysis, 1975.

—— (1927) 'Criminal tendencies in normal children', in *Love, Guilt and Reparation and Other Works 1921–1945*. London: Hogarth Press and the Institute of Psycho-analysis, 1975.

—— (1932) *The Psycho-analysis of Children*. London: Hogarth Press.

Kohut, H. (1977) *The Restoration of the Self*. New York: International Universities Press.

Malcolm, R. Reisenberg (1970) 'The mirror: a perverse sexual phantasy in a woman seen as a defence against a psychotic breakdown', in Elizabeth Bott Spillius (ed.), *Melanie Klein Today: Developments in Theory and Practice*, vol. 2: *Mainly Practice*. London and New York: Routledge

Mitchell, S. A. (1988) *Relational Concepts in Psychoanalysis: An Integration*. Cambridge, MA, and London: Harvard University Press.

Stein, R. (1998) 'The poignant, the excessive and the enigmatic in sexuality', *International Journal of Psychoanalysis* 79(2): 253–68.

Winnicott. D. W. (1958) *Through Paediatrics to Psycho-analysis*. London: Hogarth Press.

Chapter 3

'No sex, please – we're British'

Sexuality in English and French psychoanalysis

Susan Budd

When I was an undergraduate at the LSE in the 1960s, I used to walk past the theatre at the bottom of the Charing Cross Road where the Whitehall farces used to play. For a long time there was a poster outside which advertised the play with this curious name. It was long before I had any particular interest in psychoanalysis, but I was intrigued by the name of the play because it was so contradictory – rather like saying, whatever you do, don't think about elephants. As I remember it, it was black with some curious part-objects floating about on it – a glass of champagne held by a manicured hand, a woman with bright red lips and permed blonde hair, a fleeing leg with a froufrou of petticoats – could there even have been a toff with a top-hat and monocle, or am I transposing that from somewhere else?

All of these were images referring to the body and sex in a knowing way; images of images. They are not directly seductive, like, say, the paintings of the body by Caravaggio or Rembrandt just round the corner in the National Gallery, which are representations of the reality of the flesh and desire, painted by men who could both acknowledge their own and assume, in a way which is neither exhibitionistic nor voyeuristic, that both the subjects of their paintings and the eyes which would view them would share their acceptance of such realities. They are images which are formalised and clichéd references to ideas about sexuality as caricature.

My thesis is that the Anglo-Saxon attitude to sexuality has had considerable influence on the development of psychoanalytic theory in Britain and America.[1] In particular I believe that it has helped

1 I use 'Anglo-Saxon' as a convenient shorthand to refer to those countries – Britain, America, Canada, Australia, etc. – which share a common language and some cultural elements stemming from their common origins. The term is not entirely

foster the dominance of object relations theory and self-psychology. Every body of ideas can only be thought about in the context imposed by a particular time and place. How was Freud domesticated for Anglo-Saxon consumption?

A hundred years ago, Freud's starting point was the process by which the mind represses and distorts thoughts produced by desires which we cannot accept. These unacceptable desires stem from our instinctual life. The two great classes of instinct which he believed we learn to moderate or suppress are the sexual drive, and the imperfectly understood death instinct, sometimes equated with aggression. Throughout his life, he rebuffed attempts to rewrite his theory of sexuality, especially of infantile sexuality, as a theory of the vicissitudes of love or emotional dependence. He wanted to keep a link for psychoanalysis with biology, with the body and with the promptings of the body. If you read the early reactions to Freud when the news of his work reached Britain, he was seen above all as someone who saw sex in everything; as though, if he hadn't existed, sexual fantasy would never have been invented. And it was partly the Bloomsbury group's interest in sex which made them the translators and champions of Freud.

The advertising industry in Britain from the 1930s on was quick to recognise the importance of what Freud had to say about sexual symbols, and developed an iconography of sexual symbolism which they assumed, quite rightly, would influence the buying public. The symbols on the poster were drawn from that tradition. And so we get the champagne glass with its liquid, the blood-red lips, the phallic cigar, the petticoats which mimic and conceal pubic hair (Bowlby 1993).

But as psychoanalysis took root in the London soil, it changed its emphasis in several ways. Many of these changes were linked to the theories of Melanie Klein, an outstandingly gifted clinician who came to live here in the 1920s and laid great emphasis on the way in

appropriate, because probably the majority of psychoanalysts from these societies are wholly or partly Jewish. But it is part of my argument that we imbibe from our milieu our sense of what makes a particular theory congenial without noticing that we are doing so; fish do not notice the water in which they swim. It is also true that several of the leading British object relations theorists – Suttie, Bowlby, Winnicott, Fairbairn, Guntrip – were not Jewish or cosmopolitan emigrés, but came from various parts of the long-established, often provincial English or Scottish middle class. Could this be one reason for their stress on social factors in the genesis of the psyche?

which the very early fantasies of babies live on relatively unchanged in the unconscious lives of adults.

Her ideas chimed in with and influenced those of the small group of English analysts to such an extent that when refugees from Vienna began to arrive in the 1930s, they found that thinking in England had changed so much that some of them thought it was no longer psychoanalysis (King and Steiner 1991).

I suggest that we can link together several themes which caused the change. The attitude to biological and genetic factors characteristic of object relations theory; the ambivalent attitude to the body in both Freud and later psychoanalysis; the characteristic focus in Britain on both child analysis and what is believed to stem from very early experience, and therefore the focus in psychotherapy and analysis with adults on supposedly very early fantasies – often described as pre-oedipal, but, I would argue, pre-sexual; and a British attitude to the erotic life which assumes that if we have good object relations, our sexual lives will not trouble us. In all of this, like most English people, my implicit contrast-class is with the French.

French psychoanalysis tackles these themes very differently, and of course, our fantasies about French sexuality have dominated our perception of the French nation, and ended up, in caricature form, being alluded to in my theatre poster. In the language of cliché, the toff with the top-hat and the monocle surely had a nice little French mistress tucked away in St Johns Wood, or had received some of his erotic education in Gay Paree.

What the poster conveyed so vividly was something George Orwell had commented on as part of the English attitude to sex in his analysis of the dirty postcard. He thought that there was a characteristic national emphasis on smut rather than sex, a kind of knowingness which is pornographic and voyeuristic, whereby sexuality in oneself can be denied by turning a mocking eye on the desire of the other – 'ooh, you are naughty' – rather than a humour which is based on a sexual knowledge which we *ac*knowledge, which is our possession, which, once we are old enough to have it, like the fruit of the tree of knowledge in the garden of Eden, changes everything for ever. The bodies in the seaside postcards, you will remember, are of girls, enviously flat-chested, or rounded and attractive and aware of their power, who metamorphose after marriage into vast sexually experienced creatures, with enormous breasts and thighs and voracious sexual appetites. They tower over small men, anxious about the size of their penises and capacity to keep them up, get them in and get them out again. The postcards reflect a childlike and frightened view of sex and the mother's body.

As the recent reaction to the exposure of the sexuality of public figures shows, there is still something very odd about the Anglo-Saxon attitude to sex. Under the cloak of righteous indignation, there is a desire to shame and punish the powerful which conceals envy and anxiety. We deal with it by trying to deny any kinship with those unfortunates caught in the flashbulbs' glare.

They do things differently there

It would be most unjust to say that the characteristic emphasis on constantly pointing or alluding to sexuality in others whilst denying it oneself is the only influence on Anglo-Saxon psychotherapy and psychoanalysis. At the same time, when I found myself trying to define something which is making me uneasy about the attitude to sexuality which is current in British psychotherapeutic circles, I found the poster came into my mind's eye. It reminded me of the anxieties which have been expressed recently by André Green and Pearl King, two eminent French and English psychoanalysts, about the over-dominance of contemporary psychoanalysis by what is termed the object relations tradition (Green 1995; King 1996). ('Object' in psychoanalytic theory means other people, to whom we relate as the objects of our instinctual desires; but this tradition of thought has gradually eroded Freud's original meaning, and object relations has come to mean something more like interpersonal; that the world is made up of our emotional relations to others, so that a large part of therapy is concerned with the exploration of the relationship with the analyst. Thus much that was previously of interest is now less in focus, at least as we are encouraged to report our cases. In this chapter I want to focus on the switching of attention away from adult sexuality.)

This trend in psychoanalytic theorising has affected even French psychoanalysis. André Green in Paris has apparently been having the same experience as I have:

> when we listen to the material presented by some colleagues . . .
> the manifest presence of sexuality – either through dream mate-
> rial or unconscious fantasy, or even in the reports of the patient's
> life and relationships with others – is interpreted in a way which

bypasses the sphere of sexuality to address object relationships
of a supposedly deeper nature

(Green 1995: 873)

Nonetheless, a cultural climate in which the erotic can be thought
about more clearly and carefully does seem to have influenced the
development of French psychoanalysis.

In the recent volume of interviews with French psychoanalysts,
She Speaks/He Listens, edited by Elaine Baruch and Lucienne
Serrano, two American feminists and professors of literature, we can
see how the Anglo-Saxon attitude to sex looks, viewed from the other
side of the Channel. Several French analysts were struck by the difference of attitude between themselves and their American colleagues. They laid stress on the inherent differences in sexuality
between men and women, and on something which is forever
unrealised, tragic, unreachable. Gerard Pommier, for example, saw
masculine and feminine desire as fundamentally different. Feminine
desire is marked by feeling rejected and abandoned by the father; and
this very desire provokes sadism in men, who find feminine suffering
arousing. The editors comment 'This is a far more pessimistic and
sexually differentiated view than Kernberg's' (an eminent American
psychoanalyst) 'which holds that the two sexes arrive at the same
place at the end of the journey toward love, however different their
routes' (Baruch and Serrano 1996: 12).

Similarly, for Didier-Weill, the split between (m)other/whore can
never be ended. 'Americans are more optimistic about love – and sex.
They tend to think that with a few minor changes, men and women
can move to harmony just around the corner.' And Kernberg thinks
that 'French psychoanalysts have been exploring the nature of the
erotic much more systematically than analysts in other countries'
(Baruch and Serrano 1996: 14, 156–62). The influence of Lacan on
psychoanalytic thought is stronger in Latin countries – Europe and
Latin America – than in the Anglo-Saxon countries and Germany.
Where it has taken root in England, it is in academic courses on
psychoanalysis, or feminism, or literature, rather than in the major
clinical trainings.

The Lacanian influence both stresses the links of psychoanalysis
with philosophy and literary studies rather than with therapy, and
sees the experience of men and women as necessarily different, dis-
crepant, and tragic in that the gap between the Ideal and the Real
can never really be closed. The origins of sexual desire are in the real-

isation of lack, of unbridgeable difference between ourselves and the other, brought about by the intervention of both the Father and the Law (the *nom/non du père*). From this alienation, the mother-gone-away, springs language.

This way of thinking is not only derived from the late Freud of *Civilization and Its Discontents*, but also reflects the impact of Structuralism, strong in the European intellectual milieu but less so in the Anglo-Saxon countries. Structuralism addresses itself to the question, What is inherent, innate, in the human psyche, and will emerge as akin to deep grammar in any circumstances, and what is contingent upon particular experiences and culturally generated ways of understanding them, however transformed by fantasy? This question is central to psychoanalysis; for example, in thinking about the difference between men and women, reality and fantasy, the innate and the acquired, sexuality and perversion. I would argue that these issues have begun to be addressed by Anglo-Saxon psychoanalysts less because of the influence of Lacan than because of the growth of sociobiology and neuropsychology as rival explanations of human nature.

I return to this question in the final section of the chapter, but in the meantime it is worth noting how differently the object relations tradition and French psychoanalysts see normal human sexuality. The French lay stress on the inherent differences in sexuality between men and women, and on something which is forever unrealised, tragic, unreachable. Guyomard, for example, thinks that much follows from the difficult acknowledgement of the weight of the Real – ie. the intrinsic difference between the desires and points of view of men and women – which he believes that many American analysts try to minimise. Maybe, he thinks, women desire fusion more than men do – they idealise from close up because of the original close-ness to the early mother, whereas men fear it. Maybe not just our early experience, but bodily differences themselves, condemn us to experience desire differently. It follows from this that we must always be alert to the sex of our patients, and not inadvertently transpose our own experience onto someone of the opposite sex (Baruch and Serrano 1996: 18). Several of the French analysts interviewed commented on the 'feminising' of psychoanalysis: the changing emphasis which brings mother–baby relations to the fore as the prototype of all human exchanges.

When I have heard therapists talking about which sort of patient they find the hardest to understand and empathise with – is it someone from a different race? or someone whom they find morally repugnant – a child-abuser or a fascist? or someone whose experience is hard to imagine, like being born blind? – I have never yet heard anyone say that they find it hard to understand the physical experience of the opposite sex. And yet in listening to student psychotherapists, especially women, describing how they see and talk to young male patients who are sexually very active, I sometimes find myself thinking that they have resorted rather quickly to interpreting their sexual behaviour as if it was a derivate of a pre-oedipal rather than an oedipal wish. The active sexuality of young men is seen as Don Juanism; an anxious infantile desire to reassure oneself by entering as many mothers' bodies as possible and then panicking and moving on.

Maybe women therapists unconsciously generalise from the experience of most women, who enjoy sex more if it is within the context of a relationship where they feel safe and known, whilst failing to realise that for many men, sex with a stranger is extremely enjoyable and the way you get to know them. If they enjoy sex with you, you feel incomparably validated because actions speak louder than words. (Perhaps it's not just the sex of patient and therapist which is at issue; it's also that the middle-aged forget the intensities of youth.) When I gave an earlier version of this chapter to a group of psychotherapists, I was struck by the contrast in the discussion between the circumspect and detached comments of the women and the man who straightforwardly owned his counter-transference feelings of sexual attraction to a woman patient.

I have noticed that stories about doctors and therapists who end up having sexual relations with their patients nearly always involve a male therapist and a female patient. Such relationships are – rightly – condemned. But I have also heard several accounts of women therapists who have abused their patients in a subtler way, by making them into their children. In the extreme case the therapist – perhaps rather old and lonely – has demanded a part in her patient's real life, or takes the patient into her home. It is interesting that such cases are less castigated; as if it is harder to see mother-love, however inappropriate, as harmful, than it is to see sexual relations between therapist and patients as abusive.

Such feminisation of psychoanalysis, by exalting the mother–infant relationship, de-emphasises what is more specific to male experience: castration anxiety and the particular relationship of a boy with his father. The Oedipus complex has become understood in a more general way, as being when the child has to accept that two people to whom he or she is attached have a relationship with each other which excludes them. Juliet Mitchell suggests that the move toward a de-gendered version of object relations theory may be influenced by a decline in the proportion of children in England and America who are brought up in households where the biological father is present throughout childhood and adolescence (Mitchell 1997: 28–9). The father is doubly absent; both as a permanent member of the household, and specifically as a man, rather than as someone who is a substitute caregiver when it is his turn to look after the children. She suggests that the emphasis in Kleinian theory on the cruel, primitive superego may well be because in such a situation the Oedipus complex cannot be successfully negotiated, a process in which the real presence of a father-figure is crucial so that the child can develop a more benign and flexible superego which can help successfully sublimate the instincts.

The beast in man

Psychoanalysts are privileged, just as the outside world thinks we are, to hear how people really, really feel and act about sex. What strikes me above all is the wide range of variation; some people at the start of therapy talk about sex much of the time; others never. But men do seem to talk about sex more, and to see it as something which defines and makes a successful relationship. They are often preoccupied with how well they feel they are performing, and how their partner responds. With women the emphasis is usually quite different; they are more preoccupied with the relationship as a whole, and with their feelings about having or not having children. Interestingly, I have heard from a few highly attractive women with an active, 'male' sexuality, who seek for and enjoy casual sexual encounters, that the men they proposition seem to be afraid of them more often than they respond enthusiastically.

It is foolhardy to make generalisations about human behaviour, but these tendencies have an obvious link with what evolutionary biologists think are the biological givens, the neo-Darwinian strategies for each sex to most effectively perpetuate its genes. Women want to attract and hold a mate to protect them while they bring up offspring; men have to choose between intercourse with as many partners as possible, or deciding that their success on the open market will be limited, so they should find one woman and have children by her.

To argue in this way from inferred instincts creates considerable anxiety; probably in the readers of this chapter as well as in its author. Freud pointed out that Darwin affronts our narcissism by treating us as members of the animal kingdom, but as Mary Midgley puts it, 'we are not just rather like animals, we *are* animals' (Midgley 1980: xiv). In other words, if animal sexual behaviour can be successfully explained in terms of instinctual drives, then, however muted and overridden, these instincts are alive in us too.

It has been all too easy for sociobiologists to assume that whatever is, is inevitable. The history of the application of evolutionary ideas to human behaviour is littered with this kind of error. The twentieth century saw continuous debate over how far human beings – or even social animals – are what they are because of their genetic inheritance, or because they had been moulded by the social circumstances they were born into. The rise of the social sciences favoured the plastic view of man; the millennium seems to be marked by the return of explanations based more on biology or neurology. The history of social Darwinism itself shows that our assumptions about human nature are thoroughly relativist. Nonetheless, all theoretical explanations of human behaviour must contain assumptions about human nature. Matters become even more heated if we consider the differences between the sexes. 'Unmaternal mothers', 'unmanly men'; these oxymorons point to the powerful feelings aroused by challenges to particular gender conceptions.

One could write the history of psychoanalysis in this way. The first analysts were nearly all men, and centred their discussion of sexual difference on the possession or lack of a penis. The next generation of analysts were far more likely to be women, mothers and feminists, and Kleinian theory, with its stress on the importance of the child's fantasy of the mother's body, which contains both breasts and vagina but also the penis, was naturally very attractive to them. Guyomard thinks that Lacan was part of a third generation of analysts who had to cope with powerful women like Anna Freud, Marie Bonaparte, Melanie Klein and Jeanne Lampl de Groot, who were making psychoanalysis into a woman's field (Baruch and Serrano 1996: 76).

Freud wanted to root psychoanalysis in biology. I became interested in psychoanalysis partly because I felt that the view of human nature current in the social sciences was over-socialised. I was encouraged in this view by a paper by Dennis Wrong, an American sociologist, who argued, 'that material interests, sexual drives, and the quest for power have often been overestimated as human motives is no reason to deny their reality'. The twentieth century has seen the rise of *Homo sociologicus*, perhaps at its apogee with Margaret Mead's remark that 'Human nature is almost unbelievably malleable, responding accurately and contrastingly to contrasting cultural traditions.' Inevitably, psychoanalysis was affected by the general emphasis on the learnt, culturally relative explanations of human behaviour, partly because neo-Darwinian explanations had become so discredited by their use in eugenic and racialist circles. To quote Wrong again, 'in the beginning there is the body. As soon as the body is mentioned the spectre of biological determinism raises its head, and sociologists draw back in fright' (Wrong 1961). And not only sociologists.

The rise of object relations theory can be seen in this way; it sees the baby and the child as existing in a world which is above all made up of its relations to other people. At the extreme, the baby becomes a *tabula rasa*, responding to the particular experiences, good and bad, which it has with its parents, uncomplicated by instinct or its derivate, unconscious fantasy. Such a baby is innocent; the adults are always to blame. Almost no psychoanalysts think this; but a version of some Anglo-Saxon psychoanalytic thought can be translated in this way. But psychoanalysis has to take account of the fact that human beings are both organisms and persons. It was the centrality of sexuality to psychoanalysis which distinguished it from other psychologies, as a means of relating the body to the psyche. Freud made the drive superordinate to the object; object relations theory has reversed the process (Gill 1994: 139–54).

What I am arguing, put very crudely, is that maybe in Britain psychoanalysts such as Donald Winnicott, Ronald Fairbairn, John Bowlby and Melanie Klein were read in a way which reinforced a national uneasiness with the nature of genital sexuality, which involves two different bodies, an acceptance of desire and a loss of control, and a complex interplay between bodily drives and a relationship to another human being.

Bowlby did stress the role of evolutionary biology and the instincts in the child's development, but focused on attachment; the drive to stay close to the object to feel safe. Winnicott did refer to adult sexuality as heir to the excited, ruthless feelings of the infant, but he has become remembered for his insights into mothers and babies, and the regression of adult patients to very early states of feeling and being in order to feel more authentic. Fairbairn seems to have thought that psychic activity begins with object-seeking rather than pleasure-seeking, and that if the baby or child's bodily impulses are received reasonably kindly, sexuality is not problematic – so nothing gets repressed and no troublesome unconscious fantasies form. Melanie Klein retained the idea of instinct, but put the Oedipus complex, i.e. the end of instinctual development, so early that genital sexuality never really gets separated from oral and anal fantasy. The concern to redress the previous centrality of castration anxiety and penis envy by emphasising the importance of women was more important than the classical emphasis on stages of psychic development.

One reason, perhaps, why British psychoanalysis has been so comparatively ready to abandon instinct for object relations theory is that because we have always accepted lay, i.e. non-medical, analysts from the beginning a high and ever-rising proportion of analysts have been women. The long and expensive medical training which is the precursor to analytic training in many countries would have deterred many women from entering the profession. Lack of a medical or biological training makes it easier to overlook the instinctual component in human behaviour, and has led to instincts being contrasted with object relations, instead of the two being seen as inseparable and mutually influential. Many of the pioneers in British psychoanalysis were women involved in education and child development; not only Anna Freud and Melanie Klein, but Isaacs, Riviere, Brierley, Sharpe, Payne, Milner and Searl. And Winnicott and Bowlby were paediatricians.[2] Psychoanalysis was most easily accepted in Britain as a way of dealing with the problems of women and children, rather than as part of the rite of passage to membership of the intelligentsia, as it apparently became in New York or Paris.

Guyomard thinks that if psychoanalysis becomes the domain of women and children, questions of sexual difference and paternity tend to be put aside in favour of the dominance of mother–child relationships. The analyst,

> little by little, risks retransforming her analysands into little children before the moment when the question of sexual difference was posed. Like many other social professions that deal with childhood, for example, teaching, there is a way of thinking

2 I am indebted to Victoria Hamilton for this and other helpful comments.

that holds that psychoanalysis should be performed mainly by women. That would mean that something maternal takes over; at the same time there would be a kind of subterranean disqualification of the psychoanalytic function . . . . We are dealing here with the weight of the social order. Psychoanalysis is threatened by . . . forgetting that it is not only dealing with the maternal. It concerns desire, that is, the connection with the other sex, with the relation to the mother and to the father. It concerns the question of death, of jouissance, of madness, and certainly the maternal, but not only the maternal.

(Baruch and Serrano 1996: 76–7)

His Majesty the Baby

I would link the French awareness of the limitations of the object relations tradition to the current English tendency to interpret material within a rather de-instinctualized version of the mother–baby transference. The various expressions of instinct and feeling toward the therapist are talked about in terms of 'your baby self'. To my mind, this phraseology is being used to disavow both the fact that the feelings are being expressed by and towards two people who are actually adults, and that they are powerful and related to instinctual life, both sexual and aggressive. I think it feels easier to cope with if both therapist and patient can think of them as being expressed by an innocent and helpless baby homunculus within the adult patient. André Green puts it thus: 'These ideas are consequences of the fact that we think of patients as babies. The anal, oral, or in other terminologies, the depressive position and the schizoid-paranoid positions, being older or deeper, are equated with being more important' (1995: 874).

If students are taught to focus on the transference to the mother-analyst, they will of course conceive of the patient as an ungendered baby. But patients are not babies, and I think that it can make them feel both frightened and triumphant if their real adult sexuality is overlooked in this way, let alone everything which was added in as they became toddlers, children, adolescents, and finally adults of one sex or another. Their changing bodies brought changing instinctual emphases. The effect of concentrating on the interaction between patient and analyst at the expense of reconstruction is to move away from castration anxiety, realised differently by each sex to parents of either sex, towards a general ungendered persecutory anxiety about both parents. (This is connected with uncertainty as to whether the sex of the therapist really matters, or whether the transference turns us completely into either sex.)

The tendency to talk as if all patients were at a baby stage is not only true of women therapists dealing with male patients, but perhaps it is commoner amongst them. Their interpretations often contain an assumption that once the patient's object relations are improved, their sexuality will give them no problems. Unfortunately, this is not always the case, most especially in sexual perversions, where often the most that can be achieved is to enable the patient to remain sexually inactive rather than acting in ways unacceptable to him (it is mostly a him) or us. The French would argue that the realisation of our sexual natures continues to be a problem for all of us, and Green quotes Freud at the end of his life, reflecting on the intrinsically lacking, unsatisfying aspect of sexuality, and *doing so in French*. 'There is always something lacking for complete discharge and satisfaction – en attendant toujours quelquechose qui ne venait point' (Freud 1941: 300).

As Freud grew older he became more pessimistic about the intrinsic conflict between sexual instinct and fantasy and what could be realised in reality. In a masterly summary of these issues, Dana Breen pointed out that 'for some the real Freud is the one who separates psychoanalysis from biology, while for others the biological substratum is basic to an understanding of sexuality. This is an inherent contradiction and duality which lies at the heart of psychoanalysis and sexuality – the study of unconscious meanings and fantasies which have the body as their seat' (Breen 1993: 37).

Pearl King has argued that the current English preoccupation with object relations and 'here and now' interpretations takes away the potential of looking at the patient's history, of their changing instinctual needs as they grew older, and of the relative contributions that their internal objects and the external world are making both to their relationship to the therapist and to their relationships in the external world. To focus exclusively on the transference makes us ignore many things which Freud and others thought were crucial to psychoanalysis, amongst them free association (if the patient knows we always interpret within the transference they'll stop talking about much else); the repetition-compulsion, which is based on instinct; the idea of developmental stages which affect bodily experience; and the operation of instinctual impulses (King 1996).

A final example

You can often find in second-hand bookshops a book by Ian Suttie, *The Origins of Love and Hate*, first published in 1935, a few days after the death of its author, a Scottish psychiatrist who had just come to London to work at the Tavistock Clinic (Suttie 1935). In John Bowlby's introduction to a reissue of the book in 1988, he grouped Suttie with the object relations school; with the Hungarians after Ferenzi, with Winnicott, Guntrip, Fairbairn, Kohut, Sullivan and himself, all of whom believed that the most important influences on human development were how children were treated by their parents, in particular by separations from or losses of parent figures. Psychoanalysts were quick to note that this emphasis downplayed infant sexuality. Money-Kyrle (1936), reviewing the book for the *International Journal of Psychoanalysis*, commented that his views 'will be well-received by all who wish to underestimate the extent of infantile sexuality', and doubtless this contributed to its popular success in Britain. I briefly outline Suttie's views, as they seem to me characteristic of a particular Anglo-Saxon take on sexuality.

Suttie described at length how he came to reject Freud's outlook. He thought the 'need-for-companionship', for love, was more important than sex; the need for security was more important to the child than sensual feelings of pleasure, and the basis of social life. 'Hate and aggressiveness are merely the result of thwarted love.' Love was 'essentially a state of active harmonious interplay . . . genetically independent of genital appetite'. He felt that the influence of Darwin would change psychoanalytic thinking, together with accepting that man was by nature essentially social, and the work of child psychologists which showed that the important figure in the child's early life was not the father but the mother. Play and cultural achievements were replacements for our mutually caressing relationship with her, produced, not by our instincts, but by our prolonged immaturity and our lack of instincts. Hate is a development of separation-anxiety. 'Evolution has left man with so little definite biological guidance in the form of instinct.'

Suttie argued that there was a taboo on tenderness, in the society as a whole and between therapist and patient, based on cultural pressures on child-rearing which made children ashamed of their infantile dependence and forced them to try to grow up quickly. He thought that psychoanalytic theory was changing, placing more emphasis on the earliest period before mother and child were differentiated; on sibling-rivalry for the mother's affection, on men's jealousy of women rather than penis envy. Most crucially for my argument, he also thought that if we tolerated the expression of tenderness, human sexuality would become non-problematic. The absence of sexual taboos would free the sexual impulse and lead to its 'satiety in marital intercourse'. 'Mating would be satisfactory, and man would have a natural tendency toward monogamy.'

I feel that here Suttie exemplifies exactly what French analysts are struck by: a complacency about the nature of human sexual experience linked to a de-instinctualized and watered-down version of psychoanalysis; and I would argue that this perspective has affected the understanding of psychoanalysis as it has become acculturated in Britain.

Where does this leave us?

Psychoanalysis is accused at times of supporting biological determinism – *vide* the debate over penis-envy, or biology as destiny – but at times it is seen as a psychology which describes the creation and modification of the psyche by the individual's experience. The American anthropologist Abram Kardiner, for example, one of the foremost exponents of the culture and personality school, approved of psychoanalysis, despite thinking its assumptions about human nature were too influenced by its central European origins, because he saw it as a psychology which acknowledged the plasticity of the psyche (Kardiner 1945). He thought that very little was inborn in human beings; for example, 'it is an error to deal with gregariousness as a biologically determined trait', whereas now we think of babies as instinctively object-seeking from birth, and there are good biological reasons in terms of their likelihood of surviving to make them so.

Object relations theory has many strands, and many of them are correct and have changed psychoanalysis for good. Research into infancy and early childhood shows clearly that babies are related to others from the beginning, and that indeed, the need for security and for love is crucially important. But we all grow older, and as we do, our bodies, intelligences and emotions change irreversibly. We are not whom we once were, and I think that we too glibly assume, firstly, that interpretations aimed at supposed states of very early experience are the most powerful and effective ones; and secondly, that if we cope with pre-genital aspects of object relations the later ones will turn out all right and our sexual lives will be trouble-free; and that in therapy we can somehow get past the adult, to whom we are talking in words, to the totally different being that we were in childhood. Our life's experience after the first year or so of life is not just an overlay, or the prison round the growing boy. One of the greatest British cultural achievements is our children's literature; the capacity of both writer and reader to remember and empathise with how it felt to be a child. But if we assume that childhood really was like that, or that we can speak across the years directly to the child within, I think that we are throwing psychoanalysis away. At its best, psychoanalysis is an infinitely subtle and complex way of exploring the web of memory, desire, construction and reconstruction that we have built up around us to give our lives meaning. It exists not only in our minds but also in our bodies. They remember our earliest experience and speak, in the form of what we enjoy or find repugnant in sexual experience; in the content of the exact routines that are needed to achieve orgasm in sexual perversion; and most dramatically of all, in the physical symptoms which remember and proscribe sexual satisfaction.

Every society, every time, must see psychoanalysis through its own lens; truth, Max Weber said, is like a diamond. As it revolves, each facet catches the light. We are dazzled by its illumination and sparkle, but the shine conceals all the nearby facets from us. It is only as it continues to revolve that slightly different facets can be viewed. I am not arguing that the English object relations perspective contains no truth, but that we need to be aware of the cultural bias which has fostered it. Psychoanalysts often brush such considerations aside, believing that our insights in the session take us deeper than mere social conditioning, into the universals of human nature. But all our thought – just as that of any experimental scientist – is necessarily shot through with our assumptions about the world. Psychoanalysis, with the emotional penumbra that it carries, is particularly likely to founder on the rocks of relativity, and even more so if it persists in maintaining that they are not there.

References

Baruch, E. H. and Serrano, L. J. (1996) *She Speaks/He Listens: Women on the French Analyst's Couch*. New York: Routledge.

Bowlby, R. (1993) *Shopping With Freud*. London: Routledge, ch. 7.

Breen, D. (1993) *The Gender Conundrum: Contemporary Psychoanalytic*

Perspectives on Femininity and Masculinity. London: Routledge.

Gill, M. M. (1994) *Psychoanalysis in Transition: A Personal View.* Hillsdale, New Jersey: Analytic Press.

Green, A. (1995) 'Has sexuality anything to do with psychoanalysis?' *International Journal of Psychoanalysis* 76(5): 871–83.

Freud, S. (1941) 'Findings, ideas, problems', *Standard Edition* 23. London: Hogarth.

Kardiner, A. (1945) *The Psychological Frontiers of Society.* New York: Columbia University Press.

King, P. (1996) 'What has happened to psychoanalysis in the British society?', unpublished paper given to the Psychoanalytic Forum.

King, P. and Steiner, R. (1991) *The Freud–Klein Controversies, 1941–45.* London: Routledge.

Midgley, M. (1980) *Beast and Man: The Roots of Human Nature.* London: Methuen.

Mitchell, J. (1997) 'Sexuality, psychoanalysis and social changes', *International Psychoanalytic Association Newsletter* 6(1): 28–9.

Money-Kyrle, R. E. (1936) Book review: '*The Origins of Love and Hate* by Ian D. Suttie', *International Journal of Psychoanalysis* 17: 137–8.

Suttie, I. D. (1935) *The Origins of Love and Hate*, republished in 1988 with a foreword by John Bowlby. London: Free Association Books.

Wrong, D. H. (1961) 'The oversocialised conception of man in modern sociology', *American Sociological Review* 26(2): 83–93.

Chapter 4

The madness of love
A Jungian perspective on sexuality

Jean Thomson

Jung is not usually associated with sexuality. In contemporary psychotherapy, therefore, 'Jungians' seem considered either, negatively, to be less able to deal with sexuality in the transference, or, more positively, to be free of the prejudices arising from Freudian views on perversion. The words 'Jung' and 'sex', for many psychotherapists, seem to connect only when they think of Jung as having been a sexual transgressor.

The view of Jung as transgressor has evolved in the context of the dynamic conflict between the groups which form the broadly psychoanalytic world. It has been a matter as much of the establishment of political power around a theory of human relationships, as of the castigation of wrongdoing. I am, therefore, going to discuss a situation which illustrates the evolution of transference and libido theories by talking about the story of the relationship between three of the early figures in the history of psychoanalysis. What happened between Dr Jung and Dr Spielrein, and how Dr Freud became involved, has become part of psychoanalytic folklore, indeed it forms a myth in the oral history of the time. My account is a kind of case history of how a modern myth can grow from a touching and remarkable story belonging to the early years of the twentieth century when the foundations were being laid for psychoanalytic practice as we know it today. The vicissitudes of the relationship between the three protagonists not only show how differences in libido theory arose but throw light on the emotional involvement we now call transference.

Context

The names of the originators of psychoanalysis tend to become symbolic of an aspect of psychodynamic theories. Few of us explore the biographies or know much of the thoughts and writings of more than one or two of historically famous analysts. Amongst them, Freud, now a definition rather than a person, remains associated with sexuality. Despite criticisms, Freud is, to the general public, the good guy of sex, preaching understanding and continent sexual behaviour but warning of the dark and violent passions which lie beneath civilised exteriors. Jung, popularly, by contrast is linked with the spirit (rather than the flesh). In fact he researched the *relationship between mind and matter* as a scientist and clinician at a time when there was a belief that there *was* no link. He was fascinated by the vast universe of the human imagination, which he gradually came to think enabled humans to 'know' their origins. Freud gradually dissociated himself from these wider spheres and built work based in practical, clinical observations of individual patients. Through studying patients and also himself and his friends, he was able to define a context for his work as the individual's personal development in the family. Jung, while becoming increasingly interested in individuation, continued to keep clinical work in the context of culture and spirit. His ideas are thus less easy to apply in the consulting-room than those which have evolved from Freud's work.

For a few years Jung and Freud came together and shared their ideas, and then they took different psychotherapeutic pathways. Sabina Spielrein, a woman, patient and later psychoanalyst, was a significant figure in the early movement although by now her work is almost forgotten. Freud's emphasis on detailed work of analyst and patient enabled psychoanalysis to survive through all the political ideologies and wars of the twentieth century. He concentrated on the family life of the individual, emphasising family influences rather than state or culture. In 1913, when Jung and Freud finally repudiated each other, Freud's supporters formed a 'brotherhood', which had a defensive aspect and held them together through the First World War and then the gradual coming to power of the National Socialist movement in Germany. This Brotherhood, as Phyllis Grosskurth (1991) and John Kerr (1994) recount, bonded strongly and emphasised psychoanalysis as a clinical treatment for psychological disorders, funded by private fees. It avoided the wider political arena.

Jung himself remained much more involved in the socio-political developments of the time. Most of Freud's analytic circle were Jewish, and one of the reasons Freud gave for welcoming Jung to join him was that he was not. No doubt, as anti-Semitism gathered, as a non-Jew it was safer for Jung to continue to place psychological development in its cultural and religious context. The break between the men was not connected with race on either side, but Jung's efforts and some of his statements as a psychiatrist in Germany have resulted in accusations of racism and anti-Semitism which discredit him as much as the accusations about sexual transgression. It is difficult to know how much of this is valid and how much his participation was the result of mistaken ideals about influencing the regime and maintaining the presence of psychoanalysis as a treatment for the people. In the early 1930s Hitler was immensely popular and still giving Germans hope. National Socialism was still associated with International Socialism as a remedy for social injustice (Watson 1998). Some of Freud's other associates such as Adler and Reich had earlier broken away from Freud, not so much for theoretical reasons about analysis, but because they felt that psychoanalytic treatment and, later, training should be for the widest range of people. Adler thought treatment should be free for all (Kerr 1994). These debates exist to the present day and the fact is often ignored that disputes which appear to be about clinical differences are actually about political ideas. Certainly, it is clear that whatever his faults as a man, Jung committed himself to keeping psychoanalytic thinking in its political and sociological context as well as a theory for clinical practice.

In the course of this history, 'Jung' (like 'Freud') became less a description of one man than a mythology combining fact and oral history. He became the Shadow of the psychoanalytic movement. Sexuality and madness, perceived unconsciously as psychic dangers, are often projected onto Jungians, leaving the rest of the psychoanalytic world to claim the capacity to hold to rational boundaries and professional ethics. The ultimate in contemporary ideology is to portray Jung as a sexual transgressor, an idea which emerged in the split which occurred between the two men in 1913, after which Freud's colleagues formed a close, closed group around him. This group's activities came to represent Freudian ideas. Discrediting Jung helped, and his involvement with Sabina Spielrein played a part, then and now, in establishing the boundaries for psychoanalysis.

As the letters between them show, the relationship between Jung and Freud was intensely erotic as well as intellectual, as was the relationship between Jung and Sabina Spielrein (McGuire 1974). Physical feelings are now recognised to be part of eros and thus of what make human fantasies about relating interesting and exciting. The mystery of the Jung–Spielrein relationship remains, however.

Did they or did they not actually act on sexual desire and have a physical sexual relationship? It is on this that the doubts about Jung's behaviour hang and why the whole story is relevant to our worries and fears in modern psychotherapy about power and sexuality in the transference and about the nature of abuse.

In the 1900s when the concepts were beginning to be understood as we are familiar with them today, Jung experimented and researched treatment of psychotic patients, using discussion and word association tests, at the Burgholzli Hospital in Switzerland while Freud was developing psychoanalytic treatment in Austria. They debated then as we continue to debate now the nature of transference and how to hold to boundaries which will protect our patients from exploitation. This is relevant for any professional or personal relationship where one party is in a position of power and responsibility over another.

Libido and sexuality

How do Jungian and Freudian views on libido differ? Jungians generally think of libido as energy (life energy) of which sexuality is a part, rather than of libido as being equivalent to sexuality. In his invaluable summary of Jungian psychology, *Jung and the Post-Jungians*, Andrew Samuels (1985) quotes R.D. Laing (1967) as saying that Jung stated 'the schizophrenic ceases to be schizophrenic when he meets someone by whom he feels understood'. The nub of transference theory could be said to be the vicissitudes of *feeling* understood for both therapist and patient.

Libidinal energy motivates curiosity and creativity and stimulates the human imagination. It involves the whole body/mind/emotional being. Jung's wide appeal to those puzzled by simplifications about the purpose of sexual life are often drawn to his interest in the spiritual dimension but rarely seem to see that Jung was also evolving a social theory. His ideas explain the power of sex in the erotic attractions of everyday life, which are the glue of social interactions. He put reproductive needs into a wider context and implied that the establishment of an ego syntonic with what Jungians view as the Self, the inner core system, is related to experience from conception to death within each culture. We cannot be conscious of much of this until physical maturation allows the development of consciousness, and even then much experience remains unverbalised.

The myth of 'Spielrein and Jung'

An eminent psychoanalytic colleague said to me recently with a mischievous smile: 'Of course, Jung had affairs with his patients.' It seemed that he was referring to the book by Alberto Carotenuto (1984) which had brought Dr Sabina Spielrein out of the obscurity into which she had fallen. I read this and other accounts and thought that her fate was that of many women who compete in the professions. Her work had been lost in her involvement in personal relationships with competitive male colleagues. All that is now remembered in psychoanalytic folklore seemed to be that she was once a patient of Jung's.

As I pondered on this and her time in the Burgholzli psychiatric hospital where Jung was her psychiatrist, I recalled a brilliant attempt based on her life story, to *imagine* the pervasive psychotic realities of such a hospital. A play, *Sabina*, by Snoo Wilson, depicts Spielrein in 1904 in the asylum where Dr Jung is a psychiatrist. It is not a factual account but an imaginative plunge into the world of institutional projective identifications. This 1998 production by the anarchistic Theatre Workshop at the Bush Theatre in Hammersmith, London, gave some idea of what young Dr Jung was up against as he tried to understand the world of dementia praecox, as psychosis was then called. The production succeeded, although not to everyone's taste, in creating the atmosphere of madness in a confined group, a dynamic environment where it becomes difficult to know who is deluded and who is more obviously rational. Of course, the ideas about madness which the author calls upon, the notions of collective projective identifications through which unconscious fantasies take over, were not conceptualised at the time.

My own understandings of the play are informed not only by Jungian psychology but by ideas I took in as a group relations practitioner. According to these the emotional life of an institution is formed of the psyches of the individuals which comprise it in such a way that the inner life of the individual is in constant unconscious interaction with the external groups of which he or she is part. The groups themselves form histories and emotional beliefs and create a sense of a whole culture. The groups and the institution can be analysed and to some extent understood, just as the individual can be analysed as influenced by inner and outer experience. The play therefore to me seemed to be an example of what Jung described as Active Imagination, a picture which demonstrates verbal and non-verbal processes in a group.

In the tiny theatre, in a room above a pub, the audience sat on tiered, narrow benches around the circular stage space, almost amongst the players. For me, a fearful and confusing feeling of sense and non-sense evolved, of restriction and confusion. The permeable boundary between the acceptable and the unacceptable, the perverse and the normal, the funny and the tragic, the sexual and the aesthetic, drew players and audience into an atmosphere of institutionalised madness in which Jung's and Sabina's inner and outer worlds started to feel interchangeable. This atmosphere reminded me of the community at Shenley Psychiatric Hospital (Hertfordshire) in the 1960s, where staff and patients lived as a community in villas on a large estate of gardens where most patients could wander freely, although some were in locked villa/wards. The aim was to understand psychotic and bizarre behaviour. The effects of institutionalisation on staff and patients created a feeling of interchangeability, in the sense that it was acknowledged to be difficult often to know who was patient and who staff. Living in that enclosed setting the effects of institutionalisation on staff and patients could be seen in a way impossible in our dispersed society.

Applying this sort of idea to the play, I thought that *Sabina* managed to depict what we can learn about transference through the temptations of working with patients when the erotic, as a need for emotional connection, can be felt as a sexual imperative impossible to resist. Then it can so easily translate into a belief that physical action will be the best course. The play portrays a forbidden sexual relationship between a doctor and his patient. As it takes place in the atmosphere of fantasy, where no-one knows what is really happening or what is imagined to be happening, Wilson ably shows how the rumours about Jung could have begun (and indeed demonstrates the hazards of spending time alone with a patient whose erotic fantasies pervade the analysis). The play exemplifies the compulsiveness of sexuality.

The performance was, in other words, a powerful dramatic illustration of emotional engagement, a case history of the madness which in other circumstances might have been called a love affair. In the play Dr Jung is a solemn young psychiatrist already married and working at the Burgholzli Psychiatric Hospital in Zurich. He is in communication with Freud by letter. Encouraged by the director of the hospital, Eugene Bleuler, he is studying psychotic patients, trying to understand what they were trying to convey through their delusions and hallucinations. Her sex-obsessed parents bring young

Sabina to him. We are told she is a 'hysteric', borderline psychotic, manifesting in obsessive sexuality, mainly masturbation, and anal preoccupations. The kind of drug therapy familiar to us nowadays was not developed until after the Second World War, so in 1904 when she was admitted to the Burgholzli aged 19, it would be a madhouse indeed with an atmosphere of authoritarian repression and pervasive psychosis. Jung was experimenting with psychotherapy. Sabina, albeit in the throes of unrestrained sexualised hyperactivity, is an attractive girl, and in the play Jung sits by her bed trying to discuss her feelings and fantasies, while she wildly masturbates and tries to seduce him. Eventually (in the play) he is seduced and they have a passionate physical relationship. Sabina calms down and becomes more accessible to talk and less taken over by her delusions and her compulsive sexualised release of tension and withheld energy. Through the relationship with Jung, she begins to contain and understand her feelings. He, too, learns from the experience and, as the psychotic element in their passion decreases, he realises that he must bring the relationship to an end. He refers her to Freud and her parents take her to undergo psychoanalysis in Vienna.

This is a fictionalised version of the Spielrein story which Alberto Carotenuto unearthed in 1984, and which John Kerr wrote about at greater length ten years later, and Zvi Lothane in 1999. Wilson rearranges facts and dates to suit his creation. I have described his play because it conveys so well the confusion for all involved in the Jung–Spielrein relationship. As she recovered, Sabina was able to emerge from her immersion and take a cognitive look at herself and her therapist.

The life of Sabina Spielrein

The play is the artist's imagined version and some of the facts of the matter are due, in order to put Dr Spielrein and Dr Jung back into the history of transference and sexuality. Some of Spielrein's diaries and letters are reproduced in Carotenuto's book and more are being published, so my facts will be brief. The diaries show that some of her symptoms began in childhood and that she received psychiatric treatment from age 14. The various sources state that Jung treated her in the Burgholzli in 1904 and later in his private practice in Zurich. After she left hospital (in 1906), she studied medicine at Zurich University. The relationship with Jung gradually changed from patient to student to colleague. They discussed work and read each other's papers. Jung and Spielrein did not have a physical affair while she was in hospital and they may never have consummated their deep attachment to each other. She moved to Vienna in 1912, having completed her medical degree, including psychiatry. Seemingly disillusioned with Jung, she went into analysis with Freud. Later she became a psychoanalyst and was the second woman admitted to the Vienna Psychoanalytical Society (up to then closed to women). In 1907 Jung had designated her case as one of 'psychotic hysteria' (Carotenuto, ibid.) and in correspondence with Freud, she is then and later talked of by both men either as a patient or as 'a little girl'.

As a medical student Spielrein studied her own files for material for her paper: 'The psychological content of a case of schizophrenia'. This no longer appears in 'specialised literature' on schizophrenia, perhaps because it 'bears a Jungian stamp' and was thus 'a casualty of the ostracism which subsequently struck Jung' (Carotenuto 1984: 141). She did soon publish another major paper, incidentally showing that her relationship with Jung and the experience of her illness contributed to her realisation of the interconnection between destruction and creativity, pain and love. This paper, 'Destruction as a cause of coming into being', translated and published in the *Journal of Analytical Psychology* in 1994, is a remarkable and intricate exploration of psychoanalytic theory. It is part of the mythology that she is said to have given Freud the idea for the death instinct while she was in analysis with him. Jung's capacity to wrestle with her psychotic delusions gave her the serious attention and understanding she had never had before. She is influenced by Darwinian ideas (held by Bleuler and his influential Zurich group of the time) and demonstrates that destruction is part of sexuality because it is part of our biological heritage. Cellular structures unite to develop but they also destroy and are destroyed as they come together. Humans behave as part of a species, as well as striving for consciousness and an individual ego. This paper was presented in 1911, seven years from her admission to hospital.

In 1923, finding that she was not given the recognition she needed in psychoanalytic circles, she returned to Russia. She had been married in Vienna and had a daughter, Renate, before separating from her husband. He returned once she was back in Russia and they had another daughter, but then her story peters out. Etkind (1994) comments that 'she combined great achievements with tragic failure'. She joined the Russian Psychoanalytic Institute until Stalin shut it down.

She had a post in the Moscow State Institution and later in Rostov, where her child studies paralleled those of Klein in England. However, if she published anything analytic there is so far no trace, although more of her papers are being discovered (Kerr 1994; Lothane 1999). She was a supervisor and influential figure with, for example, Piaget (her patient for a short time in earlier years). She is thought to have challenged a Nazi officer (in German, of course) in a synagogue in Rostov in 1941. She was then killed, as were her two daughters. She was 56. This murder is portrayed in Wilson's play.

Her diaries show how much Spielrein loved Jung and it is clear that he loved her (Kerr 1994; Lothane 1999). She continued, after joining the Freudian group, to make links between Freud's and Jung's work. She was the only person to do so once the break had occurred (1913) when the rest of the group seemed intent on discrediting Jung. As a young girl she was sure she was destined for great things but the various opinions about her seem to see these solely as 'grandiose delusions', part of a psychotic symptomatology. I wonder if a young man's intellectual aspirations would have been so dismissed. Uniquely, Jung seems to have taken her intellectual ambitions seriously. The psychotherapy with him in hospital eventuated in her living on her own in Zurich and applying for the medical training, which she completed successfully, including the specialisation in psychiatry.

Bruno Bettelheim, referring to Sabina Spielrein in the introduction to Carotenuto's book (1984), says: 'It was what she experienced with Jung that cured her . . . Jung's behaviour and attitude, as conveyed to her in their relation – call it treatment, seduction, transference, love, mutual daydreams, delusions, or whatever – was instrumental in achieving this cure' (p. xxxvii). Jung can be said to have recognised his treatment of her as abuse and gone into flight. But discussions taking this view and, therefore, condemning Jung, seem to me to lose the question I am discussing here, the nature of transference and whether it is a process or a fixed state.

Carl and Sabina were gripped at least for a time in the madness of love, the passionate attraction which outside the therapist–patient relationship would have had quite different connotations. If there was a physical relationship, it was between 1908 and 1911 – well after her release from hospital, and their intimacy raises the question of when a patient ceases to be a patient. My colleague who said, with the mischief in his eye, that Jung transgressed, was touching on this issue. He was not, interestingly, commenting on the fact that Jung was a married man at the time. By trying to dialogue with his patient, Jung had gradually helped her re-find the cognitive powers she had lost during her adolescence. The word-association tests aroused her interest and curiosity and she began to shift from preoccupation with her bodily functions and aim for intellectual achievement. His own emotional interest in her no doubt helped to engage her as someone of interest. But later Jung was unable to deal with what he himself began to think of as a professional deviation and blindly reacted with denial of her as anything but his patient. The play *Sabina* portrays a physical affair in hospital and it was easy, as a member of the audience, to imagine how this delusion could exist in such an atmosphere. We can suppose that Dr Jung was tempted to 'act out'. Certainly, he was in love with Sabina at least some of the time of their long friendship. Being 'in love' with a patient is now regarded as a normal part of analysis (Searles 1959), as long as the analyst does not act on his or her physical feelings but retains the knowledge that this is part of the transference and is in the cause of the task. The feelings then become available for 'interpretation'.

Transference and sexuality

What had been the matter with Sabina Spielrein? How was it that she was in a state diagnosed as psychotic hysteria, yet within two years was able to leave hospital and study at a university? Now that we have reached the twenty-first century, severe breakdown diagnosed as psychotic is known to be quite common at the time of adolescent transitions and can be followed by full recovery as the individual works through the trauma of the maturational crisis. This is the daily experience of those who work with A-level and university students. Sabina, ignorant of what was happening to her body and emotionally in turmoil, was 19 when she was admitted to the Burgholzli. In her era, a girl exhibiting flamboyant sexuality could not have 'chosen' a more embarrassing way to draw attention to her unhappiness. She was a girl of her time in a Russian family, 'the first child of intelligent, well-educated, well-to-do Jewish parents'. Such a family would have strong views about their daughter's behaviour. Thinking of the family as a group or system in which the individual grows, the (unconscious) choice of symptoms is usually that which the family will find intolerable (Box et al. 1981). As a young child, Sabina had a sister who died (Bettelheim 1984; Carotenuto 1984) and we can speculate that this may have contributed to the fears and fantasies about her body, particularly about faeces, which she developed as a child. She believed in her own intellect until her adolescent sexual preoccupations. If there should be a balance in the personality between thought and feelings, between logos and eros, it is clear that this was lost. Her cognitive capacity, which had been evident in diaries, was swamped by feelings. Carotenuto calls her 'an intelligent, paranoiac woman patient' in the Burgholzli. Her adolescent maturational processes following a childhood of disturbed fantasy, I conjecture, were the seedbed for her becoming crazed with a desire for which she could not define any specific aim, which made no 'sense'. Cultural repression had, in addition, denied her the ego which told her she was clever and could have a powerful place in adult life. A young (pretty) girl, then as now, was not supposed to harbour such ambitions.

Jung, also full of youthful idealism for his psychotherapeutic ideas, treated her as a patient rather than as a dumb girl, although privately he also had a patronising view of her femininity. As her therapist, he treated her as an equal, investigating her state through his word-association tests and talking with her about herself. He wanted to explore the nature of delusions and hallucinations. Being treated to a sympathetic dialogue, with the aid (as we now know) of morphine, appealed to Sabina's reason and she was (fortunately) able to make the links which enabled her to reconnect with her environment, thus suggesting now that she had been in an adolescent transitional crisis. The play shows how this could have been.

Jung was attracted to his patient. Projective identification, in which it is impossible to disentangle who is who until the therapist is able to regain the capacity to think (Bion 1979), becomes even more of a hazard in an institutional atmosphere of psychosis than between individuals. However, he did maintain the professional distance, at least while she was a patient. I have been interpreting the play's action mainly from a group perspective, but the play's action can equally be understood as a projection of Sabina's psychotic inner world. As she calmed, she could contain and face the physical terrors she had experienced in learning about her body as a child and a young woman. She had been ignorant of sex and had only her huge imagination about her experiences. She only discovered the facts about sexual life when she studied medicine.

As she recovered, Spielrein strove to extricate herself from being seen as Jung's patient, while he became caught in the moral and ethical dilemma of being too involved with someone he had treated for a serious disturbance. Rather than transference, which was a new theme in psychoanalysis at that time, Jung was concerned about his ethical position as a doctor. Yet he was apparently consumed by the sexual desire which drew him to his patient. The question arises: does the power relationship of an incestuous bond ever modify? Can it be or become a more equal relationship and if so can the decision to have a sexual relationship become a legitimate choice? Jung helped his patient by treating her as having something valuable to contribute to their work together and ultimately as a professional like himself. She became a colleague – but did she remain ethically and in transference terms still his patient? The search for enlightenment remains to this day, muddled by the continued fear of the power of sexual desire and a consequent silence in discussing what really goes on in love relationships.

From a Jungian point of view, Sabina's energy flowed away from logos (reasoned, differentiated thought), into a physicality which suggests the archetypal eros of the collective unconscious – desire for connection but no capacity to differentiate. The homeostasis of her psyche was unbalanced and mind, body and feelings became a chthonic mass. The *coniunctio*, the sense of fusion, which draws individuals into sexual intercourse as a means of fulfilling this instinctual need, is also the basis on which the psychotherapy relationship holds the therapy couple together through the vicissitudes of analysis. Out of this fusion comes creative change. Other than in sexual intercourse, the creativity is symbolic rather than physical. The psychotherapist and patient unconsciously form an (incestuous) pair and, through what we call the transference, engage in the miseries and conflicts which preoccupy the patient.

As Searles (1959) so vividly depicts, the analyst can be delusively in love with his or her patient – actually, he says, *must* at some point be in love with the patient if the analysis is to work. In Jung's terms, if the transformative process is to take place, the *coniunctio* is there, binding analyst and patient in the transference relationship. In my view, by involving himself with his patient in hospital, Jung made himself a guinea pig to research his ideas about analysis. As a girl in late adolescence, Spielrein had met someone by whom she *felt* understood. This implicated her whole being in an unconscious rather than conscious way. In Wilson's play we could see how the therapist could be seized by the *coniunctio*, the sexual imperative, and have to act out the sexuality. In reality, the imperative was not consummated in physical sex. However, the whole relationship formed part of the experience Jung was able later to bring to bear on his understanding of the power of libido when it is not distributed within the structures of the self. In a paper I wrote (Thomson 1999), the erotic is described as a forceful archetypal need to make links (relationships), to see 'the other' not as separate and different but as the aspect of self which is required to make life complete. This can be applied to creating a work of art or to the need for a love relationship.

For Jung, eros was a feminine principle, but this is a part of all human beings. Men, as well as women, have their eros factor. Logos, described by Jung as a masculine principle, represents the capacity to separate and differentiate. As such, it can be seen to be needed by women as well as men. I am suggesting that Sabina's breakdown can be characterised as the loss of her logos capacity in a deluge of eros, surging through her as a result of her maturational hormonal development. Through the transference (*coniunctio*), Jung enquired into her mental processes – 'what on earth was going on in the mind of this creature with such sexual and anal fantasies', he might have thought and patiently tried to find out. Her emotional balance was gradually righted and the sexual eros diminished to allow her to engage in less exhausting forms of relationship.

Final comments

In this chapter, I have written from broadly psychoanalytic theory which includes Jungian psychology and now informs, consciously and unconsciously, the way we think about states of mind and feeling. Much of Jung's extensive writings anticipate group relations theory and family therapy, as well as his insistence on individuation as the main aim for individual life (Jung 1963). His personal views on sexual behaviour were strict and it is clear that his feelings for Sabina Spielrein shocked him, although he later involved his wife, Emma, in accepting his long relationship with a colleague, Toni Wolff. However, he did work out clear views about libido as a general life energy.

I hope it can be seen that the temptation which faced Dr Jung as psychotherapist in the 1900s is an example of our concerns about what constitutes abuse. Teachers, doctors, parents, as well as psychotherapists – and all in categories installed for the protection of the vulnerable against the powerful – are at some time tempted by the sexual eros. One way of dealing with temptation is to deny it. Another is to project it onto others. Although Jung fell into the temptation of denial, he suffered from his conflicts and out of his suffering he has given us some concepts which enable it to be recognised that parts are always parts of whole systems. We must struggle to see how opposites can live together in the same world.

Before the First World War, as a young doctor in Switzerland, Jung was full of hope and enthusiasm for psychoanalytic ideas and his own work on the relationship between individual, culture, mythology and society. His involvement with Spielrein engaged them both in the struggle of youth with adult reality, struggles which arouse fantasies and fears in those who observe 'unacceptable behaviour'. It seems that although Spielrein still had hard times ahead of her and a tragic death at a comparatively young age, her long relationship with Jung was necessary to her recovery from 'psychotic hysteria'. As he coped with the disintegration of the hopes of his younger self, Jung lost his credibility in the culture of psychoanalysis and I believe that he has become a convenient scapegoat upon whom to project the repudiated behaviour of forbidden desire. Looking at the relationship from the present day, we can regard Wilson's play as a case history of an inner world of psychotic fantasy, or as a representation of the kind of psychotic wonderland by which a patient is taken over and which hovers to ensnare those who work in psychiatric institutions. As Jung later suggested, that this is so is due to our common archetypal inheritance, our capacity for erotic connections. This kind of transference can blow up in the private consulting room as well, and cause otherwise rational psychotherapists or counsellors to believe that they will only help their patient by acting on their sexual desires.

In this early psychoanalytic threesome, Freud maintained his professional integrity, his authority as a doctor/analyst; Spielrein is largely ignored (not an unusual fate for a woman attempting to compete in a professional race); Jung's idea of equality between therapist and patient drew him into an involvement he could not handle and which has provided later psychotherapists with a Shadow to repudiate. His integrity was permanently damaged, less by the 'affair' itself – for many analysts before and since have had dubious liaisons with those in their care (Kerr 1994) – but because he became confused and took a path of dissimulation and lies. This was institutionalised into the split between Jungians and Freudians. Most of Freud's successors seem simply to accept that Jung was an outlandish sexual outlaw, mad or at best a woolly-minded clinician, apparently with the corollary that Freudian analysts are pure and unsullied.

Jung is largely ignored by psychoanalysts but unlike Spielrein he will not fade into obscurity. Jungians continue to learn about Freud and other psychoanalytic theories and try to bridge the split from the 1900s.

Working with training organisations in the psychotherapy and counselling fields, I find that teachers will say (sometimes it seems with pride): 'I don't know anything about Jung' but subsequently reveal that they think him to be prejudiced and deviant as well as woolly and interested in religion rather than attending to clinical work. That he acknowledged his illnesses and entry into altered states of consciousness is taken to prove that he was mad and should not be taken seriously. Yet he wrote about 'the wounded healer' and I find that trainees in particular identify strongly with this idea. Most of us come to psychotherapy training through physical or psychological difficulties. Regrettably it often seems more possible for trainees to admit this than those who have climbed into membership of their training bodies, have finished being analysed, and have come to believe it a career block to admit any form of 'weakness'. 'When swimming with sharks, you better not bleed' often seems to apply to psychotherapists' associations as much as to more obviously competitive groups. However, as Jung pointed out, we need our wounds if we are to be effective as therapists. We must risk the danger of the lurking sharks and admit that our work requires subjectivity as well as efforts to be objective. After all, it is part of our psychotherapy frame that we 'learn from experience'.

So this chapter is not a defence of Jung. He was a human being who had many faults and had a major strength in acknowledging his own weaknesses and subjectivities. My view is that 'Jung' has provided the Shadow for psychoanalysis as far as both sexuality and madness are concerned. The group which formed in 1913 after the split between the two men began a process of preserving Freudian methods of psychoanalysis against those of others interested in similar ideas. Discrediting Jung, up to then a strong candidate to take over Freud's role, supported the group by exclusion of his work. His involvement with Sabina Spielrein played a part then and now in establishing that his psychotherapy was not true psychoanalysis. In this way, Dr Jung's involvement with Dr Spielrein is still relevant as we continue to debate the nature of transference and how to hold boundaries which will protect our patients from exploitation. It is relevant for any professional or personal relationship where one party is in a position of power and responsibility over another.

Jungians, as Spielrein did, continually seek for the common ground in psychotherapy. Can we hope that eros, the connecting principle, and logos, the capacity to think, will enable a balance in the feelings we share in common? Although the methods of psychoanalytic psychotherapists and Jungian analysts are increasingly homogeneous, there are still many fundamental differences. As Carotenuto (1984) points out, Jung worked from becoming part of the flow of the relationship with his patients, using his feelings and perceptions subjectively. His approach is now recognisable as 'working with transference and counter-transference', and its dangers are better understood. It can more easily be combined with the methods for maintaining boundaries and avoiding 'incest' in ways unknown to the original therapists. At the same time the apparent freedom for sex which is now part of everyday life has increased awareness of exploitation. I hope that I have illustrated how Jung's own experiences have given ways of understanding how to work with projections and maintain integrity.

References

Bion, W. R. (1959) *Experiences in Groups*. London: Tavistock.

—— (1979) *Attention and Interpretation*. London, Maresfield.

Box, S., Copley, B., Magnagna, J. and Moustaki, E. (1981) *Psychotherapy with Families: An Analytic Approach*. London: Routledge & Kegan Paul.

Bettelheim, B. (1984) 'Introduction' to A. Carotenuto, *A Secret Symmetry: Sabina Spielrein between Freud and Jung*. London, Melbourne and Henley: Routledge.

Carotenuto, A. (1984) *A Secret Symmetry: Sabina Spielrein between Freud and Jung*. London, Melbourne and Henley: Routledge.

Etkind, A. M. (1994) 'How psychoanalysis was received in Russia 1906–1936', *Journal of Analytical Psychology* 39(2): 191–202.

Grosskurth, P. (1991) *The Secret Ring: Freud's Inner Circle and the Politics of Psychoanalysis*. New York: Addison-Wesley.

Jung, C. G. (1946) 'Problems of modern psychotherapy', *Collected Works* 16. USA: Bollingen Foundation; UK: Routledge & Kegan Paul.

—— (1963) *Memories, Dreams, Reflections*, autobiography. London: Fontana, 1983.

Kerr, J. (1994) *A Most Dangerous Method: Freud, Jung and Spielrein*. Great Britain and Melbourne: Sinclair Stevenson.

Laing, R. D. (1967) *The Politics of Experience*. Harmondsworth: Penguin.

Lothane, Z. (1999) 'Tender love and transference: unpublished letters of Jung and Spielrein', *International Journal of Psychoanalysis* 80(6): 1189–204.

McCormick, K. (1994) 'Sabina Spielrein: biographical note and postscript', *Journal of Analytical Psychology* 39(2): 187–90.

McGuire, W. (1974) *The Freud–Jung Letters*, abstracted by Alan McGuire. London: Picador.

Samuels, A. (1985) *Jung and the Post-Jungians*. London: Routledge & Kegan Paul.

—— (1993) *The Political Psyche*. London: Routledge.

Searles, H. (1959) 'Oedipal love in the countertransference', *Collected Papers on Schizophrenia and Related Subjects*. London: Maresfield Library, 1986.

Spielrein, S. (1911) 'Destruction as a cause of coming into being', *Journal of Analytical Psychology*, 1994 39(2): 155–86.

Strachey, J. and Strachey, A. (1985) *The Letters of James and Alix Strachey 1924–25*, ed. P. Meisel and W. Kendrick. New York: Basic Books.

Stevens, A. (1990) *On Jung*. London: Routledge.

Thomson, J. (1999) 'Eros: the connecting principle (or the complexities of love and sexuality)', in D. Mann (ed.), *Erotic Transference and Countertransference: Clinical Practice in Psychotherapy*. London and New York: Routledge.

Watson, G. (1998) *The Lost Literature of Socialism*. Cambridge: Lutterworth Press.

Wilson, S. (1998) *Sabina A Play. Theatre Workshop Production*. Unpublished.

Chapter 5

Of bodies and babies

Sexuality and sexual theories in childhood and adolescence

Ann Horne

> I leaned against the receptionist's window in the clinic, directly facing the patients' toilet. My very first training patient, 3 years and 9 months of age, was in there. Fleetingly I recalled a colleague telling me that Anna Freud had named the lavatory 'the resistance room', as I wondered what to make of this particular expedition. Noises of faecal evacuation sounded and resounded. There was a childish giggle. 'I'm making pooh babies!' Triumph!

The concept of infantile sexuality remains one of Freud's most important legacies. It is important, however, that we do not equate this simplistically with adult sexuality but recognise that here we are encountering a proto-sexuality, the capacity in the infant and child for passionate, wholehearted and sensuous relationships. There is a risk in applying to children the same words we use of adults and adult functions: the distressed and traumatised 8-year-old who externalises onto other children his experience of violence and sexual violation is not a 'paedophile' or a 'perpetrator' – the terms are not, at that age, either helpful or accurate. Yet, in our reconstruction of childhood experience from adult psychoanalysis or therapy, we frequently assume that fantasies – for example, of incorporation or castration – in childhood have adult equivalence. Yes, children theorise and fantasise about their bodies and sex; but this occurs minus the overlay of adult knowledge and experience that informs the adult patient on the couch and transforms the childish fantasy in the adult. Sometimes, indeed, this theorising happens in a way that consciously excludes knowledge:

> Ordinarily the child builds up his representational world (Sandler 1962) – his inner world, including his perceptual world

– partly on the basis of his own observations, partly on the basis of what is presented to him by others (and particularly by his parents), and partly on the basis of his own fantasy. But if these sets of information are contradictory he may attempt to resolve the contradictions by denying the evidence of his own eyes. Or, if information from any one of these areas produces too great a degree of pain it may be suppressed and the child may rely more heavily on information from other areas.

(Hurry and Sandler 1971: 380)

Thus the limitations both of the child's knowledge, and of his emotional freedom to take specific information on board, will have an impact on his theorising.

The body ego

If we consider the body as the first ego or psychological self for the infant, the capacity of the adults to affirm and value that self for the baby really matters. Holding, feeding, receiving and accepting the infant's sensual exploration of his body and its functions, are important in the integration of the body into the psychological sense of self. The following extract from a parent–infant observation demonstrates a little of this:

Lisa, age 6 months, lay close to her mother's breast and gazed into her eyes as the nipple of the bottle played with her mouth. Enjoying this, she smiled at her mother and accepted the bottle. As she sucked, her right hand came up to the bottle and began to explore the feel of her mother's fingers on it. She stroked these, rather dreamily, seemingly enjoying the touch. Her mother stroked her fingers with one of her own. Lisa stopped sucking and held her mother's gaze. 'She's enjoying her feed,' said her mother. 'Isn't she?' – to Lisa. Lisa gurgled contentedly and resumed sucking. There was no urgency, simply seeming contentment.

A colleague who observed the child of Sikh parents reported that part of the care of their son involved massaging and oiling his body, a process delighting both mother and son. The delimitation of outside/inside involved in this affirmation of the body is important, but equally important is the idea that the body and skin is acceptable to the object, and that being a little girl or a little boy is a source of pleasure to the carers.

It follows that the most primitive of defensive manoeuvres available to children, in the ongoing absence of an attuned and affirming object, will be body-based, physical ones, and that the infant will respond to anxiety, distress or 'surplus stimulation' (Hoffer 1950) by recourse to the body. An earlier vignette from the observation of Lisa, at this point aged 3 months, shows this way of coping in a fairly mild situation:

Lisa was being bottle-fed by her young 17-year-old aunt who was simultaneously conversing with another relative. Lisa's mother was elsewhere. The bottle was being held at an angle that did not allow Lisa to suck the milk. She gazed for quite a time at her aunt's face, as if trying to engage her with her gaze. A few noises of protest followed. The bottle moved about, sometimes allowing her to feed, sometimes not. Finally Lisa stretched her legs right out, bent up her knees, arched her back, twisted her right leg beneath her left and stretched out her arms, as if trying to find a balance that allowed her to control the flow of the liquid. She gobbled it down, not her usual feeding pattern.

Having tried gaze and sound, Lisa gave up on alerting and contacting her object and tried physical strategies to gain control of her rather random feeding. Although this was a minor episode, it shows the recourse to the body that remains available to the child. Such a defensive pattern may linger in later childhood and adulthood, when it represents an incapacity to retain the idea of benign objects in mind. As the physical body, with its drives and imperatives, is the basis of the adult sexually functioning body, how the infant is allowed to experience the body matters greatly for later development.

In an early study of autoerotism in the first year of life, Spitz surveyed 170 children for three autoerotic activities – genital play (the term 'masturbation' being felt to represent more organisation than the age of the group would indicate), rocking and faecal play. The importance of the mother–child relationship not unsurprisingly emerged. Spitz concluded:

> It was found that autoerotic activities are a function of the object relations prevailing during the first year of life. They are absent when object relations are absent; when object relations are so constantly contradictory that object formation is made impossible, rocking results. When object relations change in an intermittent manner faecal play results. When object relations are 'normal' genital play results.
>
> (Spitz with Wolf 1949: 119)

The capacity, therefore, to cathect the body-self is affected very early by the reliability of the object. Indeed, thumb-sucking as a self-consoling activity in the absence of the object can be seen as an eroticisation of the oral impulse – breast, equated with mother, is replaced by a part of the self (Kris 1951).

The toddler

Developmentally, much emphasis has been placed by theorists on the second year of life. As the acquisition of mobility makes the world a very different place for the toddler, the growing competence of the physical self gives further and greater opportunity for exploration of the self and others.

The gratification that the infant receives from the parents in their admiration and affirmation of the body is internalised and, in the toddler stage, a narcissistic exhibitionism leading towards such internalisation is found. Children will present their bodies for approval and homage, delighting in the response of attentive and appreciative adults. In early toddlerhood, once sufficient mastery is gained, clothes may come off at will and it is some time before any sense of alternative propriety is gradually gained. As the ego ideal develops through internalisation and identification, embarrassment and propriety appear. The wish to show and be seen, however, may then appear symbolically or in displacement. I recall my nephews, at the ages of 3 and 4 years, each spark the other into uncontrollable helpless mirth by whispering, 'Knickers!'

In the development of girls there comes a sense of internal space for babies and intercourse. In boys, a sense of the body having boundaries grows as they assume the pathway towards a penetrative adult sexual role. In classical theory castration anxiety in boys follows the discovery of the anatomical difference between the sexes, with penis envy the parallel in girls (Freud 1905). Today, we may think more not only of the equation of 'penis' and 'power', or what the penis and male potency might be said to stand for, but also of the envy experienced by boys of the child-bearing capacity of women. In our awareness that developmental gain contains loss, we have to keep in mind that one of the major losses that the toddler has to begin to negotiate is that of the wish to have and to be both sexes (McDougall 1995). This is a blow to omnipotence and a real narcissistic hurt, but a vital developmental step.

It is also important to think on the role of aggression in the process leading towards adult sexuality. 'At origin aggressiveness is almost synonymous with activity; it is a matter of part function,' states Winnicott, linking this to motility and separating muscularity in the infant from intent to destroy (e.g. in chewing the nipple at feeding) (Winnicott 1950–5). How parents respond to the toddler's growing sense of agency has an impact on the later capacity to integrate this into the developing self. Aggression is necessary for adult functioning in the world and a concept of one's potential, especially in relation to the capacity for intercourse and sexual relationships, and fusion with the growing sense of self is important. The reader is directed to Parsons and Dermen, who give a lively account of the role and necessity of aggression in childhood in relation to the violent patients whom they have seen (Parsons and Dermen 1999).

Such developmental tasks do not arrive in a set timescale. Children retain a fluidity in the positions they adopt in relation to sex, gender and the body, and it may not be helpful to see stages to be achieved by specific ages (Coates 1997; Dahl 1993). A developmental process, however, is under way and failure in the integration of a body self, aggression or in dealing with loss may cause gross difficulties with sexuality in adolescence and adulthood. With such a perspective, one can see how gross a trauma the experience of sexual abuse (or physical violence) must be in childhood, and comprehend a little of the struggle of violated children to integrate a damaged body-self into the changing ego.

Early theories and fantasies

Ideas about the penis almost always, at some stage, include the idea of the phallic mother. At first, this occurs because it is assumed by little boys that everyone must have a penis. The discovery of difference can lead to a variety of theories, depending on the age and development of the child: the female penis has been castrated, or, on observing little girls, it is simply late in growing and will appear later. Indeed, even the discovery of the penis may cause transient anxiety in boys – Casuso gives a delightful vignette of his 10-month-old son's relief at having his plastic pants replaced, theorising: 'for him, at that time, through his discovery of body boundaries by sight and hand, the penis was not only alien but also particularly disturbing in its strong sensations because of its erotic sensitivity' (Casuso 1957: 174).

Amongst the early and typical sexual theories of childhood, the equation of 'baby' with 'faeces' or 'penis' is common. Dependent on the influence of oral, anal and phallic development, conception may present as a process occurring in the mouth, through kissing, and with birth being also an oral event. The explanation that 'Mummy has a baby in her tummy' can be received extremely literally by the toddler who already knows that things get into the tummy via the mouth – and the theory that eating and birth are connected is born. Why Mummy ate the baby is more difficult to answer; perhaps the knowledge that she is 'growing it until it is ready to come out' is the more benign part for the toddler to concentrate upon. Similarly, ideas that 'Daddy planted a seed in Mummy's tummy' are often construed as 'Mummy ate Daddy's seeds' and the child arrives at an oral explanation for sex, intercourse and conception. Equally commonly, theories of mixing urine and faeces to conceive babies appear, often alongside the idea of an anal birth. The vignette at the start of this chapter illustrates one toddler's attempt both to understand the mysteries of life in the light of his own single-minded logic and knowledge, and to defend against his envy of the child-bearing capacity that he does not possess. Hermaphrodite, he need envy no object – 'I'm making pooh babies!' One finds 'pee' babies and the capacity to give birth by urination amongst such theories, too. This wish to have a baby appears both in boys and girls pre-oedipally (Jacobson 1950; Mack Brunswick 1940). Indeed, the fantasy is often very alive when the toddler's mother is pregnant, when the small child becomes convinced that he or she, too, has a baby in his/her tummy – or several, to outdo Mummy!

Fantasies of intercourse often contain much that is dangerous or sadistic. The idea that the man hurts the woman can be compounded by the toddler's discovery of menstrual blood and a therefore damaged Mummy; or in intercourse Daddy has castrated Mummy, hence she has lost her penis. Adult enjoyment of intercourse cannot always be stealthy and silent, and the small child develops his own theories about noises that sound as if someone is being hurt. Witnessing the primal scene may add to this but the toddler has usually been able to collect enough information for some theory to have been generated minus this. One fantasy that lasts a long time, reviving again at adolescence, is that of the *vagina dentata*, that intercourse is castratingly dangerous for the male. Equally powerful is the fear of engulfment, a primitive anxiety and one also revived when puberty brings enforced bodily change.

A note on gender

It is generally accepted in the psychoanalytic literature that a 'core gender identity' is established in children by around 18 months of age. By this is meant a primary sense of being a boy or a girl. The developmental period of early toddlerhood is, therefore, critical in such establishment, and separation anxiety, loss, trauma, abandonment, omnipotence, identification and dis-identification, and fear of merging, all feature as key influences when things go wrong (Horne 1999). 'Gender role', however, remains more fluid (de Marneffe 1997). Although the contemporary Freudians have done much work on a developmental line for gender, and delineating points on that line (e.g. Tyson 1982), other observers point to a continuing fluidity of possibilities in children, a curiosity about gender roles and the capacity to play with ideas of gender (Coates 1997; Dahl 1993).

Oedipal longing and legacy

The passions, renunciations and rejections of the oedipal phase, preceding identifications and turning to the external world, are well catalogued. Dis-identification from the mother, ambivalence in the relationship with the father (admired and feared as possessor of the mother and a potentially castrating rival for her) give way to closeness and identification with father in classical theory about boys. With girls, decathexis from mother, and passion for father who equally has to be renounced as a partner, paves the way for identification with the mother. The modern focus would centre on the realisation of parental partnership and sexuality, three-person relationships, and on the boundaries between adults and children. As Hamilton states, 'In *some* cases this realisation is experienced as a castration or narcissistic blow' (Hamilton 1993: 273). Winnicott's description of being 'all dressed up and nowhere to go' encapsulates the dilemma of the oedipal child (Winnicott 1964: 156). The capacity of the parents to keep alive for the child the idea of a parental relationship matters, whether in single-parent or two-person relationships, as the child moves to coping with the idea of 'three', from dyadic relationships to triadic.

Post-oedipally, and following the developing identification with the same-sex parent, it is critical that children also experience an affirmation of gender and appreciation by the opposite-sex parent. In many cases of gender dysphoria in childhood and adolescence, not only is such affirmation absent but an identification with the opposite-sex parent has at times been encouraged – boys identify with mothers, girls with their fathers. It is also vital that affirmation of the opposite-sex child does not become sexualised, that in affirming the son the mother does not seduce him.

Observations from nursery and from child analysis

The following material illustrates some of these themes. I am indebted to the Director and staff of the Anna Freud Centre, London, for permission to use it. The first two vignettes are of nursery children aged between 3 and 5.

A Jonathan asks the observer to unbutton his overalls, then says, 'I have a willy. Boys have willies and girls have . . . (pause) . . . I don't know what girls have.'

B All the children are in a circle in their swimsuits, ready to use the pool, but Lily is still in her underwear, playing. The teacher reminds her to get ready quickly. Lily takes off her clothes and stands naked in the middle of the circle, then puts her pants between her legs. Michael laughs and points at her, saying loudly, 'Look at Lily!' Mary says to Lily with disgust, 'You're rude!' but Lily is unfazed and stands there for quite a long time before fetching her swimsuit. Robert then shows the observer a scrape on his chin and leg, telling her he fell off his bike and even his tooth hurt from the fall. Michael comes up to the observer, his finger stuck out, showing her he is hurt (there is not a scratch), and another boy pipes up that he's hurt, too. Then Robert turns to Joanna and says, 'I have a willy.' Joanna responds proudly, 'And I have a vagina!' Zoë calls out from the pool that she has a vagina, too, and two other girls shout out the same. Robert then says he has a bellybutton and adds, 'Everybody has a bellybutton,' but Lily says she doesn't.

Lily's exhibitionism demonstrates her lack of a penis – with a consequent range of anxious and displacement activities. The knowledge of the vagina is interesting: for girls, much about the sexual organs has to be taken on trust – the womb and ovaries are not visible and breast development is yet to come (Joyce 2000).

The following two extracts are from child analyses.

A Judith (3 years 4 months) became very ambivalent towards her mother and frequently cast her in the role of a witch or a bad wolf who had to be placated with sweets. She had a positive oedipal fantasy that the female analyst lived in the house opposite with the male doctor whom she had seen for assessment. She thought he was the analyst's 'father' and that they had no other family. She then noticed a log in the garden opposite and imagined that a daddy bear and a baby bear were sitting on it together, hastily adding that there was a mummy bear there as well. Later, she wanted the analyst to pretend to be Daddy Santa Claus who brought her presents at night – she imagined making a baby with the daddy-therapist by peeing. Four months later she asked if the therapist remembered the story of the daddy bear and the baby bear on the log. The analyst talked about her wish to play love games with the daddy, and spoke of how, when she was grown-up, she could have a daddy-husband all to herself and play nice games with him. Judith looked very pleased, then soberly remarked that it was a very long time to wait!

B Richard (7 years 8 months) had positive oedipal wishes to share his mother's bed without Dad being there, and to steal Dad's penis. Castration anxiety became intense and he feared father's retaliation. He told his therapist that Dad scared him by talking about robbers, and the therapist suggested that sometimes children got scared that Dad might rob them of their willies. He agreed, but said, 'What about a father being scared that his son might rob him of *his* willy? Dad wouldn't like it.' He then played games with big and little rockets, and showed his fear of the woman being dangerous and damaging during intercourse – 'If I have a bigger willy, more will break off!'

So just what's latent about latency?

The dramatic pace of body changes and hormonal influence of infancy and toddlerhood slows in the latency period. The latency child is in pursuit of fairness, mastery and the acquisition of self-control, following the passions and renunciations of the oedipal resolution. In classical theory, this is control of the instincts and sexual drives – perhaps now we think especially of passion, emotion and sensuality. Sexual curiosity and theorising continues, but becomes more a matter of private speculation and peer group conversation, out of sight of the grown-ups. 'Doctors and nurses' and games designed to encourage bodily exploration are, after all, early latency games. Children at this stage retain curiosity about the sexuality of others but may well be offended when family members bring this too close to home. Maternal pregnancies may arouse an element of embarrassment and it is easier to engage curiosity with the outside world than in the intimate cauldron of the family. Oedipus is, as yet, not too far away. The curiosity about the kind of sexual adult (or sexually ready adult) one will become also continues as the following vignette from the 1950s demonstrates:

> Three 7–8-year-old girls were accompanying each other home from school. The subject of their intensely serious conversation was what kind of breasts they would like to have when grown-up. There appeared only to be two choices: either rather provocative, like Jean Simmonds, a starlet of many films, or ample but certainly not causing any frisson in the beholder, like Ma Broon. (Ma Broon was the matriarch of an extended Scottish family in a Sunday newspaper cartoon.) They opted unanimously for Jean Simmonds. The criterion was an idea of something sexual but as yet nameless, a potential self.

This conversation was notably serious – no-one found cause for giggling – and held in the absence of both adults and boys. The anticipation it presented felt daring and they quickly resumed safe chat about the school day. Interestingly, the subject had been stirred by the return of their class teacher after the Easter holiday break, now married. *Her* sexuality may have been coped with by the displacement of the vital 'breast' question. That it occurred in a 'same sex' group was also not surprising: the preference for same-sex friendships and play partners in early latency may well be one result of a regression to phallic-narcissistic concerns in the aftermath of the oedipal rejection (Furman 1980).

Earlier childhood theories may well linger, as they do with us all, and require analysis as Sandler and his colleagues describe:

> Throughout his analysis Michael [age 7 years 8 months] insisted on having a ritual 'two kisses' on parting from his father at the clinic . . . . When he did not receive these kisses, he became agitated, and in the end his father would provide the 'magic'; thus he was forgiven his hostile wishes to the father. When the therapist asked him what he thought would happen if his father kissed him only once or three times, Michael replied, 'My penis would fall off. My biggest worry is that my penis-bottom will break.'
>
> (Sandler, Kennedy and Tyson 1980: 148)

One can see here the legacy of oedipal fantasies based on rivalry with the father.

Latency is also the time of the 'family romance', the certainty that there was an awful mix-up at the hospital and that one has been taken home by the wrong parents. Such fantasies both aid with the distancing from oedipal desires that is necessary for further development and contain other possibilities and identifications for the child. The idea that there is a princess or a pop and football star pondering sadly the whereabouts of their real child can often be found. Heroes and idols emerge, but frequently with a glossy, packaged sexuality that in its wrapping is safe from the realities of adolescent and adult sexual potencies. It is also in latency that the certainty that one was an immaculate conception appears (rather damaged if further siblings are born, but why believe reality) and the preferred belief that one's parents 'only did it once'.

A variety of mechanisms, especially the age-appropriate defences such as identification or sublimation, are used by the latency child to deal with the impotence of the post-oedipal position and also to counter the dangers of being overwhelmed by adult information for which they are not yet ready. Children's literature contains much about children being cleverer than adults or defeating them, with a real flair for subversion at times (Lurie 1991), perhaps as one way of coping with not yet being a sexually potent being in the adult world. Indeed, some latency jokes manage to package in one unit both ideas about sexuality and the capacity to mislead the adults, to their embarrassment:

Q. There were two Bishops in bed together. Which one wore the nightie?
A. Mrs Bishop

(Ahlberg and Ahlberg 1982)

Rhymes are created, often to contain the trauma of the adult world – violence, death, alcoholism, pregnancy, war, murder, child abuse – and to give a veneer of control over it. These may be incorporated into singing or jumping games, a long-recognised sublimation of sexuality by latency girls. The current trend to perform one's favourite pop star's songs in school playgrounds may also be seen as a rehearsal, albeit a safe one, for adult roles and adult exhibitionism. A sense of boundariedness to the body is important for boys in their rehearsal for an adult penetrative role, one reason perhaps for the seemingly relentless rush towards contact sports and physical encounters noted in any junior school playground when the boys tumble out at break-time.

As well as rehearsing for adult life, latency children are still expending energy on leaving the exhibitionism of earlier toddlerhood behind them. The awkward memories of flamboyant demonstrations of the body – often embarrassingly recounted for one's humiliation by parents and older siblings – appear in early latency in games that endeavour to make another child similarly embarrassed:

children of six or so tease others by trying to pull down their pants; they now know that they are not supposed to expose themselves, so they try to expose someone else.
At about seven, actual physical assault is replaced by rhymes about exposure. There are literally dozens of these, most along the lines of:

I see England, I see France,
I see [Mary's] underpants.

To the adult such verses seem stupid and, if one has to hear them very often, annoying. But to the child, as Wolfenstein points out, they represent a giant step toward growing up. The conflict between id and superego, between the wish to see and show off nakedness and the knowledge that this is naughty and forbidden, has been sublimated into an art. It is a very low form of art, but art nevertheless.

(Lurie 1991: 223–4)

A note on masturbation

I think we may describe masturbation as a normal activity of childhood for the purpose of discharging instinctual tension
(Lampl deGroot 1950: 155).

Masturbation is having sex with someone you love
(Woody Allen).

But is it? Masturbation may therefore beself-consoling, tension-releasing, a denial of exclusion from the parental relationship, or a way of containing impossible fantasies. The genital autoerotic activity of early childhood will encounter different responses from the adults in the child's life, with consequent impact on the degree and role of masturbation in the latency period. The child whose castration anxiety is too great is inhibited in masturbation:

the masturbation fantasy is deprived of all bodily outlet, the libidinal energy attached to it is completely blocked and dammed up, and eventually is displaced with full force from the realm of sex-life into the realm of ego-activities.

(Freud, A. 1949: 203)

Fraiberg, exploring the degree of genital arousal in girls in latency, comments on the need to find with the child-patient a vocabulary of words like 'good feelings', 'hot feelings' and 'prickly feelings' and notes: 'Once we had a vocabulary children were astonishing in their ability to describe differentiated states' (Fraiberg 1972: 445).

Fantasies in latency often centre on competitiveness and power. The capacity of latency boys to engage in group masturbation shows a phallic competitiveness only beaten by their peeing competitions, seeing who can make his urine go highest up a wall. The activity itself may become detached from the original fantasies, or become modified as in the case of the 11-year-old girl who repeatedly caressed her arms (Bornstein 1953). Hair-twiddling and nail-biting have long been viewed as masturbatory displacements. In adolescence, fantasy and reality may be of homosexual or heterosexual activity. The heterosexual fantasies accompanying masturbation move from an initially passive position (e.g. the boy who imagines being initiated into intercourse by a sympathetic older woman, a displacement of the oedipal wishes with the adult now sanctioning the wish) to an active role (Wermer and Levin 1967). In girls, the passive wish to be 'taken' by a powerful male, in fantasy, may well have had an impact on the capacity to report rape: apart from the male comment, 'She wanted it,' it may be impossible to separate the masturbation fantasy from reality. Indeed, the content of masturbation fantasy changes with growth and development and the excitement it encapsulates may end up being usefully displaced onto non-sexual ego activities.

Puberty and adolescence

We know that the character structure of a child at the end of the latency period represents the outcome of long drawn-out conflicts between id and ego forces. The inner balance achieved, although characteristic for each individual and precious to him, is preliminary only and precarious. It does not allow for the quantitative increase in drive activity, nor for the changes of drive quality which are both inseparable from puberty. Consequently, it has to be abandoned to allow adult sexuality to be integrated into the individual's personality. The so-called adolescent upheavals are no more than the external indications that such internal adjustments are in progress.

(Freud, A. 1958: 264)

Adults can harm adolescents either by assuming from their behaviour that they are adults, or by ridiculing them for their infantility. This is especially true in the sphere of sex, for in the adolescent we see the infant's evaluation of touch, for instance, going side by side with sex-play that looks adult. Sex-play has its own value, and does not at first involve long-term planning in terms of a new family setting. This adolescent phase soon passes . . . .

(Winnicott 1955: 138)

Commentators like Anna Freud, Winnicott and recently Van Heeswyk (1997) alert us to the normality of adolescent processes and the adult projections of anxiety and envy that may accompany these. Nevertheless, there remain key adjustments to be made on the way to an adult body and anticipation of an adult sexual self.

The approach to puberty is fraught with anxiety and comparisons. The girl who reaches her menarche at 9 years probably lacks the support and confirmation of her peers, while she who still hopes her menstruation will begin at 16 years can experience a desperate sense of difference. Regressive features are not uncommon in early puberty, possibly a seeking of earlier safety in the face of rapidly changing bodies.

Intimacy of body and of mind assume vital importance. Ownership of the body is a prime issue at a time when the earliest passions of infancy and early childhood are revived but with a now sexually functioning body – no longer 'all dressed up and nowhere to go' but potent. In early adolescence the reluctance to care for the body can be seen as an attempt to delay the insistence of physiological and sexual change; in later adolescence, as responsibility for and ownership of the body more surely passes from parents to young person, great attention to the body's grooming and imperfections follows. Adaptation involves reworking the oedipal experience, making the parental intimacies less intense. This includes intimacy of the mind – parents may find themselves shockingly disparaged as the realm of ideas and attitudes becomes a displacement arena for the emotional struggle to find the optimum intimate distance.

A return to bodily means of coping with anxiety can be perceived in sports, sexual exploration, discos, flirtation with drugs, alcohol, nicotine, the pursuit of fashion trends, even body-piercing – all containing a mixture of earlier mechanisms with an overlay of rehearsal for the future. The capacity to tolerate this new, fluid body-self is crucial: adolescence is not surprisingly the risk time for eating disorders and suicide in those who find the move towards establishing an adult sexual self too impossible a task.

This is also the time of 'crushes', of passionate feelings for same and opposite-sex peers and adults. Identification forms part of this process, as does exploration and integration of aspects of others into a modified ideal desired self. Homosexual exploration is an expected part of adolescence and the capacity to keep sexual object choice open has an important developmental function. The peer group provides a mirroring function with its possibilities of trying out roles and emotions, experimenting with aspects of the self and seeing these in others. A sense of transition is important, that fluidity and potential be kept open. There is a danger of polarisation, an 'all or nothing' quality in the face of so much change, that can cause foreclosure and flight from uncertainty.

Fantasies of adolescence often appear via the jokes that they tell or the comments they make in teasing their peer group. Inevitably, these centre around potential inadequacies: the size of the penis, whether it is large enough or whether it is (boastingly) too large for any female – female taunts that 'size matters' easily discomfit the unsure youth; fears of being consumed or castrated in the act of intercourse; and, in an omnipotent denial of anxiety, fantasies of sexual irresistibility. Adolescent jokes are often crude and may contain disparagement of the wished-for but feared object and of the young person's own vulnerability. There is little of the 'politically correct' in such revelations, but much of a revival of childhood fantasy and anxiety. Even swearing is often sexualised, containing themes of bleakly perceived intercourse, anality and incestuous wishes, and early and mid-adolescents enrage peers by cursing their mothers.

Conclusion

Children theorise as soon as they can symbolise – it is part of their struggle to make sense of themselves and their world. Fluidity and playfulness about bodies, gender, sex and sexuality are strengths in childhood, and a developmental urgency in the child is a strong ally to the caring parent – or the child psychotherapist. Such openness and growth, however, are easily set at risk by adult failures in affirmation, boundary-keeping and attachment.

Acknowledgement I wish to thank my colleague and friend, Marianne Parsons, for her generosity with time, thought and critical advice.

References

Ahlberg, J. and Ahlberg, A. (1982) *The Ha Ha Bonk Book.* Harmondsworth: Puffin.

Bornstein, B. (1953) 'Masturbation in the latency period', in *The Psychoanalytic Study of the Child* 8. New York: International Universities Press.

Casuso, G. (1957) 'Anxiety related to the "discovery" of the penis: an observation', in *The Psychoanalytic Study of the Child* 12. New York: International Universities Press.

Coates, S. W. (1997) 'Is it time to jettison the concept of developmental lines?', *Gender and Psychoanalysis* 2(1): 35–53.

Dahl, K. (1993) 'Play and the construction of gender in the oedipal child', in A. J. Solnit, D. J. Cohen and P. B. Neubauer (eds), *The Many Meanings of Play: A Psychoanalytic Perspective.* New Haven, CT: Yale University Press, ch. 7.

de Marneffe, D. (1997) 'Bodies and words: a study of young children's genital and gender knowledge', *Gender and Psychoanalysis* 2(1): 3–33.

Fraiberg, S. (1972) 'Some characteristics of genital arousal and discharge in latency girls', in *The Psychoanalytic Study of the Child* 27. London: Hogarth Press.

Freud, A. (1936) *The Ego and the Mechanisms of Defence.* London: Hogarth Press.

—— (1949) 'Certain types and stages of social maladjustment', in K. R. Eissler (ed.), *Searchlights on Delinquency.* New York: International Universities Press.

—— (1958) 'Adolescence', in *The Psychoanalytic Study of the Child* 13. New York: International Universities Press.

Freud, S. (1905) 'Three essays on the theory of sexuality', *Standard Edition* 7. London: Hogarth Press, pp. 125–243.

Furman, E. (1980) 'Early latency: normal and pathological aspects', in S. I. Greenspan and G. H. Pollock (eds), *The Course of Life: Psychoanalytic Contributions toward Understanding Personality Development*, vol. 2: *Latency, Adolescence and Youth*, Washington, DC: National Institute of Mental Health.

Hamilton, V. (1993) *Narcissus and Oedipus: The Children of Psychoanalysis*, 2nd edn. London: Karnac.

Hoffer, W. (1950) 'Development of the body ego', in *The Psychoanalytic Study of the Child* 5. New York: International Universities Press.

Horne, A. (1999) 'Thinking about gender in theory and practice with children and adolescents', *Journal of the British Association of Psychotherapists* 37: 35–49.

Hurry, A. and Sandler, J. (1971) 'Coping with reality: the child's defences against the external world', *British Journal of Medical Psychology* 44: 79–385.

Jacobson, E. (1950) 'Development of the wish for a child in boys', in *The Psychoanalytic Study of the Child* 5. New York: International Universities Press.

Joyce, A. (2000) Personal communication.

Kris, E. (1951) 'Observations on early autoerotic activities', in *The Psychoanalytic Study of the Child* 6. New York: International Universities Press.

Lampl-deGroot, J. (1950) 'On masturbation', in *The Psychoanalytic Study of the Child* 5. New York: International Universities Press.

Lurie, A. (1991) *Not in Front of the Grown-Ups: Subversive Children's Literature*. London: Sphere Books.

Mack Brunswick, R. (1940) 'The pre-oedipal phase of the libido development', *Psychoanalytic Quarterly* 9: 293–319.

McDougall, J. (1995) *The Many Faces of Eros*. London: Free Association Books.

Parsons, M. and Dermen, S. (1999) 'The violent child and adolescent', in M. Lanyado and A. Horne (eds), *The Handbook of Child and Adolescent Psychotherapy: Psychoanalytic Approaches*. London: Routledge.

Sandler, J., (1962) 'Psychology and psychoanalysis', *British Journal of Medical Psychology* 35: 91–100.

Sandler, J., Kennedy, H. and Tyson, R. L. (1980) *The Technique of Child Psychoanalysis: Discussions with Anna Freud*. London: Institute of Psycho-Analysis and Karnac Books.

Spitz, R. with Wolf, K. (1949) 'Autoerotism', in *The Psychoanalytic Study of the Child* 3–4. New York: International Universities Press.

Tyson, P. (1982) 'A developmental line of gender identity, gender role, and choice of love object', *Journal of the American Psychoanalytic Association* 30: 61–86.

Van Heeswyk, P. (1997) *Analysing Adolescence*. London: Sheldon Press.

Wermer, H. and Levin, S. (1967) 'Masturbation fantasies: their changes with growth and development', in *The Psychoanalytic Study of the Child* 22. London: Hogarth Press.

Winnicott, D. W. (1950–5) 'Aggression in relation to emotional development', in *Collected Papers: Through Paediatrics to Psychoanalysis*. London: Hogarth Press, 1975.

—— (1955) 'Adopted children in adolescence', in R. Shepherd, J. Johns and H. Taylor Robinson (eds), *D W Winnicott: Thinking about Children*. London: Karnac Books, 1996.

—— (1964) 'The child and sex', in *The Child, the Family and the Outside World*. Harmondsworth: Penguin.

Wolfenstein, M. (1954) *Children's Humor*. Glencoe, IL: The Free Press.

Chapter 6

Women's sexuality in the new millennium

Marie Maguire

As we move into the twenty-first century, women in our society have a greater range of choices than ever before. We are free for the first time to delay pregnancy until early middle age, to live alone or with a partner of either sex. Theoretically at least, marriage and motherhood can be combined with success in traditionally male spheres. Or we can control our fertility indefinitely, whilst remaining sexually active throughout life. Yet cultural imagery continues to depict women gaining pleasure from being attractive rather than from exercising their own desires. Many female patients describe a disturbing clash between their conscious hopes of sexual and social equality and their tolerance of painful or frustrating personal relationships. Even women who see themselves as powerful and independent in the outside world may feel that their desire does not emanate from inside themselves, but is aroused only by lovers who are remote or emotionally withholding. Other women describe inhibitions – perhaps a lack of sexual interest or satisfaction – related to unconscious fears about their own potential destructiveness. How far can psychotherapy help us to change such psychic patterns given that gender power inequalities have permeated erotic life for so long? Have such inequities become necessary to our sexuality?

The roots of gender expectations lie in our ideas about the psychological division in parenting. What is seen as masculine and feminine varies between cultures and historical epochs. But it is still true that masculinity tends to be associated with activity in our society and femininity with passivity, as Freud argued. Power relations between the sexes are in flux, but women's major sphere of influence is still over the mind of the human infant. Men may be losing their pre-eminent position but they continue to control most major cultural institutions – political, economic, legal and medical. In our society the mother is expected to look after the baby's physical needs and help her to contain and think about feelings. If the girl cannot internalise the maternal capacity to process and understand her wildly ambivalent passions and fantasies, physical excitement and desire may become terrifying – associated with a dread of annihilation or abandonment. Fathering is associated with boundary-setting and offering the child a pathway out of the symbiotic preoccupations of infancy into the wider world. The daughter – as I show later – needs to identify with the agency and potency associated culturally with men if she is to be able to acknowledge the strength of her own desire. I assume that the capacity for mothering and fathering exists in all men and women. Indeed fathers are sometimes more conventionally 'maternal' and mothers more paternal. When there is no actual father in the family, what is crucial is the mother's internal relationship to her own father and the male aspects of her psyche.

I argue that we need to integrate object relations insights about mother–daughter identification with a feminist Freudian perspective on how at the Oedipal phase a distorted view of sexual difference is structured into the personality. Outlining some quite polarised psychoanalytic perspectives on maternal and paternal power I show that no one theory offers a complete understanding of sexual identity. For instance Freud and Lacan, who gave a central role to female sexuality – in contrast to object relations theorists – also viewed women's erotic experience solely from the viewpoint of fathers and men. Drawing on the work of Luce Irigaray, Janine Chasseguet-Smirgel and Jessica Benjamin, who each seek to integrate mother and father-centred theories, I explore the way culture binds erotic desire at the crucial point where the daughter struggles to form an autonomous female identity without devaluing her own sex.

To illustrate these themes I discuss a lesbian patient who enriched her sexual life by re-owning aspects of herself previously projected onto men. Simultaneously she consolidated an internal relationship with a more consistent and nurturing maternal figure through the transference relationship. Once she had more fully explored male and female aspects of her psyche she formed a new partnership with a woman where sexual difference was acknowledged and both could move freely through a range of cross-gender identifications. In focusing clinically on a lesbian I am not suggesting that men are redundant to female sexuality in the new millennium. I would rather suggest that the entire topic of sexual orientation deserves far more clinical and theoretical attention. Ironically, at a time when many more women feel free to choose a same-sex partner, detailed accounts of successful psychotherapies with homosexual patients still remain rare in psychoanalytic literature. This might reflect the lack of a non-pathologising theory of homosexuality (O'Connor and Ryan 1993; Maguire 1995).

Penis or womb-envy? Opposing theories of female sexuality

In the twentieth century two periods of psychoanalytic controversy about female sexuality coincided with rapid shifts in women's social position. Between 1919 and 1935 Freud's theory of female penis envy provoked a vigorous debate amongst psychoanalysts about the nature and origins of all sexuality. In the 1960s psychoanalytic clinicians, influenced by an embryonic new feminist movement, returned again to those questions. What is sexual identity? they wondered. Are we born with a certain kind of male or female identity, with tendencies towards heterosexuality or homosexuality, or with a desire to produce children? Opposing factions from the first debate coalesced into theoretical tendencies which continue to dominate psychoanalytic thinking about sexual identity. I structure my survey around the 1919–35 debate, beginning with the polarised views of Freud and his major opponent, Karen Horney, on gender power relations.

Freud's theory revolves around the child's relationship to the father and the girl's struggle to come to terms with patriarchal authority and privilege, a process in which the mother becomes almost a bystander. Karen Horney accused Freud of 'male bias', of creating a theory which devalued women. Horney's view was that each sex has something uniquely valuable which arouses fierce envy in the opposite sex (Horney 1924, 1926). This argument won influential support from colleagues who later transformed the role of the mother in psychoanalytic theory. For British object relations theorists and North American ego psychologists, women – far from being deficient – have enormous emotional power based on their reproductive capacities and the utter dependence of the new-born infant. From this perspective women's influence over the psychic lives of infants is far more significant than men's political and economic power. At issue here are different notions of power and control and arguments about which parent is viewed by the child as most potent and enviable. Mother-centred theorists such as Klein and Winnicott emphasise that ambivalence towards maternal power underpins female envy of male privilege as well as men's repudiation of femininity. Most crucially for my discussion, early psychoanalytic interest in the erotic life of women has faded and been replaced by a preoccupation with their maternal function. In much contemporary clinical discussion the mother may well dominate her children in indirectly sexualised ways, but is not the subject of her own desire (Welldon 1988). Ironically, given women's increased sexual independence, there has been a long period where we have heard little about their actual sexual relationships with men or other women.

In spite of his provocative tone Freud was preoccupied with questions which are still relevant for women. For instance he noted that girls of three seemed more intelligent and lively than boys of that age. He asked how those confident little girls came to lose their intellectual curiosity and assertiveness (Freud 1933: 151). Freud did not know whether it was through nature or nurture, but he was sure that it was at the point where the little girl becomes interested in the father and men that she becomes more passive. His explanation was that the girl – unlike the boy – has the painful task of giving up her primary love-object and renouncing her active (masculine) love for her mother for a more submissive, conventionally 'feminine' attachment to her father and men. As she becomes more passive the girl often loses much of her own sexual desire. From these painful renunciations 'difficulties and possible inhibitions result which do not apply to men' (Freud 1931). The girl simultaneously has to come to terms with belonging to the less valued sex – a fate she may never fully accept. She may well turn her 'masculine' aggressive urges inwards, becoming self-sacrificial, prone to tolerating unhappy situations. Feeling a sense of internal lack, women look for a sense of value through being desired by others – especially men.

Not surprisingly, Freud thought that many girls never do become fully heterosexual, even if they think they are. They might identify with their fathers, wanting to be seen as 'one of the boys' whether they desire men or women. Or they may retain their primary attachment to the mother, becoming lesbian or establishing only a very unstable veneer of heterosexuality. 'Some part of what we call "the enigma of women" may perhaps stem from this experience of bisexuality in women's lives,' Freud observed (1931: 385). Such women, according to Freud, might marry and quickly lose interest in their husbands, transferring their love entirely to a baby. He thought this was all the more likely if they had a boy whose masculinity they could live through vicariously, but of course the mother might become just as preoccupied with a daughter.

Can female sexuality change?

Feminists have remained divided as to whose views on sexual identity were the more radical – Freud's or Horney's. They disagreed fundamentally about whether women were born heterosexual, with a desire for motherhood, or whether femininity was created through culture. For Freud the girl only begins to desire men sexually and to want their babies once she realises she can never be male. In contrast Horney argued that women are born with tendencies towards heterosexual femininity. By emphasising innate womanliness in this way Horney intended to defend women against the Freudian charge that we are all men *manqués*. But present-day feminists have pointed out that she 'threw the baby out with the bath-water', abandoning one of Freud's most subversive insights, his theory that sexual identity is formed through personal history and culture, rather than biology (Mitchell 1974).

My personal view is that we are formed primarily through culture but that anatomical differences between the sexes do impact upon the psyche, affecting our unconscious fantasies and anxieties. Because male and female bodies are constructed differently and we have different sexual and reproductive capacities, our experience of sex, reproduction and the physiological life-cycle will inevitably be different. However, I do not think that we are born with tendencies towards heterosexual femininity or masculinity. Neither do I believe that there is a core of 'real' personality that transcends culture. I am saying then that sexuality is shaped within culture but mediated through the body. Desire cannot exist outside prevailing social structures, but neither can psyche and soma ever be seen as distinct from each other. Language-patterns, belief-systems, cultural symbols and values will fundamentally determine how we interpret physiological sensation in any given society.

Lacan – a return to the father

Some feminists have turned to Lacan's theories, arguing that we need to look again at Freud's father-centred theory to understand how gender inequalities continue to reproduce themselves in our minds however family life is structured (Mitchell 1984). Attempting to reinstate the father at the heart of psychoanalytic theory, Lacan was deeply critical of the contemporary theoretical preoccupation with the mother–infant relationship.

He disagreed particularly with object relations theorists and ego psychologists who chart an ideal line of development from infantile satisfaction at the breast through to adult heterosexual fulfilment. Describing some relationships or states of mind as 'mature' or 'healthy' romanticised conventional ways of structuring sexual and family life, Lacan argued. Instead he stressed that adult sexual relations are inevitably unsatisfying because the loved one is always a substitute for the primal maternal lost object. Desire comes into existence through experiences of absence or lack (of the breast or the mother initially), not as the result of satisfaction. There is then something intrinsically painful and insatiable about desire itself. Any later experience of satisfaction always contains that first loss within it. As Freud said, 'We must reckon with the possibility that something in the nature of the sexual instinct itself is unfavourable to the realisation of complete desire' (Freud quoted in Mitchell 1984: 255).

However, Lacan's theory of female sexuality is, like Freud's, deeply ambiguous. While rejecting the idea of the 'natural' or pre-given, Lacan seems to echo Freud's uncertainty about whether women really are in some way inferior. For instance he says:

> the fact that the penis is dominant in the shaping of body-image is evidence of [an autonomous, non-biological imaginary anatomy]. Though this may shock the champions of the autonomy of female sexuality, such dominance is a fact and one moreover which cannot be put down to cultural influence alone.
> (Lacan 1953: 13 quoted in Grosz 1990 p. 123.)

Certain feminists argue that neither Lacan nor Freud were supporting patriarchy. They were simply describing what they saw around them: a world where women were second-class, their social position entirely unenviable (Mitchell 1984). But in order to arrive at this conclusion Freud and Lacan must be read in a very selective way. Both are fundamentally profoundly phallocentric, and focus primarily on male subjectivity.

The need for a female symbolic

Luce Irigaray, a French feminist psychoanalyst, claims that Freudian and Lacanian psychoanalysts see all desire as masculine. She, like

Horney, argues that psychoanalysis reproduces one of the 'sexual theories of children' – the phantasy that there is only one sex, and that is male, so that women are viewed as castrated, defective versions of men. Irigaray's project is to seek other ways in which women can speak of and for themselves.

Irigaray argues that the mother–daughter relationship is so little symbolised that it has become the 'dark continent of the dark continent, the most obscure area of our social order'. Women are deprived of their own symbols, gestures, imaginary, denied access to their own auto-erotism. And, without that 'interval of exchange, or of words, or gestures, passions between women manifest themselves in a rather cruel way' (Irigaray 1984: 103, quoted in Whitford 1989). Irigaray argues that mothers and daughters must create a new language with which to articulate their identities as women. At the moment the daughter has no woman with whom to identify.

Women do not need, Irigaray argues, to find something external to touch themselves with – a hand, women's genitals, language – as men do. 'A woman "touches herself" constantly . . . for her sex is composed of two lips which embrace continually . . . woman has sex organs just about everywhere' (Irigaray 1977: 345). 'She experiences pleasure almost everywhere . . . one can say that the geography of her pleasure is much more diversified, more multiple in its differences, more complex, more subtle than is imagined' (Irigaray 1977: 348). When Irigaray describes some typical female erotic pleasures, such as 'Caressing the breasts, touching the vulva, opening the lips, gently stroking the posterior wall of the vagina, lightly massaging the cervix', it is startlingly clear that such experiences are rarely if ever referred to in psychoanalytic literature (Irigaray 1977: 348). Instead we hear much about the power of the penetrating penis, and the smothering potential of the womb.

Obviously Irigaray is right in arguing that our culture represents all agency and power in phallic terms and there is no equivalent symbol to suggest female desire or potency. At this point, though, we also need to ask some questions about how female sexuality is shaped and mediated in culture and the psyche. Psychoanalysts have often suggested that men may find it easier to mobilise aggression and desire, because they can symbolise these powerful emotions through their more visible genitals. The penis might be imbued in fantasy with magical powers for destruction or reparation (Freud 1924; Klein 1928). Does the hidden nature of women's sexual and reproductive organs reinforce cultural inequality? Indeed, it may well be easier to control anxiety through symbolising a physical focus of sensation. This lack of anatomical anchoring could be connected with women's difficulties in symbolising our own desire as truly inner (Montgrain, quoted in Benjamin 1988). We may experience desire as more frightening and destructive because it cannot be linked to an external genital and localised in space, allowing us to visualise control of its duration. Perhaps we need a new set of metaphors for describing inner space. Maybe spatial images could be used to convey images of a female desire which is active and exploratory as well as receptive and holding. And we need ways of representing the sensual capacities of the entire female body as the site of pleasure.

Why do women tolerate sexual unhappiness?

Gender power inequalities are woven into our fundamental passions and desires at the point where we struggle to understand the difference between the sexes and the generations. The narcissistic wish to avoid confronting our ultimate helplessness in the face of psychic pain, loss and death exists unconsciously in all of us. The most important aspects of existence elude our control. Recognising that both sexes are anatomically different yet equal, would mean facing up to the fact that our mothers and all later love-objects are separate individuals beyond our control. As a defence against this girls are still brought up to maintain an illusion of ecstatic fusion with others – the traditional stereotype of femininity – while boys are encouraged to cut off from their own 'feminine' dependency needs and project them onto women.

Girls often have particular difficulty in separating psychically from their mothers since they feel they have nothing she lacks. In contrast the boy can assert his physiological difference and privileged place within culture, thus triumphing in fantasy over a mother experienced as omnipotent. Daughters who cannot overcome problematic experiences in infancy can remain unconsciously stuck in a state of ambivalent subservience towards their mothers, unable to build a viable lesbian or heterosexual identity. The girl dreads that in fighting for autonomy or expressing Oedipal rivalry she will destroy her mother – the mainstay of her identity. Or she may feel terrified of arousing her mother's envious retaliation if she is more sexually contented, or manages to combine motherhood and work in a way her mother could not. Here the parents' unconscious wishes and expectations are crucial. If the mother or father is indeed envious, the daughter's anxieties about rivalry will be greatly magnified (Maguire 1995).

Some daughters – including those who appear obsessed by disappointing relationships with men – remain tied, in a quasi-erotic way, to their mothers. Others try to cut off from early pain and deprivation by resorting to the culturally favoured solution of denigrating their mothers and their own sex. 'Basically penis envy is the symbolic expression of another desire. Women do not wish to become men but to detach themselves psychically from the mother and become complete autonomous women,' argues Chasseguet-Smirgel (1964: 118).

To the girl fathers represent difference. Male influence in the external world may appear more limited than the mother's all-encompassing emotional power. But the girl who idealises men may be fighting against a particularly virulent form of envious guilt towards both parents which can lead to profound sexual and creative inhibitions. She will then project her own destructiveness and her ensuing dread of parental retaliation onto her own female sexuality. Consequently she might be unable to enjoy sex because of an unconscious fear that her own vagina is dangerous or that any kind of penetration will damage the inside of her body (Chasseguet-Smirgel (1964: 97).

Envious guilt can leave the woman feeling profound contempt for her own female sexuality. Yet she may simultaneously be unable to fully utilise her own 'masculine' qualities if she feels paralysed by the guilty phantasy of having stolen what rightly belongs to her much-envied father. If she does allow herself success in the outside world she may sabotage her personal happiness through extreme passivity, even subservience within intimate relationships.

Jessica Benjamin, the North American psychoanalyst, explores this dynamic in her account of 'ideal love', where the woman yearns for an unattainable 'heroic sadist' – who alone can arouse her desire. Daughters who could not form an identificatory love relationship with a paternal figure are particularly prone to idealising 'masculine' qualities. They may seek out men or women who are extremely ruthless or emotionally independent so that they can experience those qualities vicariously while consciously disowning them. Distant, controlled relationships offer the woman an opportunity to surrender her will so that she can feel both excited and contained, an experience she lacked in childhood. She feels that such a detached lover won't overwhelm her or be destroyed by her intense emotion as once she feared her mother would be. Nevertheless, beneath the sensationalisation of power and powerlessness lies a distorted wish for recognition and intimacy with an equal other (Benjamin 1988).

How can a daughter separate psychically without entering into another relationship where she relinquishes her will and desire? First we need to recognise that the girl gains strength from her early identification with the mother. Then we can explore how the daughter might form an identificatory relationship with the father without idealising his sex. Theories which assume that only the father's authority can protect us from irrationality and submission reinforce the devaluation of women and motherhood. Real mothers devote most of their energy to fostering independence, inculcating the social and moral values that make up the superego. It is usually they who set limits to the child's desire for erotic closeness and wish for omnipotent control.

It is necessary then to combine the object relations emphasis on how women's second-class status is structured into the personality through early maternal identifications, with a feminist analysis of the Oedipal phase, where the girl's perception of sexual difference becomes distorted. At these two points of interaction between culture and the psyche fundamental questions arise about the girl's capacity to symbolise and act on her own desires.

The girl needs to be recognised as being like both parents psychologically. She also needs to have access to images of women as active sexual beings and agents of their own destinies. And it is women themselves who must continue the fundamental task of creating new ways of symbolising female experience.

As I have shown, some girls denigrate one parent in their struggle to resolve early difficulties and build an autonomous sexual identity. Benjamin and Chasseguet-Smirgel focus on those girls who idealise their fathers. However, I often find that my patients idealise their mothers. It will be interesting to see whether this is an increasing trend in the new millennium as women's position in society changes. The patient I discuss next dug down to the foundations of her sexual identity, meticulously unpicking and examining every one of her own assumptions and beliefs. When she first came to psychotherapy she dismissed men as generally dull and cynically self-motivated. Unconsciously she was preoccupied with ousting her father and winning her mother's undivided attention.

Rescuing the maternal object of desire

Several years after leaving college where she had won a national prize for best graduating student in her field, India had not yet managed to settle down in a permanent job. She described a series of affairs with older women who were uncertain of their sexual orientation. Often a man – past or present – stood between herself and the object of her affections.

India described her glamorous mother as leading an exciting social life with racy women friends. With her daughter she had been tantalisingly inconsistent, overwhelming her with too much of the wrong kind of attention while failing to notice when she really needed to be looked after. Gradually a picture emerged of her father as consistently loving, attentive and proud of his beautiful daughter. But he had never stood up to her strong-willed mother and had eventually become rather depressed.

In summarising her psychotherapy, I focus on how India internalised a more consistent maternal figure through her transference experiences with me, while simultaneously building on her more positive identifications with her father. This resulted in a rapid rise to a prominent professional position, and an increased capacity for emotional and sexual intimacy.

India had been brought up in a country where women were in many (but not all) respects very oppressed, yet in her extended family the women tended to be dominant. At school she found the boys very aggressive, brutally competitive. Sex in her family was never discussed, and she had grown up with the idea that heterosexual intercourse was dangerous to women, and childbirth a particularly risky venture. Her parents had put great emphasis on education, expecting her to be a career woman rather than just a traditional wife.

India soon began wondering about my sexual orientation. Simultaneously she became involved in another doomed relationship with an older woman. I suggested that affair had gained some of its intensity from feelings stirred up in relation to me. Perhaps she also saw me as a tantalising maternal figure of uncertain orientation? 'I don't know,' India said. After this the transference began to feel dead. India avoided direct interaction with me, growing increasingly hopeless and depressed. If I said anything about her feelings towards me she would change the subject or go silent.

Profound anxieties about the maternal transference emerged in her dreams. She dreamt about the therapy as a little tug-boat shaped like the female genitals. She'd been expecting a short hop from one Irish inlet to another, but as always in Ireland the skies darkened and the tug suddenly started heading out into the open sea. In the dream as in her therapy she didn't know where we were going, the water started to come over the sides and drench her and she looked longingly at more sturdy (masculine) boats associated with her childhood. 'Yes, I know your name is Irish' India said as she finished recounting the dream.

After a year of three times weekly psychotherapy I realised there was another emotional 'no-go area' – men. I knew little about India's father, she avoided men socially and was vitriolic about the shortcomings of her male colleagues. But was the absence of men in her life a problem for her? Certainly it was significant that she got into triangles where she sought to 'rescue' her lovers from unhappy heterosexuality. Was her hostility towards men compounding her difficulties at work? Recently India had got a new and prestigious job and was astonished that her male boss was so helpful. 'I just can't understand why,' she said. Determined to break some silences I said 'Perhaps you wonder whether he finds you attractive.' 'That's outrageous,' India said. 'I never think of men in that light. I don't want to discuss the idea.'

Soon after this she described a very desirable and sorted-out older blonde lesbian who would not consider her seriously as a partner. I said that she felt I would not take her seriously – that I, like her mother, related to her intensely and then abandoned her for other relationships. She gave me a scathing look and said: 'I just don't see you in that light.' Then she said, 'Just like the men.' Later she alluded again to her older blonde friend and said 'I haven't stopped thinking that SHE is attractive.'

So in a half-unconscious way she created new barriers around these no-go areas. For instance, the next session she described how a silly, flirtatious colleague, who could not decide whether she actually was a lesbian, had made a very suggestive remark in a professional context. India had felt embarrassed and furious. I suggested she might also be describing her reaction to my remark in the last session. 'Well, I just thought what you said was TOTALLY inappropriate,' she responded immediately.

Once she'd got over her shock India began admitting that the reason she hated heterosexual parties was because men swarmed round her. 'They crowd up close and steal the food off my plate' she complained. She remembered being told about male workmates who were crazy about her. At work she became extremely friendly with one of her bosses – a completely new experience for her. He was flirtatious in an entirely protective way, joked about sex and would have made a great father, India said. She even found herself admitting that she found just a few men attractive as long as they were delicate-looking, girlish and not too big. I might be amused to learn, she said, that helpful father-figures kept coming out of the woodwork and advising her. Whereas previously India's pioneering ideas had been dismissed as outrageous, now they were seen as timely, and she was achieving expert status with astonishing speed.

There had also been a sudden change in therapy, India announced one day, 'I used to think you didn't like me but you seem to be saying more,' she told me. 'I noticed you laughing at a joke I made. It reminds me of being with my father. I think we had a similar sense of humour.' I said, 'So the change is that your father has come into the room in the last few weeks.' 'That's exactly right. We've talked more about my father and men in the past few weeks than we have in the past year,' India replied. She went on to talk about her sadness that she had colluded in excluding and devaluing the men in her family. 'I always assumed that my father wanted to be left out. But did he really?' Now it was obvious to both of us that the therapeutic relationship was not going to be seen as a purely lesbian dyad. She could play the role of her father, and so could I.

'If I say that men find me attractive and I don't find them all repulsive, what then?' India repeated in worried fashion. She suspected me of pathologising her sexuality, but then decided that she'd been imputing 'wrong motives' to me. 'You're not trying to change my sexual orientation. You just want me to talk about it. I can see now that you're not necessarily expecting me to rush out and jump on the next available man.' It would be convenient, she said, if I was pushing her towards heterosexuality, but in fact, even more worryingly, she was beginning to think that I didn't really know where she was going. And indeed, India seemed to feel cast adrift from some internal mooring and was becoming worryingly desolate.

There followed a period of profound exploration of her sexuality. We discussed what desire, excitement and fulfilment meant to her. What is sexual attraction, she asked, and how does it fit in with liking the look of someone or wanting them to cuddle you? 'What if I am left with no sexual orientation?' She had cut herself off from her old unsupportive lesbian friends, many of whom were having babies, something India knew she did not want. She wanted a woman for herself. And anyway, having a baby seemed difficult enough even in the conventional way, let alone facing all the prejudice her friends were enduring towards lesbian parenthood. India even questioned whether she had 'taken a wrong path' in having sexual relationships with women. Maybe she'd have been happier in a close celibate partnership? Was sex worth the ensuing misery?

At this point some certainties emerged. India decided I must be heterosexual. 'If you are not, you're the most ignorant of lesbian culture of any I've come across,' she told me. And she now felt absolutely certain she was a lesbian. She dreamt of a couple, a man and woman who stood in the entrance hall of a big stately home, one on each side of the front door. At first they were wearing shabby tracksuits. Then they went away and reappeared, standing in exactly the same position in tennis outfits. This was repeated in every possible combination of clothes – business suits, cocktail outfits, ball-gowns, summer day-wear, winter furs. Finally they re-emerged wearing the same old tracksuits they'd started in. India had looked at the parental couple from every angle, her dream was telling us, and it was still the same dull serviceable combination it had been to start off with. Men were now fun as friends and interesting as mentors – a huge change in her life, she reminded me. But it was really women who attracted her sexually.

It is a feature of many British case-histories of the late 1990s that the patient goes through a long period of depression where new life and creativity manifests itself only through a cosseted garden or ledge of pot-plants. India was no exception. She dreamt during this fallow phase that she was in a large garden at night which had marsupial creatures, like small kangaroos with babies in their pouches, sitting on the walls, watching her. She needed an incubation period surrounded by lots and lots of Mar-supial mothers.

When every inch of her flat and roof-terrace was crammed with plants India began a new sexual relationship with a slightly younger, rather than an older woman. She reported that for the first time she was able to discuss sex with her partner. She had never been able to tell me about it before, either. But now she told me how her previous partners had wanted sex to be affectionate, satisfying but restrained, or else experimental in a rather objectified way. If India had hitherto been operating primarily in the mother–daughter sphere, it now looked as if difference – including psychic masculinity – could be introduced into her erotic life and found exciting. India had a dream about a camel and a giraffe playing with each other.

She commented that these animals would not normally associate with each other. Camels in her experience were rather cranky and bad-tempered as she could be, while the gracefulness of the giraffe reminded her of her new lover. This woman looked very feminine, but actually could be very 'laddish' in her sexual manner. She was telling me of a change in her internal objects. But disappointment ensued. Whereas previously India had sought out mother-figures, now she was being asked to step into that role herself, and she did not want to.

Finally India found a more equal relationship with a woman of the same age who was also devoted to her work in a related field. She felt they really did have common needs and values.

> In previous relationships they seemed interested in the experi-ence of lesbian sex. I feel that T really wants me. I used to get pushed into being the more male person. I wanted it a bit but then realised I didn't. They were girlies who needed rescuing. T is not a girlie. I'm not going to get polarised into my old role of being stronger, more of an 'out' lesbian. She helps me a lot whereas I used to always be the organiser. But if I'm not rescu-ing her, what are we going to do? Just enjoy ourselves? I don't think she has any ambivalence about her sexual orientation. I always used to feel I had to push the boundaries, suggest differ-ent positions or times of day. Then I'd wonder if they thought I was a sex-fiend, or think I had to have sex when I didn't really want it. But T takes as much responsibility as I do.

This marked the beginning of a protracted and eventful period in psychotherapy, as India painfully struggled to rework and consoli-date the changes she had made.

Changing female sexuality

How does a woman come to 'own' her powerful desires, to experi-ence them in her mind and body in a way which allows her to assert her wants both in sexual life and in other spheres of existence? And how can psychotherapy assist her in this?

In therapy as in childhood the woman needs to play in fantasy with a range of cross-sex identifications, accepting difference by mak-ing it familiar. We need to recognise both the 'holding' mother and the exciting father as elements which make up desire. And female sexuality will be enriched if we can re-own some of the qualities we so often prefer to project onto men.

As India developed a more reliable internal mother she felt freer to explore a buried relationship with her father. She gradually discovered her own personal authority and potency, whilst strengthening her identification with her father's adventurous nature. As she confronted her own sexuality, India dared acknowledge what she had always known – that men found her intensely desirable – a reflection of the positive oedipal attachment she had had to her father. But now India knew she was strong enough to make up her own mind what kind of woman she was. She did not have to live life as the object of male desire, or to deny the existence of men and masculinity completely. More secure in her own femininity, she could declare her enjoyment of male attributes, while recognising that they were especially pleasurable in herself and other women. Crucial to this transformation was India's discovery of a new way of thinking about and representing her own sexual and emotional experience.

Conclusion

Female sexuality must be mediated through a range of identifications which transcend stereotypical notions of gender if women are to create a psychic link between freedom and sexual desire. The girl needs a space in her mind where she can symbolise her own desire through drawing on 'maternal' containing functions, and the kind of active sexuality seen culturally as 'phallic'. She also needs to identify with the 'exciting' qualities of both sexes. Ideally she should have paternal figures (who might be female), to help her gain a sense of herself as psychically separate, and find a way out into the external world. It is crucial that parents protect daughters from their own envy and rivalry, instilling in girls a sense that they can succeed both in conventionally 'masculine' and 'feminine' activities. This parental belief in the daughter's capacity for personal fulfilment is a vital antidote to the cultural devaluation of femininity.

We must bear in mind though that female sexuality will not alter through psychological change alone. The girl will have to struggle to synthesise any sense of independent selfhood with the reality of living in a society where there are so few images of female sexuality as active and autonomous.

Expectations and wishes which are transmitted from generation to generation cohere around bodily experience. We need to understand more about how physiological sensation is mediated through culture and becomes inscribed on the psyche, so that we can read and interpret it in new ways. Only then will girls and boys come to see women as full subjects with their own needs and desires.

References

Benjamin, J (1988) *The Bonds of Love: Psychoanalysis, Feminism and the Problem of Domination*. New York: Random House.

Chasseguet-Smirgel, J. (1964) 'Feminine guilt and the Oedipus complex', in *Female Sexuality*. London: Maresfield, 1985.

Freud, S. (1924) 'The dissolution of the Oedipus complex', *Pelican Freud Library* 7. Harmondsworth: Penguin, 1977.

—— (1931) 'Female Sexuality', *Pelican Freud Library* 7. Harmondsworth: Penguin, 1977.

—— (1933) 'Femininity', New Introductory Lectures in Psychoanalysis, *Pelican Freud Library* 7. Harmondsworth: Penguin, 1977.

Grosz, E. (1990) *Jacques Lacan: A Feminist Introduction*. London: Routledge.

Horney, K. (1924) 'On the genesis of the castration complex in women', *International Journal of Psycho-Analysis* 5: 50–65.

—— (1926) 'The flight from womanhood: the masculinity complex in women as viewed by men and by women' in J. Baker Miller (ed.), *Psychoanalysis and Women*, Harmondsworth: Penguin, 1984.

Irigaray, L. (1977) 'This sex which is not one', in C. Zanardi (ed.), *Essential Papers on the Psychology of Women*. New York: New York University Press, 1990.

—— (1984) *Ethique de la différence sexuelle*. Paris: Minuit.

Klein, M. (1928) 'Early stages of the Oedipus complex', in *Love, Guilt and Reparation and Other Works 1921–45*. London: The Hogarth Press, 1975.

Maguire, M. (1995) *Men, Women, Passion and Power: Gender Issues in Psychotherapy*. London: Routledge.

—— (1997) 'Envy between women', in M. Lawrence and M. Maguire (eds), *Psychotherapy with Women: Feminist Perspectives*. Basingstoke: Macmillan.

Mitchell, J. (1974) *Psychoanalysis and Feminism*, London; Allen Lane.

—— (1984) *The Longest Revolution*. London: Virago.

O'Connor N. and Ryan, J. (1993) *Wild Desires and Mistaken Identities*. London: Virago.

Welldon, E. (1988) *Mother, Madonna, Whore*. London: Free Association Books.

Whitford, M. (1989) 'Rereading Irigaray', in T. Brennan (ed.), *Between Feminism and Psychoanalysis*. London: Routledge.

Chapter 7

Celebrating the phallus

Warren Colman

Is there such a thing as male sexuality or is it only possible to talk about sexuality in general? Are there any fundamental differences between men and women or are the differences we see merely the effect of cultural conditioning and stereotypical generalisations? The impact of feminism has been to considerably undermine assumptions about gender differences which, previously, were taken for granted. Yet once the constricting limitations of culturally imposed stereotypes are overthrown, we may be left with a potentially limitless panorama in which anything is possible and nothing that can be said about one gender cannot, in principle, be said about the other.

Thus we are faced with two possible – and prevalent – theoretical extremes: on the one hand there is the biological determinism neatly expressed by Freud's famous aphorism 'Anatomy is destiny' (Freud 1924); on the other there is a paradoxically absolute cultural relativism that denies biology any significant role in the construction of gender differences, including the different ways (if there are any) that the genders relate sexually. In this chapter, I attempt to take a middle way which acknowledges biological differences between the sexes as a limiting factor in the construction of gender and sexuality while also acknowledging that gender and sexuality *are* constructed, within these limits, in a complex interaction between psychological, physical and socio-cultural factors.

Biological sex and the limits of gender

I suggest that biology operates as a limiting factor in three inter-related ways.

1 *There are major physical differences between men and women and to assume that these differences do not also have major psychological correlations is to assume an untenable split between mind and body.* As Robert Stoller puts it, 'from puberty on into adult life, most boys are driven by their erotic physiology more than most girls are'. In terms of their different styles of erotic interpersonal relationships he suggests, in an aphorism to rival Freud 'For men – the younger the more so – engorgement dominates engagement' (Stoller 1985: 35). It seems reasonable to assume that a genetically driven imperative to inseminate as many women as possible in order to promote the survival of their own genes is the source of this psychological and emotional imperative in men. For women, though, for whom each insemination has potentially much more costly consequences (I am speaking in strictly biological terms here), it would make sense if they were genetically programmed 'to wait, forgo, refuse if they feel it appropriate' (Stoller ibid.). Such differences, though, must be seen as tendencies, statistical probabilities only and capable of being overridden by other factors in certain circumstances. Sociobiological explanations such as this operate only at the basic level of our genetic hardware; they are insufficient to explain or even describe the higher level emergent properties of our cultural software.

Nevertheless, testosterone (and adrenaline) have a lot to answer for. Males are physically organised towards high energy, focused bursts of activity (Hooke and Hooke 1993); young males especially often have an insatiable thirst for aggressive, competitive, high risk action and challenge. Furthermore, in all known economically primitive cultures, it is men who wage war while women look after the home. The ethnographic evidence strongly suggests two sex-linked preoccupations – of men with violence and of women with nurture (Hudson and Jacot 1991).

2 *Each gender has to come to terms with the physical realities and limitations of their biological equipment.* This is the aspect Freud uses to explain the differing Oedipal fates of boys and girls, especially their differing experience of the castration complex. For the boy, he argues, fear of castration persuades him to give up his Oedipal wishes and ushers in the dissolution of the Oedipus complex. For the girl, it is the realisation of her castration (as she sees it) that ushers in the Oedipus complex itself – the wish to be given a penis, transformed into the wish to be given a baby, by the father (Freud 1924). I am not concerned here with whether this argument is true or not so much

as with the kind of argument it is – Freud's explanation consists of elaborating the feelings and fantasies which the young child weaves around his perception of the facts of his or her anatomy. His approach is therefore much less determinist than the phrase 'Anatomy is destiny' suggests. Freud's argument is concerned with the psychological *consequences* which derive from the possession or lack of a penis, that is, how the child *construes* these biological facts in his or her mind.

Later in life, there are similar issues around the biological fact of women's child-bearing capacity. Questions of procreation, sterility or abortion have a much more direct meaning for women than they do for men. Whether or not they bear children, women have to come to terms with their child-bearing capacity and men have to come to terms with their lack of it.

Males also have to come to terms with the possession of a penis. For most men this becomes a taken for granted fact in the course of establishing a core gender identity in the first few years of life. Although their feelings and fantasies about their penis may be complex and problematic, as I shall explore later on in the paper, they accept that it is a natural part of their anatomic equipment. Some men do not do this, however – these are the transsexuals who believe themselves to belong to the opposite gender and for whom the penis is felt not to belong to them in some way. Would-be transsexuals (whether male or female) experience a head-on clash between their self-perception and the biological facts of their own bodies. Whatever the reason for this, the possibility of such a clash throws into relief the accommodation the rest of us have made to the gender implications of our own bodies.

3 *The biological facts act as an organising focus for a host of psychological and emotional factors that give meaning to and are given meaning by the physical facts but cannot be directly derived from them.* These include all the feelings, fantasies, images and beliefs that are built up into a kaleidoscopic patchwork in the course of a lifetime through personal experience, social interaction and immersion in the particular set of meanings generated by each culture. It is with this third factor that I shall be mainly concerned for the rest of this chapter. I shall argue that, for men, the penis acts as the central organising focus for their sexuality. In so doing, the physical organ of flesh and blood – the penis – is transformed into a symbolic image of immense power, fascination and mystery – the phallus.

Archetypal masculinity and the phallic complex

Freud has been rightly criticised for his phallocentrism – the belief that the penis is an ultimately desirable object, the lack of which consigns women to a position of inferiority and lack. But the problem with Freud's theory is not the emphasis he gave to the penis but that he assumed that what was true for men was also true for women. In my view, men *are* phallocentric: their relationship to the phallus is central to their gender identity. Most, if not all, men's feelings and fantasies about their sexuality cluster around the image of the erect penis, which thus becomes the central image in what might be called the phallic complex. The phallus represents the whole range of feelings and fantasies associated with male sexuality and is therefore much more than the penis itself. As an apocryphal remark of Jung's puts it 'the penis is a phallic symbol'.

Nevertheless, the basis for male phallocentrism can be found in the biological organisation of male sexuality, even if that does not define its content. The male's sexual and reproductive functions are entirely located in his genitals, whereas for the female these functions are more widely distributed. A woman's genitals are merely the portal of entry for the reproductive activity that takes place deep inside her body in her ovaries and uterus. This wider distribution means that female sexuality is more appropriately symbolised by the whole body, whether this is conceived as woman's body or mother's body, than by the genitals alone.

As a consequence of this differing sexual and reproductive organisation, male sexual arousal is also much more localised. Since the man's role in procreation is confined to insemination, it is not surprising that erection, penetration and ejaculation arouse intense excitement which is capable of sweeping all other considerations aside. As a result, male sexual arousal is much more readily available to be utilised in the service of defence against other painful emotions than is women's, and it is this, I believe, which is the source of the much greater frequency of frankly sexual perversions amongst men. When we speak psychologically, we can readily see that women are just as perverse as men in the way they twist and distort psychic reality, for example, or in their capacity for sado-masochistic internal object relations, but it is the means they use to express these perverse ways of thinking and feeling that are different.

As I have said, the phallus is not merely the penis – it is a symbolic representation of male sexual feeling and phantasy. As an image, the phallus is usually much larger than the physical organ since it represents the psychic situation rather than the physical one. Images of giant phalluses appear in many cultures: as the appendages of Hermes and the phallic god, Priapus, in Greece and Rome; as the lingam in India; and as the penis gourds worn by the tribesmen of New Guinea. In our own culture such images have been relegated to the secret alternative world of pornography. One of the clearest expressions of this occurs in the satirical pornography of the eighteenth-century artist Thomas Rowlinson, in which men are depicted as no more than huge erect cocks slavering after any woman in sight (Tang 1999). All these images represent not so much what men *look* like when they are aroused as *what they feel like*.

It is at least plausible that there is a biological basis for the feeling of tremendous strength, power and invulnerability often associated with male sexual arousal. Genes that have the capacity to generate such feelings would be promoted by natural selection since those males possessing them would be more likely to overcome whatever obstacles appeared in the way of inseminating females, including competition from other males and female reluctance. What I am interested in here, though, is exploring the psychological uses to which these basic emotions might be put. *Any* situation of weakness or threat can be compensated for by invoking the emotional power of sexual arousal, symbolised in the totemic potency of the erect phallus. In this way, the instinctual component of male potency can be transformed into images and fantasies of male omnipotence. The men who walk around wearing only penis gourds are apparently flouting the strength of their big cocks; in fact, they are revealing their hidden sense of insecurity and threat for which the big cock is used as compensation. This doesn't only apply to New Guinea tribesmen, of course: so-called civilised society has countless symbolic derivatives of phallic potency. A great deal of male competitiveness is conducted in the symbolic language of who has the biggest cock. Schoolboys test this out quite literally, showing off their penises, measuring them with a ruler and competing for who can pee furthest and even ejaculate furthest. Later on, it often has to do with big numbers – it seems to me that most of the promotional advertising for computers, for example, is based on this premise: the biggest hard-drive, the fastest processor, the more RAM. Who cares whether you really need it – doesn't it make you feel good to have all those big numbers under your fingers? The same is true for other machines, like cars – and, of course, for money. He with the smallest wad pays for the drinks. In all these situations, the underlying issue is anxieties about *power*. The dragooning of sexual arousal into overcoming feelings of helplessness and powerlessness reaches its most extreme form in rape, where the sexual act is merely a means to the main aim of asserting power over a feared object by inflicting humiliation and/or revenge upon them. A particularly revealing form of this is where apparently heterosexual men demonstrate their homophobia by raping homosexual men.

Creative and destructive aspects of the phallus

The phallus is felt to be an instrument whose tremendous power has both creative and destructive potential. It is frequently symbolised as a weapon or a tool and this symbolism works both ways round: on the one hand, the universal male preoccupation with violence and warfare invokes sexual symbolism through the association of swords, knives and spears with the penetrative phallus; while on the other, men frequently symbolise their sexual activity in terms of tools, weapons and screwing etc. While this symbolism is often drawn upon as evidence of the destructive quality of men's sexual fantasies, it is important to remember that weapons and tools have positive and constructive functions as well. Men make things and bring things together using screwdrivers, for example, and in a society where warfare is necessary for self-defence or for the future prosperity of the group, the capacity to wield a sword may likewise be very positively construed.

There is an interesting example of this kind of archetypal imagery in *King Lear* (1963), in which the bastard son Edmund seems to identify himself with the erect phallus. Early in the play he proclaims:

> Edmund the base
> Shall top th'legitimate. I grow, I prosper,
> Now, gods, stand up for bastards.
> (I.ii.20–2)

Later on he instructs the soldier despatched to kill Lear and Cordelia: 'to be tender minded | does not become a sword' (V.iii.32–3). In these invocations we can see how the stiff hardness of the erect phallus is associated with destructive power while the tender, flaccid state is hated and despised as unbecoming weakness.

In the play, Edmund stands for the ruthless power of unmodified nature. As an illegitimate son, his rights and, at times, his very existence are denied and, typical of unconscious contents, he therefore remains in a primitive state that threatens the social order. He seeks to overthrow the weakened old father, King Lear, as well as his own father, Gloucester. In him, the phallus is a weapon of conquest and destruction, teeming with life and virility but seeking its ends with a ruthlessness that amounts to pure evil.

Almost identical imagery can be used to indicate the almost mystical creative properties of the phallus. Jung quotes a passage from Goethe's *Faust* concerning the key that 'unlocks the mysterious forbidden door behind which some wonderful thing awaits discovery' (Jung 1912/1952: para. 180). The key is unmistakably phallic in character:

Mephistopheles:	Here, take this key
Faust:	That little thing! But why?
Mephistopheles:	First grasp it; it is nothing to decry.
Faust:	It glows, it shines, increases in my hand!
Mephistopheles:	How great its worth, you soon shall understand.
	The key will smell the right place from all others;
	Follow it down, it leads you to the Mothers!

Further evidence for the centrality of the phallus in the archetypal masculine comes from Jung himself in a most vivid example of a highly numinous experience. In his autobiography, Jung recounts a childhood dream in which he found his way into an underground cathedral-like cavern. In it there was a wonderfully rich golden throne on which was standing an enormous phallus, the size of a tree trunk, reaching almost to the ceiling, with a single eye at the top of the head gazing motionlessly upward. The child Jung was paralysed with terror and heard his mother's voice call out 'Yes, just look at him. That is the man-eater' (Jung 1963: 27).

In Jung's dream the phallus is displayed in both its most creative and destructive aspects. It is an object of terror, fascination and awe. The dream conveys the potentially overwhelming magnitude of the phallus – which Jung regarded as symbolic of the life force itself – and it perhaps also indicates the enormity of his own creative powers as well as his fear that he could be destroyed by them. In a recent interpretation of Jung's dream, one Jungian analyst has commented

From the archetypal standpoint the phallus in the dream is an enormously creative symbol. For the ancient Romans the phallus symbolises a man's sacred genius, the source of his physical and mental creative powers. The phallus symbolically is the dispenser of all his inspired or brilliant ideas and of his buoyant joy of life. In classical Greece the entire Dionysian religion, and with it both tragedy and comedy, seems to have sprung out of a systematic veneration of the phallus and the male generative function.

(Feldman 1992: 266–7)

These examples all demonstrate men's enormous narcissistic investment in their penises. Here it is difficult to distinguish between the direct importance to them of a part of their anatomy capable of giving them such ecstatic pleasure and its symbolic meaning as signifier of and focus for their narcissistic self-investment in general. The same is true of the other side of the coin: their fear that any harm should come to such a valuable, yet actually so vulnerable piece of themselves. According to Freud, the castration anxiety which induces the little boy to give up his Oedipal wishes is, in fact, a *narcissistic* threat to his supreme investment in his penis (Freud 1924). In any event, the phallus is the source of intense pride or shame, depending on whether the narcissistic cathexis is a positive or negative one. Men seek to protect this aspect of themselves both literally and symbolically at all costs.

While agreeing with Robert Stoller's opinion that I quoted earlier to the effect that men are driven by the urgency of their stiff cocks, I also want to stress the *emotional* significance of men's preoccupation with sex. The commonplace assertion that men are only interested in sex while women are interested in the emotional side of relationships misses the point that men's sexual preoccupations are highly emotionally charged. While men can and do divorce sexual feelings from emotional ones, and seem to be able to do this more successfully than women, their sexual needs express a relation to the phallus which is, in itself, a deeply emotional one.

Differentiation, dissolution and the development of masculine identity

The struggle to achieve a secure identity as a separate person from which it is possible to relate without fear of engulfment, invasion or dissolution is not gender-specific. However, the form taken by these basic anxieties about relationship and the defences against them do show typical variations along gender lines. Castration anxiety is one obvious example of this. We all experience anxieties about loss or destruction of our identity and sense of self but, for the reasons I have outlined, men associate this existential loss with an attack on their genitals or, more generally, on their sexual identity. The equivalence to this in women is the fear of intrusion and violation which often takes the form of sexual assault. Thus for men phantasies about engulfment may take the form of the *vagina dentata* while for women phantasies about intrusion take the form of being raped by the destructive phallus. *Both* sexes, however, experience anxieties about engulfment and intrusion equally: the anatomical situation provides the form not the content of these phantasies. To understand the latter we must turn to the situation of their origin in early development, including the development of gender identity itself.

For all of us, self-differentiation is a precarious matter. The more secure we are in our own identities, the more secure our sense of a boundary between ourselves and others, the more capable we are of intimacy with others, since we are able to allow that boundary to temporarily and partially dissolve secure in the knowledge that we cannot ultimately lose ourselves. But the difference between men and women in this respect is that for the boy, differentiation from mother is interwoven with the experience of being of a different gender. He is able to say 'I am unlike mother because I am a boy' and, vice versa, 'to be a boy is to be different from mother'. Masculinity, epitomised by the possession of a penis, becomes the sign of differentiation and separation from mother: the phallus cuts like a sword between the undifferentiated union of mother and infant. Phallic potency becomes a totemic signifier not only of manhood but of a man's fundamental sense of identity.

In phantasy, the phallus takes on a magical power to fend off engulfment in the dark continent of the feminine. Like Edmund, many men are pricks on sticks: their unconscious identification with the phallus means that they feel themselves to be identical with their sexual potency and its derivatives. They use their gender identity and, especially, its location in the phallus as a bulwark against dissolution and annihilation – the ultimate meaning of castration. For women, potency *as women* does not offer this basically defensive function. On the other hand, since their gender identity is not built on being unlike mother it cannot be invoked as protection against loss of identity either.

This means that while both sexes may fear and therefore resist experiences of merging and loss of boundaries in sexual intercourse, the effect is different. Women in this situation become unable to risk 'letting go' and their sexual pleasure may be curtailed or blocked altogether but they do not feel that their gender identity is threatened. For men, much of this is reversed. Their resistance to merging and letting go may not affect their sexual pleasure but it curtails their emotional involvement. Women seek emotional safety in order to be able to let go sexually but their men may fear that such emotional involvement will emasculate them or, worse, annihilate them, depending on how profound their emotional anxieties are. As a result, male emotional anxieties join forces with male sexual functioning to create the familiar syndrome of 'Wham, bam, thank you ma'am'. Or, as a patient of mine informed me, 'Men don't pay prostitutes to have sex with them but to go away afterwards.'

Both sexes come to associate femininity with the experiences of merger, nurture, dependence and helplessness characteristic of the early relationship with the mother. As a result, masculinity can function as a defence against anxieties associated with these early experiences. This can perhaps be seen most clearly in phallic women, who have taken on a masculine identification in reaction against the maternal relationship. In such cases of cross-gender identification, it is not only that the mother is hated and despised in some way so that the girl does not wish to be like mother. It is also that there has been a substantial failure in early maternal containment so that strong defences against infantile anxieties associated with dissolution and merger have become necessary. I think it is revealing of the function of masculinity that it can be called upon to serve this defensive function. By contrast, men with cross-gender identifications have been unable to separate themselves sufficiently from the maternal matrix; they are usually mothers' boys who feel cut off from their fathers and therefore unable to escape the maternal embrace. In them, the regressive longing to return to the womb is strong – that is, they *seek* merger and dissolution in fantasy, while in practice they tend to fear it and run away from it. They are more 'in touch' with the feminine but at the price of having failed to develop a relationship to the masculine phallus, which is felt to be dangerous, destructive and damaging (Colman 1995).

Wimps and bastards: defensive masculinity and the feminised man

The young boy's attitude to the phallus as creator or destroyer is deeply influenced by the attitude of his mother. If she herself has a good relationship to the phallus she will welcome his phallic strivings while making it clear that she doesn't need them. While the boy may feel rejected that mummy can't marry him because she is married to daddy, he will be spared the impossible task that many dissatisfied women impose on their sons of trying to compensate for their father's inadequacy. These sons assume grandiose poses as they swing from the false glory of being mummy's special little darling to the helpless impotence of knowing that they are not really up to the Big Job without daddy's help.

The mother may also have too poor a relationship to her own sexuality to accept that of her son. These are the women who are most likely to be married to destructive, absent or impotent men so the boy's problem is compounded – his father does nothing to compensate for the attitude of his mother. He therefore has two choices – either he identifies with the destructive phallus and becomes the phallic monster his mother unconsciously sees him as or he repudiates it and takes up a predominantly feminine identification. This is the dichotomy between the wimp and the bastard, the male equivalent of the Madonna and the whore.

There is a wonderful scene in Woody Allen's film *Play it again, Sam* which perfectly captures the psychology of the wimp. Woody Allen, the ultimate neurotic, has spent the whole film trying unsuccessfully to make it with a woman. Finally, at the urging of his internal Humphrey Bogart, a fantasy figure who represents the strong creative father, he plucks up his courage to kiss Diane Keaton, the neglected wife of his best friend. Overcome by emotion, Diane Keaton runs out of the door. Allen, aghast, is convinced that she believes he is a terrible monster. The joke, of course, is the absurd contrast between Allen's obvious wimpishness – afraid even to kiss the girl – and his neurotic fantasy of himself as a monster, the destructive phallus incarnate. But the serious edge to the joke is that it is precisely because of this neurotic belief that his sexuality is dangerous, damaging and will inevitably be rejected that he is so afraid of showing it.

The psychology of the wimp involves a defensive identification with the feminine against the fear of the destructive phallus. Fear of castration may enter into this but it is not the central point. As the Woody Allen example shows, the wimp fears his *own* phallic urges as much as those of the destructive father. The unconscious image of parental intercourse is one in which the father is damaging the mother with the destructive phallus. Hence the prominence of rescue phantasies in feminised men. Many of these men enter the caring professions, seeking both to identify with the maternal role and to act as rescuers to their phantasised damaged mothers. I will not take issue with those who would argue that such fantasies of destructive intercourse are *projections* of the child's own envious and jealous wishes and that the typical lack of aggression in feminised men is further evidence of the defensive processes (including splitting and projection) that have been mobilised against such destructive wishes. But I would add that an actual parental situation in which the phallus is felt to be destructive must greatly influence the child's own fantasy life and make it difficult, if not impossible, for him to find sufficient containment for the aggressive aspect of his Oedipal wishes. This may be the case either where the father is actually destructive (e.g. in violent or abusive behaviour) or, more insidiously, where he is *believed* to be so. The mother may have a similar view to the one Woody Allen portrays: she promotes a propaganda campaign against the father and all his works (that is, his phallus) in which many fathers, wimps themselves, unfortunately acquiesce. So it is that a man whose father is a limp prick personified, grows up to believe that men are terrible monsters and so to fear his own erection, both literally and symbolically.

It is, however, the alternative route of identification with the destructive phallus that makes up much of what is conventionally taken for masculinity but is in reality a defensive caricature of it. As I have already suggested, this position is rooted in fear of the feminine. Ralph Greenson seems to have been the first to point out that a successful development of a masculine identity involves two steps: boys need to dis-identify with their mothers and re-identify with their fathers (Greenson 1968). Once both these steps have been successfully negotiated, the young man has a secure position in himself from which to relate to the feminine as other. This is not quite the whole story, but I will come back to the rest of it later. Here I want to emphasise that if men have been unable to successfully dis-identify from their mothers their masculine identification remains defensive against the ever-present threat of overwhelming femininity.

These men deny their emotional need for feminine nurture in displays of macho behaviour and grandiose posturing. They have to keep themselves in a state of permanent erection so that they can feel strong and invulnerable (cf. penis gourds). Emotional needs, seen as weak and infantile, are projected onto women, who are called 'baby' and denigrated – but also feared. Such men fear even their own sexuality since it indicates some form of need and dependence and may lure them into women's clutches. As a result, women are seen as dangerous seductresses who must either be avoided or controlled. They are sluts and whores who are 'asking for it' or who have to be covered from head to toe so that men are not tempted by them. In this polarised world, women become mere embodiments of sexuality while men are equally no more than embodiments of violence and aggression.

Alternatively – and often, simultaneously – an idealised image of the feminine is constructed from whom sexuality is barred: she who is pure, innocent and unblemished, the virgin angel Madonna, who would be shocked by the mere mention of the word 'penis'. The way these madonnas must be kept safe from sex shows just how dangerous and destructive sexuality is felt to be, although it is a moot point whether it is ultimately the devouring power of female sexuality or the murderous, weapon-like assaults of the destructive phallus that are felt to be the more dangerous.

Identification with the creative father

If the underlying problem in conventional masculinity is fear of the feminine, it might be thought that identification with the father would provide the solution. Many societies make formal provision for this process of male identification through rituals of initiation. It is significant that amongst economically primitive societies, those in which mothers and babies share the same bed for at least a year to the exclusion of father are far more likely than others to have initiation ceremonies at puberty (Whiting et al. 1966, quoted in Hudson and Jacot 1991). This evidence suggests that there is a direct relation between levels of closeness between mother and son, and the need for direct intervention by the father to disrupt it so that the young boy can take up his role as an adult male. However, it may also suggest that initiation has a defensive quality about it, especially as there is often strict segregation between men and women in such societies, along with beliefs about the dangers posed by women to male potency. Identification with the father can therefore also be a defence against femininity especially if the fathers themselves manifest a defensive masculinity with which the boy is expected to identify.

This seems to have been the problem with the men's movement that has developed in the United States and elsewhere in the wake of Robert Bly's book, *Iron John*. Bly argued that the absence in our culture of any means whereby the father can introduce the son to the world of men is one of the main reasons why men have become uncertain of their masculinity. They have lost touch with the elemental 'Wild Man', a crucial archetypal component of masculine identity (Bly 1990). Bly was reacting to the feminisation of men, in the wake of feminism. In itself, the idea of the Wild Man is positive and attractive. But it has been used, not only by feminised men, but also by traditional men feeling battered by the growing power and influence of women, as a way of retreating into the old grandiose posturing (Tacey 1997). The failure of the men's movement is that it does not face up to male *fear* of the feminine and it cannot therefore allow for a *return* to the feminine.

The apparent paradox here is that it is only when a man is comfortable with his femininity that he can achieve a comfortable sense of mature masculinity. But the opposite is also true. It is only on the basis of a satisfactory relationship to his own masculinity that he can achieve satisfying relationships with women. This sounds like a Catch-22 but it isn't. This is the point in the story beyond Greenson's two-step formula. It concerns the identification not with one parent or the other but with *the internal couple in creative intercourse*. This represents the achievement of the *conjunctio*, the conjunction of opposites that is the hallmark of Jung's concept of individuation.

In the act of creative intercourse, the phallus is not a weapon of destruction but the vehicle of life. (This is true whether the intercourse is heterosexual or homosexual, although the homosexual relation to the *conjunctio* is inevitably more complex – a factor to which I return below.) In positive heterosexual intercourse, male pride in the creative potency of the phallus is matched by female desire for it. And vice versa: male desire is matched by a woman's pride in her female body and its creative contents. Envious dependence is superseded by creative interdependence. As an internal state, this means that a man is able to relate to his own creative contents as positive and valuable. He wants to get back inside a woman, not only for the satisfaction of his own infantile needs but because he feels that he has something good and valuable to give her through his phallic activity, both literally and symbolically. This deep longing is not merely to confirm his narcissistic investment in the phallus but also to offer something of supreme value to a woman in order to repair the wounds inflicted by the phallus in its destructive aspects and to create new life.

Externally, it is of immense value to the boy if he is able to identify with a creative father who is not afraid of his love for his mother and whose phallic potency is valued by both parents. Despite the sense of exclusion, the fact that his father possesses his mother in loving intercourse gives him hope that he too will be able to receive what he needs from a woman through what he is able to give to her, symbolised by the phallus in its creative aspect. This is what I mean by 'celebrating the phallus'. It refers not only to the sexual facts of life but also to the phallus in its symbolic aspect, as a representation of male creativity and generativity. These aspects are expressed through many of the old masculine virtues such as strength, independence, rationality, aggression and competitiveness. All of these have their negative side and if they are tinged with the defensive fear of the feminine, it will be the negative aspects that get expressed. The same is true of men's preoccupation with sex. But when these qualities can be affirmed and cherished in their positive aspect, men are able to feel secure enough in their relation to women to begin to own their own 'feminine' qualities as well, such as their need for emotional support, their capacity for care and concern and perhaps also their capacity to dream and imagine.

I do not believe that the position I have outlined here is exclusive to heterosexuality. There are many complications in the network of identifications and counter-identifications that take place in the formation of gender identity and it seems likely that some of these may result in a homosexual object choice. While this obviously separates sexual desire from the image of the feminine, the essential issues remain the same. In fact, I believe many homosexual men are seeking a more positive relation to the father and his creative phallus through their homosexuality. Furthermore, many homosexual men have a more positive relation to the feminine than many heterosexual men. I hope I have said enough to make it clear that this does not necessarily make them any less masculine, even if they do not conform to conventional, defensive notions of masculinity. At the same time, homosexual culture also includes a variety of defensive versions of masculinity as well as some rather elaborate defences against overwhelming feminine identification – e.g. the deliberate exaggeration of a 'camp' persona. But just as the phallus is a symbolic as well as a literal reality, so the identification with the internal creative intercourse does not necessarily issue in its direct representation as heterosexual genital intercourse either. In the end it is the mystery of the *conjunctio* that is at issue: the capacity to be 'not just one thing', which is ultimately the position of narcissism, but to strive to develop the capacity to relate to the other. For men, whether homosexual or heterosexual, the first other is the mother and through her the other always retains something of her feminine aspect. She is the goal towards which men strive and the phallus is the most potent instrument of their search.

References

Bly, R. (1990) *Iron John.* Shaftesbury: Element, 1991.

Colman, W. (1995) 'Cross-gender identifications in heterosexual couples', *British Journal of Psychotherapy* 11(4): 522–35.

Feldman, B. (1992) 'Jung's infancy and childhood and its influence upon the development of analytical psychology', *Journal of Analytical Psychology* 7(3): 255–74.

Freud, S. (1924) 'The dissolution of the Oedipus complex', *Standard Edition* 19. London: Hogarth Press, pp. 171–9.

Greenson, R. R. (1968) 'Dis-identifying from the mother: its special importance for the boy', *International Journal of Psychoanalysis* 49: 370–4.

Hooke, W. D. and Hooke, S. L. (1993) 'The orthodox Jungian perspective on gender differences in consciousness: a re-examination', *Journal of Analytical Psychology* 38(3): 273–302.

Hudson, L. and Jacot, B. (1991) *The Way Men Think: Intellect, Intimacy and the Erotic Imagination.* New Haven and London: Yale University Press.

Jung, C. G. (1912/1952) 'Symbols of Transformation', *Collected Works* 5. London: Routledge & Kegan Paul.

—— (1963) *Memories, Dreams, Reflections.* Glasgow: Collins and Routledge.

King Lear (1963) *Signet Classic Shakespeare*, ed. R. Fraser. London: New American Library.

Stoller, R. (1985) *Observing the Erotic Imagination.* New Haven and London: Yale University Press.

Tacey, D. (1997) *Re-making Men.* London: Routledge.

Tang, I. (1999) *Pornography: The Secret History of Civilisation.* London: Channel 4 Books.

Whiting, J. W. M., Kluckhorn R. and Anthony, A. (1966) 'The function of male initiation ceremonies at puberty', in E. E. Maccoby, T. M. Newcomb and E. L. Hartley (eds), *Readings in Social Psychology.* London: Methuen.

Chapter 8

The internal couple and the Oedipus complex in the development of sexual identity and sexual perversion

David Morgan

In psychoanalysis a person's first relationships and how they are experienced are seen as the bedrock of future psychic and sexual life. This is a complex interaction between the child and the parental couple, starting with mother. Mother acts as a container for her child's fears, anxieties and desires. Her capacity to bear these powerful impulses relates to her own internal objects and external relationships.

Understanding the complexity of the child's mind and social world began with Freud's theory of the Oedipal complex. In Sophocles' myth, Oedipus encounters the parental couple, unconsciously committing patricide on his father and incest with his mother. He destroys his father, i.e. excludes him, and forms an exclusive link to his mother. The common denominator in all Oedipal configurations involves an attempt to split the parental couple, and a hope that the parental couple will manage this attack without either excluding the child or colluding. It includes the denial of differences of the generation gap, a wish to create a world where differences are eliminated.

Children's experience of their parents as a couple and the type of relationships they have as adults are linked. Freud emphasised the sexual aspect of the Oedipus complex. Its conflicts, under castration threats, were partially resolved by identification with the same-sex parent, the formation of the superego, and the establishment of the incest taboo towards the parent of the opposite sex. Melanie Klein deepened our understanding of what underpins the Oedipus complex. It is not only the threat of castration that makes the child renounce the parents as sexual objects: the active desire to love and tolerate frustration enables the child to allow the parents their creativity and to become creative himself. In Kleinian thinking the couple becomes an internal object, which develops partly from experiences with the real parents and partly through the complex interaction of love and hate, guilt, reparative feelings, towards not one parent or the other but the link between them. That the child is created by a couple is a powerful truth. At the deepest level, realising that one's life began as an act of love and ecstasy between two people is the optimal start in life.

After conception and birth, the child needs to be contained. In psychoanalysis containment means:

> when an infant has an intolerable anxiety he deals with it by projecting it into the mother. The mother's response is to acknowledge the anxiety and do whatever is necessary to relieve the infant's distress. The infant's perception is that he has projected something intolerable into his object, but the object was capable of containing it and dealing with it. He is then able to re-introject not only his original anxiety, but an anxiety modified by having been contained. He also introjects an object capable of containing and dealing with the anxiety. The containment of anxiety in this way is the beginning of mental stability. This stability can be disrupted due to the mother being unable to bear the projected anxiety so that the infant introjects an experience of even greater terror than the one he has projected. It may also be disrupted by excessive destructive omnipotence of the infant's phantasy.
>
> (Segal 1975: 134–5)

This containment includes child and mother, the child and mother's world, including her own mind and needs, father, friends and other helpmates: from the beginning of life there is an interplay that involves at least three people. The child learns that this is manageable or feels excluded and vulnerable, leading to conflict and anxiety.

Within this constellation the child projects into mother an image of its own anxiety. If mother is experienced as an object that cannot manage more than one relationship at a time, the child may feel that only an exclusive relationship is possible. The mother's needs or her involvement with others – other children or partner – can be experienced as intrusive, threatening to exclude the child. This interplay is the beginning of a complex inter-dynamic social relationship. The object is explored intimately to discover in it the capacity to bear conflict, which the child as yet cannot. Recognition of the parental sexual relationship involves relinquishing the idea of sole and permanent possession of mother, leading to a profound sense of loss, which, if not tolerated, may become a sense of persecution. How this is experienced underpins all future mental and emotional life (Britton et al. 1989: 83–7).

To cope with this profound sense of loss the child needs to project his own terror of abandonment into his objects. When his projection is met, the child is enabled to work through the feelings of love, hatred and guilt, which he projected into the couple. Then the link between the mother and the father is seen as positive and creative, rather than destructive and excluding.

The mixture of a person's reality and phantasy concerning the parental relationship affects and underpins the quality of all their future relationships, the nature of their anxieties and defences, and profoundly affects their capacity for creative thinking. In phantasy, the parental couple can be experienced as coming together in lively and pleasurable or destructive ways and these will determine the way a person experiences things coming together in his own mind, his own thoughts, or relationships. The capacity to think and to relate to a parental couple are thus connected. Thinking about the other, in this case the parents, is the prototype of all future mental and sexual life: how I think about you thinking about me affects my own thoughts about myself. Klein suggested that this process of thinking about their parents and how they feel responded to, begins in the earliest moments of life. The infant always relates to an object such as the breast, or other parts such as the mother's mind, but there are always other objects, atmospheres and presences representing the other. The infant's experiences of these interactions form the child's attitude and relationship to this unfolding experience, laying the foundation for the urge and capacity to learn, to know, to relate to reality. Klein later described this as the depressive position – a realisation of the real world outside the self, the difference between internal and external. The Oedipus situation is an exploration of the other beginning with the child's recognition of the parents' relationship in whatever primitive or partial form. This is followed by rivalry with one parent for the other. It is resolved when the child relinquishes his claim on his parents by accepting the reality of their sexual relationship.

Britton et al. (1989) designated three positions within the triangular situation: (1) the child's separate link with each of the parents; (2) the observer of and non-participant in their relationship; (3) being observed by them. Accepting this link, that couples get together to make babies, is difficult: it excludes and exclusion can only be managed by attacking and destroying any representation of the parental couple, or, as in schizophrenia, by attacking all links so that nothing gets together to make anything else.

Anxiety becomes the parent's responsibility, to be resolved in the parent's mind or heart before it is returned to the child. For it to be digestible and helpful, the child has to feel that the parent has been able to ameliorate these powerful feelings in a non-persecutory way. This interaction is the foundation of all future intercourse: if I put part of myself into the other, how it is received involves exploration, tenderness and love, as well as sadism, penetration and hate. The parents' capacity to resolve this dilemma depends on their own Oedipal experiences. If the parent is a member of a mature couple in their own mind, including their own internal couple and relationship to a partner, a child's phantasies need not be denied or acted out. This capacity, or later *in loco parentis*, the analyst's capacity, to think rather than act, communicates that there is help at hand: there is another object in their mind to which they can turn so they are not overwhelmed, unlike the child.

In analysis this conflict often occurs: a patient angrily retorts in a Friday session about the weekend, 'when you leave me, I feel you don't give a damn about me, you are with your family and they are more important to you than me'. To reassure the patient would be a lie: the analyst's family, in reality, is more important to him than the patient, particularly at the weekend. The patient would triumph over the analyst's family, forming an idealised transference with a lonely old analyst who had nobody else but her. Confirming the patient's fears that she is meaningless is equally untrue; our patients mean a lot to us, analysis is an intense attachment. The painful triangular reality can be recognised, hopefully in a helpful way, by saying 'You feel that because I have people in my life other than you, you no longer feature as an important person in my mind at all.' In this way the analyst meets the patient's projections of her rivalry and jealousy by thinking both about her and the others in his life without excluding her. A link is made rather than destroyed. A patient recently responded to a weekend by dreaming of a couple on a train bound for Russia. He was relieved to discover that the train was in fact bound for Middlesex, a county adjoining his – representing the bedroom next door – making a link between himself and the parental couple.

Over many such interactions, an internal model of mental intercourse can be established, representing the parents' good sexual intercourse, tolerating anxiety, dependency and separateness. When I have an anxiety I can turn for help in my mind to a creative intercourse with my wife, analyst, supervisor and psychoanalytical theory. If this is a creative experience, thoughts and ideas can interact in a kind of healthy intercourse. Conversely, a bizarre or predominately destructive couple, or analyst who is vulnerable and alone, might have little capacity to turn to another: this can lead to damaged, perverse or inhibited forms of relating and thinking. This constellation is frequently found in inexperienced clinicians who, from kindness or the need to reassure the patient (themselves), allow an unanalysed positive transference to develop as if to meet the patient's fantasies of their total devotion. This can lead patients to believe that an overly involved therapist has met their projections, or therapists to identify with the projection by thinking they are indispensable to the patient. Alternatively, the analyst may respond in over-rigid ways, encouraging the patient to conform.

A patient group illustrates what happens when the internal couple becomes pathological: patients with various problems show the many permutations or perversions of this early blueprint. In these cases we can discern a continuum from the earliest breakdown in Oedipal relations – such as fearing engulfment by mother in the absence of father, or an attacking mother personifying her child's projections of his own appetites – to later developments where the relationship to mother is fairly resolved but the connection to father is faulty.

- A transsexual man wants to remove his old man (penis) surgically and fulfil his wish to become a woman. He portrays his mother as encouraging him to become a woman, and his father as violent; he wishes to dis-identify with his father and identify with mother by literally getting inside her.
- Further along this continuum is a transvestite man who imagines getting in and out of women's clothes at will. He does not want to stay inside a woman's body forever as it becomes a claustrophobic trap threatening to engulf him. However, he uses it to make his wife feel second class and triumphs over her as his accomplice. In his internal couple mother is frightening and powerful, over-involved with her son, sometimes exciting him, sometimes ignoring him. Meanwhile father is inadequate and uninvolved.

- A homosexual man cruises, exposing himself to AIDS by compulsively engaging in unprotected sex. He has a good relationship with mother, but feels his father was dictatorial. A sexually abusive father-figure, a priest, compounds the picture of frightening men. This provides an unreliable internal couple, leading to negation of women and identifications with sexually sadistic men.

These permutations in sexual orientation clearly resonate with an adult's conception of his parents' interactions.

Analysis with patients is, I feel, a way of exploring the other in an attempt to resolve these conflicts. The analytic mind that encourages lively intercourse must be positively narcissistic, able to meet its own needs, able to relate to others, and, consequently, able to think about the patient. Initially any hint of others in the analyst's life is seen as destructive and excluding, repeating the earliest experience of the breast: the patient often lives in an all or nothing world, feeling that when his object has others, he has no-one. In reality, if the analyst had no one but his patients, they would be left with an impoverished object unable to help anyone, let alone himself. But the mind projected into the analyst is incapable of thinking of the patient, oneself and the other: it is as if the patient has not experienced a mind with room for all three. This is a projective identification of the patient's own conflict and the analyst is only equipped to respond when his needs – such as family, partner, friends, his own analysis – provide him with experiences of being thought about and an internal world involving intercourse and links with others. This world does not preclude others; indeed a good relationship with another, like the mother with the father, creates the resources for caring for another, rather than becoming over-dependent on the child. This latter might seem desirable to the child but generates confusions between the child's needs and the parent's needs.

Various permutations of the internal couple

Case Study One

A young woman with a needle phobia, starting analysis, dreams that mother sends her to a man for a series of painful injections. It appears from her history that her parents married precipitously after the death of her maternal grandmother when mother was 16 years old. Her parents separated upon the patient's 16th birthday. She dealt with losing the couple by taking the absent father's place and becoming her mother's partner. She thereby denied her father's absence, disposing of her need for a strong father by destroying him and projecting her own needs into her mother. She felt that psychoanalysis was a cruel invasive treatment, that I would use my potency to harm her. This young woman feared intercourse because she feared giving up the potent feelings she derived from looking after mother. She feared becoming a victim of an unscrupulous analyst, who would use her to carry his own pain, whilst making himself feel stronger at her expense, thereby re-enacting what had happened when her parents' marriage ended. The analysis involved undoing this without making her feel I was using my position to hurt and rob her.

Case Study Two: A transsexual phantasy

Toni requested a meeting feeling that an assessment might help her confusion over her sexual identity. She told me she was a girl but was confused by wishing to be a boy. When she arrived for her first meeting with me I met a person who could have been either sex. I felt some confusion, in my counter-transference, about whether a boy or girl was peeking out at me from behind this figure. She said she had always been confused about her identity. She had considered a gender reassignment but felt this was too drastic and she knew that it took more to change sex than an operation; in fact it was really rather impossible. She knew it was about something else but didn't know what. She also said that her breasts had not developed and her periods had not started although there were no medical reasons for this.

Her earliest memory was of her father dying when she was two. She told me, proudly, that he was a successful architect and some of his buildings were still standing. Her mother had remarried. Before this Toni felt that she looked after her mother. She did well academically, and won all the races against the boys. She became so good at tennis that she was banned from the all-men's tennis championship because she could have won. She was now a computer expert.

She told me in a rather touching way that, since the age of 4, she had been fascinated by astronomy and begged her mother for a telescope. Since then she had bought three telescopes, each bigger than the one before. Now she had a very large one. She was sure that there was life out there somewhere in the universe and that she would find it someday. She said this with enthusiasm, yet I felt enormously sad and tears came to my eyes. I found myself thinking about my own children whom I hadn't seen all day.

The patient's first communications in psychoanalysis are often the most telling; all are incontrovertible facts *and* communications about the patient's internal world, connecting us with the patient's unconscious. Toni is telling me about her confusion, ostensibly about her sexual identity, and she tells me the story of her life as she sees it. It involves a mother, and a father who dies before she feels they know each other. Her mother is depressed and Toni feels responsible for her, becoming in some ways her partner and caretaker. One understanding of this would be that her loss of her father, and guilt that her rivalry with him for mother killed him, is projected into her mother who is understandably depressed at this time. Toni avoids her own feelings by adopting the position of mother's partner, the lost father, feeling like a male. Her own need for father is expressed by identifying with him, attempting to keep him alive by taking him into her own body. The telescopes are symbols of potency, as is her sad search for life in space, for the lost father. My own counter-transference reactions to the story suggest that she is unconscious of her sadness over the loss of, and her confusion about, the absent father. I interpreted that I felt she longed for her father to fill the empty space his absence created; that she dealt with this feeling by caring for her mother who also missed him. One way of caring for her mother and herself was to become a male that both of them lost, and keep him alive in that way. She looked thoughtful for a moment and said, 'Phew, that's a bit Freudian.' She was right: I was thinking about her problem as an unresolved Oedipal situation. She managed her pain and confusion by freeze-framing a part of her mind and body at a time when the conflict over her own sexual identity occurred.

Case Study Three: An unresolved homosexual anxiety

Mr C. loved his wife very much but he was obsessed by thoughts of golden-haired young men with whom he was driven to perform oral sex. He had these thoughts only when making love to his wife. He found them depressing, felt paranoid about them and wondered if he had an unconscious wish to be gay. Mr C. said he loved his parents. He was the eldest, close to his mother, but longed for a closer relationship with his father. His father, a sporting person, seemed to devote all his energies to his younger son, a 'blonde hairdo' surfer type. Even though Mr C. was more successful than his brother he felt that his father never gave him the recognition he deserved. Exploring this in the transference revealed his craving for recognition from his father and me. He dealt with his rivalry with his brother for father by projecting the unwanted feelings into the woman, giving all his desire at moments of intimacy to the golden boy image that his father had idealised. Exploring this with me helped him feel that I was not seduced by this idealised image that he felt he had to suck up to, and that I could appreciate a real him. Consequently he felt more attentive with his wife and after a while his ambivalence towards her disappeared, as did his homosexual longings. He felt his father did not provide an alternative to his mother's love. Feeling rejected by father, he turned against his wife (and probably his mother), joining his father's latent narcissistic longings expressed through his golden boy son. Discovering that his rivalrous and desirous feelings towards his father's favourite boy underpinned his longings for the gay encounter enabled him to feel sad about his father's apparent immaturity but enabled him to love and appreciate his wife again. He later talked to his father who told him that he had always felt inferior to his own brother, whom his father had loved more than him. He was mortified to learn that he maybe recreated this with his son.

I will end this chapter with a detailed analysis of a patient with a perverse phantasy in which the analysis of the internal couple played a significant role. I will highlight the use of the transference in bringing these conflicts to the fore, and how the analyst's mind recreates the patient's earliest conflicts, leading to some reparation of the couple in the patient's mind and consequently an improvement in his capacity to relate socially and sexually.

Case Study Four: Psychoanalysis of a transvestite phantasy

Mr D. is 30 years old and started analysis five years ago. He came into treatment feeling confused and depressed because his wife refused to continue to participate in his transvestite activity and was threatening to leave. He felt she was unreasonable and was attacking him. In addition, he wanted to be a writer but he only wrote articles for women's magazines, which were always rejected. He lived on a trust fund left to him by his mother's father, in a house that was purchased for him. He paid for his analysis from this fund. He was aware of feeling depressed and lethargic, as if all the energy was in everyone else. I gleaned that Mr D. had felt lonely in his early childhood. He remembered having a rubber sheet that comforted him as a baby and child. I feel that this could be seen as his defensive retreat, to a reliable object which he could control and use to comfort himself. This attachment to materials intensified later into a secret wish to dress up in his mother's clothes. He described a sense of calm that would descend on him at these times.

Mr D. is the eldest of three children. His father was an accountant who abandoned the family when he was implicated for fraud. Mr D., who was three at the time, did not see his father again until, as a result of his analysis, he decided to find and confront him. Mother appears to have become depressed and unavailable when the marriage ended. Mr D. felt it was his responsibility to put away childish things, and set an example to his siblings by caring for his mother. He can remember how responsible he felt on the one hand, and on the other hand, feeling numb and desperately trying to hold onto reality. He found the experience of putting on and taking off his mother's clothes extremely gratifying, relieving him from confusion.

His mother remarried when he was fourteen, to a man he respects but whom he experienced as a disciplinarian. When he changed his name to his step-father's he felt further distanced from his own identity. His step-father encouraged him to study at school and this helped him get to university. However, he soon found the work dense and difficult and barely got his degree. He felt increasingly lethargic and started a postgraduate degree in philosophy. He found Western philosophy impenetrable and retreated into Indian mysticism. He tended to attract younger students, becoming something of a guru in the students' union. He dropped out of this course eventually, suffering from migraines and unable to think.

He married a student from abroad who became very dependent on him. She was sexually abused by her father when she was five. Within this relationship they regressed to an internal world inside his house, living on his trust fund. He drew her into his transvestite activities, dressing up as a woman and masturbating in front of her. He felt this gave him power over her which comforted him. Here we see him projecting his needy infantile self into her whilst he becomes the provider. His wife's subsequent refusal to participate in this arrangement distressed him. His fragile world was collapsing. He described feeling almost catatonic with depression, raising himself from this torpor only to eat or evacuate.

He spent a great deal of time at home trying to write articles for women's magazines: a concrete form perhaps of getting parts of his mind into women. However, they were always rejected. In frustration he berated his wife, often violently, for being stupid and lazy. He was able to do this partly as she was still a student, as stuck as he was. He kept her financially and threatened her with eviction. Since they married their sexual relationship was minimal except for the transvestite activity. She seemed at first willing to play the voyeur to his exhibitionism, presumably re-enacting her own abuse by her father.

Here we can see Mr D. projecting his infantile self into his wife. She has to stay in this position lest she threatens him with awareness of his own needs, whilst he retains the power to look after her or abandon her. Thus, his own experiences are reversed and projected into his wife, who was always frightened that he would leave. As we can see, the damaged or absent maternal object is replaced almost entirely in phantasy by the subject so that whilst he feels in control, other people like his wife are reduced to the role of an accomplice. He reverses earlier experiences of deprivation through putting them physically and psychologically into the body and mind of the other. He aims to evacuate his unwanted parts so forcefully into the other that the communicative aspect of the projections is unlikely to be recognised. His wife's experience of abuse made her an available recipient of his projections.

In the first year of analysis Mr D. was increasingly fearful about his needy self surfacing. He became enormously anxious about becoming addicted to his analysis, which he said was an arrangement that would rob him of his autonomy. He felt that I was intent on seducing him into a relationship with me so that I could use him entirely for my own ends without considering him. He was convinced of the accuracy of his perceptions and oblivious to the irony that they contained a mirror image of how he used his wife. I interpreted these anxieties saying that he feared a rather empty analyst whose own life was so devoid of any real substance that I derived my only comfort by seducing and controlling my patients into providing me with the feelings of power lacking in my impoverished life. He was interested in these observations and curious at my willingness to be explored as such an unattractive figure. He become less anxious and more able to explore what realities these accusations might have.

Analysing the internal couple around the breaks was crucial in managing his acting out. As he became more aware of his dependence on me, his fury with his wife increased. After a Bank Holiday weekend he felt enraged with her saying she was a bloodsucker. It was as if she was a parasite that he felt like killing to protect himself. He comforted himself through dressing up and masturbating. Thus, he simultaneously projected his own emerging dependency into his wife whilst he, in phantasy, became the mother. He then felt ambivalent about returning to his analysis, wanting to stay in bed rather than attend sessions. I showed him how, at these times, I am the abandoning father leaving him alone with his wife/mother into whom he projects his own needs. He can avoid needing me, both by gratifying himself and by evacuating all his neediness into his wife. He fears my return because the analysis will put him in touch with his own needy self and a vengeful me who feels robbed by a 'him' who has taken over my qualities and put his wife in the patient's position. I also connected this ambivalence and fear to his mother's second husband who pushed him out of the nest.

As I encouraged him to think about, rather than enact, these things he became very critical of his analyst. He attempted to take his feelings outside the analysis and dump them into his wife. However, he felt less convinced by what he was doing to her and she seemed more able to resist it. He furiously attacked me, certain of my perverse aims: 'Wasn't Freud a charlatan anyway?' He voraciously devoured negative reports in the papers and quoted Masson at me. He was also at these times fond of calling me 'a complete cunt'. I was eventually able to take up his anxiety that I was unreal. I was a man dressed up in the clothing of psychoanalysis, a discredited theory used as a way to control him. He responded by attacking his wife again. She was infuriating, driving him mad with 'his' incessant demands. He was unaware of this slip. I said that although he located this needy baby-self in his wife, he was also aware that these feelings belonged to him: he feared his need for me would drive me away (like his father), so he put them into his wife where he could control them. I thought he was searching for a mind which could contain and understand his evacuated feelings of abandonment and loss rather than become identified with them, like his mother and wife, or reject him by walking out, like his father.

After the third year there was an important development. His need to project the unwanted aspects of himself into his wife, who was becoming stronger, abated. He became terrified that he was going to slip into a massive depression. He dreamt of falling, of losing his grip, of being lost at sea with a lighthouse in the distance, of losing himself in the underground. These dreams suggest original fears of disintegration, of the overwhelming mother and the distant unavailable father who might have been able to throw light on his predicament and save him. His fears of being engulfed by a void felt palpable and we were confronted by the possibility that he might break down. Mindful of the attacks that he might make on his wife, I feared she could become the recipient of his breaking-down self. He had a powerful wish to impregnate his wife, despite her wishes, thinking this would provide relief from his own feelings. I showed him that he wished to get rid of his childlike feelings in his analysis by putting them physically into his wife, impregnating her with his split-off self, enacting the transvestite's wish to occupy mother. Thus his wish to evacuate this part of himself into the mother/wife was contained in the transference with me, rather than being enacted, leading to a possible conception. (How many children are created for this reason?)

At this time he had a dream confirming his emerging baby-like feelings and his wish to be rid of them. He is living in a flat on the set of *Eldorado*, the soap opera that flopped. He is with his wife. He thinks it is wonderful but a child looks into the window of the flat and he feels terrified that it will get in and take over. The flat is taken over by lots of children and he and his wife are overwhelmed. I said that his dependency with me frightened him because he feared that I might not be able to cope.

A week later he reported a second dream. He is again in a flat in *Eldorado* with his wife but this time he is aware of being frightened. The whole set is on fire. He realises this is just a superficial film set and, as it is about to collapse, the Prince of Wales rescues him. As soon as they are out of danger, the Prince (a reference to my Welshness or baldness, and let's face it, not a great family man) is occupied with two children. I said that although Mr D. felt rescued by me from the dangerous illusion that he lives in with his wife and mother, I quickly abandon him, like father, for people I deem to be more interesting than him. He knows that he needs his father's help to leave the phantasy world where he has been living with his mother but, like his father, I will leave him for other children. Around this time he discovered where his father lived and, amidst great pain and sadness, found he was remarried with two children.

As a result of meeting his father and the gradual strengthening of his wife and me in his mind, his terror of his neediness returned. He dreamt that his wife was a vampire. She bites him and he becomes a vampire too. I feel this vampire is a perverse image of the blood-sucking baby. The source of evil is now in them both. They search a jungle for the source of evil to save themselves. They see a huge stone statue of Orson Welles, the outside shell crumbles and it comes alive. They become aware that this is the source of all evil. In the dream he attacks it and cuts it to pieces. I feel this dream illustrates Mr D.'s dilemma. He needs an object into whom he can project the cannibalistic parts of himself but he fears they will then hunt and kill him. I said to him that when I leave him, he becomes frightened and confused by his relationship with his wife, as he did with his mother when they both felt like needy children. He is aware of how much they need a third person, like the 'Third Man' (hence Orson Welles) to help them. However, rather than a helpful person who can think about this with him, I become full of the cruelty that he fears so much, so he can justifiably destroy me.

At this time he decided to get a job. He now only used the cross-dressing in the breaks. He seemed to be aware that I might be able to think about his needs rather than be overwhelmed or rejecting of him. He had reached the point where he could explore the realities of his projections in his analyst, rather than put them into an object which could not help him understand, like his wife or mother.

During a weekend break, having berated his wife again he also had a dream. He is on a working holiday in the USA, in the desert, and is worried that he is short of money. It becomes rather like a 'Mad Max' movie. His mother appears, as if by magic, with a credit store card for Selfridges. After initial relief he is shocked to find a credit limit of fifty pounds. I said that he deals with the painful reality of losing his father and me by rewriting a mad story of himself and his mother, living in a state of perpetual bliss, which he can use like his cross-dressing, to avoid doing any real work. However, he is aware that this makes a limiting desert of his life. He responded by saying that he had told his wife that he had made a will that no one could benefit from including her. He had been surprised when she cried. I said that rather than understand this problem in himself, he makes out that other people are interested in free-loading on him. His belief that he is taking care of others is a way of avoiding getting on with his own life, recreating his time with mother when she might have depended on him. His wife then has to tolerate having his dependency needs being pushed into her whilst he has none at all.

Now that Mr D. can hear my communications, he is more aware

of his own destructiveness. In a Friday session he presented material that was about painful separation and the role of the internal couple in his internal world. He dreamt that he was going away with me but that I give him a false address. He runs to the station but sees me leaving with my wife and realises he is being left behind. I said that it was painful when, like the false father, I leave him. He feels that if things were different I would take him with me. I felt he was more aware of the importance of his analysis and beginning to be aware of an Oedipal couple. On Monday he reported a terrifying nightmare about death: 'My mother is dying of cancer. I have a child and I am trying to take care of it. My fear is that he is dying too. I take some of my mother's medicine and give it to the child.' I said that during the break he was so furious with me for leaving him that he kills off his analysis. He then discovers that not only is his analysis dying but also the life that he has started here with me. His fears of dying surfaced and his feelings of dependency, on his wife and analyst, intensified.

In a final weekend dream he demonstrates his psychotic anxieties and his dependency on me. He dreams he is sitting on top of a monument that changes suddenly into a collapsing black industrial chimney. Someone passes him a rope and he climbs out. I said that on the weekend he climbs on top of his analysis but becomes frightened of being stuck inside something dead and collapsing about him, the dead body of the triumphed-over mother. He is relieved by the return of his analysis on Monday because it and I are still alive. I believe this dream reflects a change in his view of the internal couple: instead of being left inside the dead body of a mother he is rescued by a father with a penis. Now he is more aware of what he does to his objects, taking over their good qualities and evacuating what is felt to be bad into them. I think he is genuinely relieved and hopeful that someone can save him from this.

The analysis has helped Mr D. to feel that I can bear becoming what he projects into me long enough to explore and contain these elements. He has less need to evacuate into an object that is unable to understand him and is able to project into someone who is better able to understand his communications and return them to him in a digestible form. An important part of this work is the capacity of the analyst to bear the projections long enough for the patient to discover whether the analyst corresponds to them or not. They can then be interpreted to the patient, who can begin to symbolise them (rather than enact them) through other forms of communication

Chapter 9

Genital and phallic homosexuality[1]

Steven Mendoza

Introduction

This chapter tries to show how psychotherapy or counselling is done with homosexuals as it is with any other clients. This is because sexual orientation does not determine or even, to a reliable extent, indicate, any special disturbance requiring particular treatment. Homosexuals present for psychotherapy the same difficulties of quality of life, inappropriate emotions, difficulties in relationships, frustrations of ambition or difficulties of behaviour as any others. They hope for and need ordinary treatment and to be treated as ordinary, which they are. The psychotherapist or counsellor, however, will need to be on good terms with his or her own homosexuality to do this work properly. This is a matter of analysis and self-analysis, including our capacity for honesty and courage in the analysis of the counter-transference. To support that, I suggest something of Meltzer's account of homosexuality which includes the normal gender identi-fications which are essential to the dissolution of the Oedipus complex. Conversely, perversity is also discussed. It is suggested that perversity is independent of object choice, choice of the object of sexual fantasies or choice of the partner in sexual activity.

Psychoanalysis does not have a very good explanation of homo-sexuality. Meltzer, indeed, suggests that we might dispose of it altogether as a diagnostic term because such a wide range of per-sonalities, healthy and otherwise, subtends it. Freud characterised homosexuality as inversion, meaning the choice of a partner of the

---

1 An earlier draft of this chapter was published under the title 'Genitality and geni-tal homosexuality: criteria of selection' by Steven Mendoza, *British Journal of Psychotherapy* 13(3) 1997: 384–94.

same sex instead of one of the opposite sex. By this he distinguished homosexuality from the perversions which he defined as variations of the aim of sexual activity or actual variations of the object rather than the mere inversion of the choice of object. This distinction of homosexuality from perversion lays the ground very early for the treatment of homosexuals as capable of benefiting from a conventional psychotherapy, that is, one which analyses relationships in terms of the balance between hate and love, or perversity and creativity.

I go over Meltzer's thinking about homosexuality in terms of gender identities and fantasies, conscious and unconscious. I shall try to show that if we think about the meaning of the basic principles of psychotherapy we will find that they apply equally whether we are homosexual or not. Indeed the problems, both presented and emergent, are the same: whatever our orientation we have the same difficulties in reconciling ourselves to our need for a love object. We can assess the homosexual for psychotherapy in terms of criteria of personal development and integration, of the capacity to love, of the capacity for depressive position organisation, exactly as we do all other prospective patients. I think we need to think these things through in order to have the courage to work psychotherapeutically in this way. My approach is largely theoretical, seeking to show how we can think about homosexuality by applying carefully a basic knowledge of the Oedipus complex and its dissolution.

The first section, 'Genitality', utilises the idea of genital love and Meltzer's idea of 'good', polymorphous, and 'bad', perverse, sexuality to propose the possibility of loving sexual relationships between those of the same sex. The next section, 'Homosexuality as an Oedipal defence', proposes homosexuality as serving, sometimes, as a defence against incestuous anxieties, protecting loving feelings. The section 'Phallicism and sexuality' considers the basis of sexuality on physiological imperatives manifesting psychically as impulses toward objects. These may be mobilised, using Dr Meltzer's ideas, in a polymorphous or perverse organisation. Where there is disturbance, loving sexuality may be blocked by destructive impulses or it may be blocked by inhibitions arising from fears of destructiveness.

The section on 'Accommodating the Oedipus complex' looks at the therapeutic needs of the loving, infantile parts of the personality and the way that perversity seeks to get rid of these parts. This is because the nature of perversity is basically narcissistic. There is some discussion of the need to safeguard the treatment by a proper analysis of the therapist's own homosexuality to guard against projections into the patient. There is also a review of the significance of gender identifications in the alliance with the parent of the same sex. The purpose of this section is to trace the dissolution of the Oedipus complex from the primary object relation through to the homosexual alliance with the rival parent of the same sex.

Genitality

In the *Three Essays on Sexuality* (1905) Freud uses the term genital stage to approach the concept of maturity. He says that the orientation to the phallus in both sexes is given over to procreation. He really does seem to mean that the penis is seen by both sexes as simply the means to the conception of children. He writes as though the eroticism of the polymorphous stage of development is left behind. Laplanche and Pontalis (1973) point out that this very biological approach is given over in subsequent analytic writing to the ideal of genital love. The idea of a genital love as against a biological drive to conceive seems to restore the idea of the object and a hierarchy of relations to it. Freud's original formulation of a metapsychology[2] of behaviour driven by unconscious impulses is elaborated into a theory of mind consisting in an inner world of objects and object relations.

As soon as we consider the idea of a love that is genital and not merely phallic, we can think about a drive that is psychologically mature, even if its object is one with which union is not procreative. A homosexual, limited to his or her own sex, may be capable of a love of the other in the sense of a whole object which may be called genital. Such an object would be related to in the depressive position, it would be an object perceived objectively. This means a love which is capable of putting itself in the place of the other, capable of agape. Where the phallic organisation sees the object merely as a means to drive satisfaction the genital organisation wishes for the satisfaction of the other as well as the self. This capacity to identify allows a satisfaction conferred by the satisfaction of the other. This is the use of projective identification for a mature purpose.

* * *

2 Metapsychology is Freud's theory of the unconscious causes of conscious psychological process and observable behaviour, that is the body of psychoanalytic theory.

Donald Meltzer (1979), in *Sexual States of Mind*, is trenchant, not to say polemical, in his reservations about classical psychosexuality:

Freud's differentiation of source, aim and object in infantile sexuality seems stark if not moralistic. He elevates heterosexual genitality to a unique position, as if it were the only aspect of infantile sexuality fit to survive into adult life. Abraham's clarification of the distinction between part- and whole-object relations enriched the conception of genital sexuality, but did nothing to alter the quantitative and normative attitude implied. Instead of clearly defining the state of mind involved in the adult love relationship, it tended to exalt an act of genital coitus, rampant on a field of pregenital foreplay, a sort of coat of arms of the sexual aristocracy.

(Meltzer 1979: 65)

He presents psychoanalysis as emphasising the psychic organisation of the genital stage of development to the exclusion of the psyche of the polymorphous stage. He suggests that sexual pleasure and the love and security that should attend it is dismissed by classical psychoanalysis as mere 'pre-genital foreplay'. He contrasts the polymorphous with the perverse thus:

A term like 'homosexual' can now be given a clear metapsychological definition, if desired, to distinguish it from the manifestations of infantile bisexuality, although there is much to be said in favour of throwing it out as a waste-basket term, as I hope to show, in favour of a more definitive elucidation of the terms polymorphous and perverse in psychoanalytic theory. . . . we can establish the terms polymorphous and perverse as having definitive references to good and bad sexuality respectively.

(Meltzer 1979: 66)

Infantile bisexuality suggests here the identification of a little boy as a girl and his phantasy of intercourse, as a girl, with the father. Equally it implies the identification of the little girl as a boy and her phantasy of sex, as a boy, with the mother. An adult engaging in an overtly homosexual relationship as a manifestation of such an infantile bisexuality phantasy would be excluded from the term 'homosexual' by his or her sexual difference from the object in phantasy. A 'clear metapsychological definition' of homosexuality, then, might be that the unconscious phantasy would have to be one in which both partners were of the same sex. It may be helpful to note here that bisexuality is used to denote the capacity to have *identifications* with both sexes and not to denote the predilection to have *sex* with partners of both sexes. The polymorphous, I think, refers to the way eroticism in the polymorphous stage of psychosexual development pervades all the zones of the body. At the genital stage, as sexual feelings become stronger, they concentrate in the genital zone. Meltzer seems to me to remind us that polymorphous, or polyzonal, eroticism persists in mature, genital sex itself and not as mere 'pregenital foreplay'. Meltzer's distinction of adult polymorphous sexuality from childhood, of regressed or fixated kinds, is elaborate (1979: 67).

Where he writes of the polymorphous and the perverse I understand his distinction to be in terms not of the zone or object of eroticism but of the *aim* of the drive. I think he means that the polymorphous is driven by the desire to give and receive pleasure and the perverse by the need to control the object out of fear or to punish it sadistically in a retaliatory and envious way. I certainly think that Chasseguet-Smirgel (1985), in *Creativity and Perversion,* construes the perverse as a pathological compromise seeking to retain an element of omnipotence at the cost of love. Omnipotence, having all the power, cannot have love because in love we depend upon the consent of the loved one to love us back, as Blake (1977) says:

> What is it men in women do require?
> The lineaments of Gratified Desire.
> What is it women do in men require?
> The lineaments of Gratified Desire.
> (Blake 1977: 158)

Meltzer seeks to rehabilitate infantile polymorphous impulses into adult sexuality which, I think, may be regressive not in a pathological way but 'in the service of the ego' (Kris: 1935): regression as play, creativity, pleasure and love. Meltzer goes so far in his defence of infantile elements in adult life as to write:

> A well-integrated bisexuality makes possible a doubly intense intimacy with the sexual partner both by introjection as well as a modulated projective identification which finds its place in the partner's mentality without controlling or dominating.
> (Meltzer 1979: 67)

I understand this to mean that the capacity to identify with the sexual partner's experience of intercourse may depend upon a healthy surviving bisexuality and that this can double the intensity of intimacy: 'If I can tolerate the homosexual fantasy of being the object of my own love making in my identification with my partner then our sexual life may be the richer.' I think this has implications for psychotherapists and counsellors as well as lovers. To work with homosexual patients we need a tolerance of our own bisexuality with its uncomfortable intimation of homosexuality *and* our homosexuality itself, metapsychologically different as we saw Meltzer propose earlier.

I think we need to remember when reading this passage the primary nature of projective identification as a means of communication between infant and mother. We also need to bear in mind the persistence and indispensability of this mode of communication in adult life. Such communication is possible when destructive intrusive modes of projective identification do not predominate over the mode of projective identification as a means of communication. Indeed, it is precisely when intrusive modes predominate in this way that the perverse supersedes the polymorphous. This is a primary diagnostic distinction and our understanding of it can give us confidence in diagnosis, in understanding the working of our client's mind. We need to be able to distinguish healthy projective identification from perverse, that is to say, destructively motivated, projective identification.

Meltzer (1979: 67) says, as quoted above, that a doubling of intensity of intimacy with a sexual partner may be made possible by a well-integrated bisexuality allowing introjection as well as modulated projective identification. A psychotherapist may also need to be able to use introjection as well as projective identification, and for him too this may depend upon a well-integrated bisexuality: we need to be able to take inside us a sense of the partner's pleasure. Thus a man may need to be able to allow into himself the desire to be penetrated by a penis and a woman may need to be able to allow the equivalent, desire of a female body and the drive to penetrate it. Where bisexuality is not well integrated there may be difficulties in accepting homosexuality in our patients and our colleagues as well as ourselves: all require of us that we be able to tolerate our own capacity for homosexual fantasy. From Meltzer we can infer the reassurance that this may not be an indication of our suppressed inversion but a healthy aspect of polymorphy. But more than that I think it requires us to be in touch with the wish to engage sexually the parent of the same sex. Such a fantasy is homosexual *per se* but may be heterosexual in the phantasy of a man offering himself to the father as a girl or of a girl offering herself to the mother as a man. Here, perhaps, we have some sense of the intricate distinctions between bisexual and homosexual and the confusion between inner and outer realities. As we have seen before, overtly homosexual behaviour may be heterosexual in phantasy or vice versa.

Meltzer writes encouragingly on the inadequacies of the term homosexual as a category. After a classification of all the disturbances of sexual life in seven categories subdivided under the rubrics of perverse and polymorphous, he comments:

> It is important to note that any one of the above may give rise to a sexual pattern deserving the descriptive term 'homosexual', which illustrates its virtual uselessness in psychoanalytic nosology.
> (Meltzer 1979: 67)

For me this implies that it is not what we do in sex which matters, nor whom we do it with, but why we do it. If we do it to revenge ourselves upon or to control, or to humiliate, or to appropriate the object we are perverse. If we do it out of love and the innocent pursuit of pleasure, our own and the other's, then we merely draw upon our healthy polymorphy, 'good sexuality'.

Homosexuality may, if it allows a genital relationship, be a more healthy compromise than a heterosexual relationship fixated by hate in the paranoid schizoid position. A state of mind having to protect the good by splitting it from the bad bars us from the integration of the depressive position. We are then limited to a phallic organisation fraught with sadistic potential. I am suggesting here that Melanie Klein's formulation of the paranoid schizoid position might be seen to include development of the psychic implications of Freud's phallic stage of psychosexual development. Her depressive position would then include the development of the idea of genital love, itself a development of Freud's genital stage. To take the example of a heterosexual congress pervaded by a homosexual fantasy: such a fantasy may be implemented as a perverse attack upon the mother and her intercourse with the father. Alternatively it may be a polymorphous expression of love of the parent of the same sex to support a loving conjunction with an external object.

Homosexuality as an Oedipal defence

Generally the Oedipus complex is organised around the wish to possess the parent of the opposite sex. We are familiar with the idea of homosexuality originating in the terror of the castrating reprisal of the parent of the same sex. Women, but men too, might flee from the failure of love with mother into premature sexualisation by investing, cathecting, sexual energy in father.

In men this object choice is denigrated as a pathology which shows that homosexuality is a bad thing, primitive, fixated in the narcissistic, and therefore having no potential for three person organisation. Again I offer for speculation another logical possibility: that an inversion of object choice may serve as a defence allowing a relation to an object in the depressive position precisely because it *is* homosexual, that is to say, not the same sex as the object of Oedipal contention, the parent of the opposite sex. We may consider the possibility that homosexuality might sometimes function as a defence allowing love to survive the vicissitudes of the Oedipus complex, albeit at the expense of a complete working through. This is not to suggest that homosexuality is never perverse in its organisation but that it may sometimes be a choice of object intended to protect the parental couple rather than to denigrate it; denigration being, of course, the disposition characterising the perverse.

This may be easier to consider if we remember the prevalence of pathological functions in heterosexual relations: promiscuity, regression, orgastic impotence, miscegenation, sadism, schizoid terror of annexation, all offer themselves as paradigms of failure in marriage and other heterosexual relationships. Where heterosexual relations may be subject to these vicissitudes homosexual relations may find a compromise which evades them.

Such vicissitudes may obtain where the nursing relationship between infant and mother has been too difficult. Or they may obtain where the Oedipal relation of the child to the parental couple has been too difficult. Then the heterosexual relation may never escape phallic fixation. Conversely a homosexual relationship may allow a genital love of the object which is paradoxical in its apposition of genitals of the same sex.

A clinical example suggests just such a possibility. Gilbert's mother threatened to leave the children and go off with one of her many lovers if they were not compliant. She threatened to have the dog put down if the children did not exercise it. Gilbert was the youngest child and only son in a family of four children. He held himself to be homosexual by constitution having never experienced any other orientation. He hates his mother as a whore, deceiving his father by her peccadilloes and by her concealment of the paternity of the eldest child. He fears her as selfish, vindictive and murderous. There were persecuting older female transference figures, 'wicked witches', as he called them when they were drawn to his attention. He longs for the love of a father who was away from home at work for most of the time. He was referred to psychotherapy for panic attacks and an overwhelming fear of death. He appeared to have an infantile personality disorder but one which allowed trusting regression in the transference to a male therapist and in his relationship with an older male lover he had lived with for some years. In the course of therapy he became increasingly capable of gratitude to his lover. The relationship developed a strong attachment in the face of ambivalence in the depressive position such as would have been a good outcome in the analysis of someone in a heterosexual relationship.

For him a heterosexual orientation might be overwhelmed by paranoid forces where in his homosexual orientation he can find a transference from an internal good object realised through the thought of an absent father. His orientation can be seen as allowing development in and through a sexual relationship *because* the object choice is inverted.

Phallicism and sexuality

I have looked at what genitality can mean generally and with respect to homosexuals. I have contrasted genitality with 'the phallic'. I have tended to imply that the phallic is bad, in the course of contrasting sexuality that is perversely phallic with polymorphously organised genitality. I want now to consider the nature of the phallic itself. Essentially it is primitive and developmentally neutral in its disposition toward the object. It may serve destructive perverse purposes or it may be employed polymorphously in the search for pleasure.

I think of the phallic as the theatre of drive. Freud described an id consisting in drives aiming to derive a desired reduction in tension by action on particular objects. This drive theory has been modified by the psychic complications of object relations. But object relations themselves still depend upon the cathexis of libido to objects. Object relations emphasise the psyche and the inner world where Freud sought a metapsychology of unconsciously determined behaviour. While the phallic knows only drive satisfaction, the genital, in its love of the other, is committed to object relations. But the genital, with its love of the object, must take its drive to possess the object from the phallic. We desire not only the object but the object's desire of us. We 'require' 'The lineaments of Gratified Desire' (Blake), the visible traces of passion written in the face and in the bodily disposition of the lover. And there is the element of sexy sex which is purely phallic and bent passionately on possession and climax.

The aspect of love which is excitement must therefore be *the containment of phallic drive within genital regard.* We wish to take and be taken with the absolute commitment of the phallic to its goal. The sexual problem of marriage is so often that the phallic excitement is lost from the relationship and excitement finds only the unknown other.

I would trace back the concept of the phallic to the biological substrate upon which the unconscious is got: that is, everything we learn from ethology about the basis of sexual behaviour. We have seen (*The Economist* 30.8.97) how animal sexual responses are oriented to sexual triggers. These are usually bodily configurations of form, pattern and colour, sometimes calls or scents. Studies of other animals show that we *may* respond to very simple stimuli, signals of gender and readiness to conceive. In these cases the general stimulus pattern may be sufficient without even the suggestion of the whole body of the sexual object. In the same way babies were shown in my elementary psychology course to respond to the simplest display suggesting the maternal smile. Here is the simplest possible configuration of a part object. Desmond Morris has suggested the equivalence of breasts and buttocks, lips and vulva.

It is helpful to think of the genital as the object related and the phallic as the drive directed. Psychology is organised hierarchically: ethology underlies the operant conditioning of B. F. Skinner. The operant underlies the dynamic metapsychology of Freud. Within the dynamic, the drive directed underlies the object related, the development of Abraham and Klein and its special elaboration by the 'British School'.

Fairbairn writes of pleasure as being 'essentially to provide a signpost to the object' (1952: 33). He says this in the course of arguing for the redundancy of the concept of id. He is drawing attention to the exigencies of dependency. But I do not think it disposes of Freud's formulation that finding an object includes an impulse toward the object seeking positive or negative gratification. Object relations mediate impulses for Klein where for Fairbairn they supplant them. Impulses, I believe, may be physiological or emotional but they are always of the nature of id. That is the usefulness of the term id. I have to think of adult eroticism as needing neurological climax: without passion object relations seem too disembodied. I do not see that any polymorphy of organisation would reverse secondary sexual development. As we try to find what is true and necessary in Fairbairn we can see how easily the need to recognise psychic reality can lead us to deny biology. I do not think survival is the only motive human beings have. We still have strong drives to gratification and defences against insecurity in object relations which depend upon addictive adherence to drive satisfactions.

The *rapprochement* of object related and drive directed metapsychologies gives us the flexibility that patients need us to have. This requires us to be aware of our defensive tendency to project the promiscuous and phallic, which we want to disown as bad, into the homosexual. To do so leaves us only the *goody goody Sunday best sexuality* of genital love supposed in false morality (Bion: 1962b) and isolated by incestuous fears from its proper phallic expression. Woody Allen asks about this: 'Is sex dirty?' and answers: 'Only when it is done properly!' *Suck* magazine put it even more succinctly when it said: 'Sex is wet stuff.' Some practitioners need to disinhibit the phallic. Some need to bring the phallic into the service of the genital. Both these splits are engendered by anxieties and limit tolerance of abnormality (McDougall 1978).

Accommodating the Oedipus complex

In this section I give a précis of genital love in terms of relating to an object in the depressive position. I suggest that this is a psychology pertaining to the number three and not pertaining to gender. Previously I have tried to show genital love to be the capacity to maintain the depressive position in relation to a sexual partner. I have tried to show how homosexuality inverts the choice of object but sometimes, nonetheless, remains capable of achieving genital organisation. The homosexual in treatment may have such integration of personality. But in any therapy we usually need to analyse two impediments to the introjection and actualisation of a good internal couple: the fearful and the angry impediments.

In development the negotiation of rivalry with the father, so that a parental couple can be internalised, is usually called the dissolution of the Oedipus complex. Here I have used the term accommodating instead to emphasise the ongoing compromise which I think is a truer view of the fate of the Oedipus complex than the view that it is dissolved. The internal parental couple is the model of linking. Linking is also in the nature of the Container containing the Contained, which Bion (1962c) calls container/contained. He says that container and contained are commensal, each existing by virtue of the other, the container containing only because it has a content, the contained existing only because the container makes its existence possible. We develop the capacity to think and to love to the extent that we can bear to internalise a parental pair. If we cannot bear that then every thought, every feeling is testimony to the unbearable pairing that leaves us out.[3]

If we can internalise a parental pair then we can be parents ourselves. When homosexuals can parent, even though they cannot procreate, this has diagnostic implications for their organisation and function. The capacity to parent is as significant a criterion of successful development as any. It is through the organisation, or development, of such a faculty that patients can be seen and helped to mature in psychotherapy. I consider parenting here merely as a criterion of maturity and not at all with respect to the division of labour between gender roles nor matters of gender identity. Procreation is a biological function but parenting is a psychological one. To parent requires us to cognise the child in the depressive position, that is, as a whole object. We must also put the priority of the interests of the child over our own interests. Usually this is called love.

I think the clearest understanding of our infantile needs comes from Guntrip's (1968) theory of the fear of ego weakness and the alliance of the self with Fairbairn's antilibidinal ego. Guntrip holds that as adults we fear the weakness of the ego which prevails in infancy: we fear that in discovering it we will find our adult faculties of autonomy, discretion and effective action to be no more than infantile omnipotent phantasy. We fight against our inclination to a proper regression, substituting for love the identification with Fairbairn's (1952) 'internal fifth column', the saboteur, the anti-

---

3 See David Morgan, Chapter 8, for a detailed account of the significance of the 'parental couple' in the mind [editor].

libidinal ego. This mind has recourse to a sadistic organisation to reinforce a feeling of power. In it we contemplate ego weakness with fear and with a painful shame of dependency. This can make it difficult to respond properly to the need and vulnerability of our children. Thus in parenting we meet with the test of our mature acceptance of our own regression: the accommodation we have made to the Oedipus complex.

Psychotherapists have to be wary of their own or their counter-transferential resistance to contacting such feelings of weakness. This kind of resistance can hide behind a clinical emphasis on the omnipotent and sadistic aspects of narcissism. Here it is important to have a proper appreciation of Klein's (1946) references to the fears of annihilation of the early ego and to its actual weakness. This also has a bearing on Rosenfeld's (1971) treatment of fear of the libidinal infantile component. He uses the term 'dependent libidinal self' where Fairbairn refers to the 'libidinal ego'. Rosenfeld says: 'it is essential to help the patient to find and rescue the dependent part of the self from its trapped position inside the psychotic narcissistic structure' (1987: 112). This, then, is the purpose of analysing envy. If we are not clearly on the side of the loving parts of the self *the analysis may be as persecuting as the processes it seeks to disclose.*

Balint (1968), in *The Basic Fault*, is striking in his attribution of the mother–infant relationship as mediated by the infant's primary love rather than the mother's love. We have been reminded of this more recently in Meltzer and Harris Williams's (1988) account of the infant's apprehension of the beauty of the breast. All of the ills that psychotherapy seeks to remedy seem to me to derive from the principle that it is the weak parts of us that love and that the strong parts of us have to dare to serve them.

Our attitude to the weak, needy, loving parts of the self seems to me to be paramount in the practice of psychotherapy. In work with homosexuals we depend upon the analysis of our own homosexual component to protect them, and us, from the projection of perversity into them. By perversity, in this context, I mean the destructive denial of infantile dependency expressed as sex which is anti-love, what Bion might designate −L instead of L. Instead of projecting perversity we need to find a loving attitude to our own needy parts and to those of the patient. Psychotherapists who identify as homosexual will have the same need to assimilate their heterosexuality as the need to assimilate homosexuality which practitioners who identify as heterosexual will have.

If we can identify with the infantile part of the self then we can relate to a good object: the narcissistic organisation is circumvented and we can serve as a parent, a lover or a therapist. The child in us is a vulnerable and therefore hidden true self. It is libidinal but it retains the original sense of vulnerability. The creative cannot defend itself because it must be open to the whole potential of reality. The true self is therefore vulnerable. The lives of many artists attest to this. Creativity requires the analyst to be receptive in the field of transference/countertransference to projective identifications. This incurs the same experience of vulnerability. Self-analysis may not have an absolute power to protect but it does affirm the power of 'K', where the self can bear the truth. By 'K' I mean here the real knowledge that Bion (1962a) says comes from learning from experience, the sometimes painful or chastening process that can happen when our love of truth prevails over our inclination to deny our doubts about ourselves.

This is an account of defences against vulnerability. But fear of infantile weakness is not the only cause of pathology. There is also Klein's attribution of envious omnipotence as the motive of attacks upon the vulnerable, loving, knowing, functions of the self and the object. The loving intercourse of the internal parental couple may be apprehended as the link. Perversion may be organised in a narcissistic mode as an omnipotent attack upon that link. But however necessary it may be to recognise perversity when it arises it is also important to recognise simple, that is to say, unperverse defences against infantile fears of annihilation. The proper analysis of these fears is essential where health and development are in question. The survival of the capacity for primary love is paramount.

Where Balint assumes primary love as a matter of course, Meltzer and Harris Williams (1988) indicate, in *The Apprehension of Beauty*, what an overwhelming experience it can be. They say it may precipitate splitting as a defence against being annihilated by depressive anxieties rather than as a defence against envy.

Insofar as our relation to the true self is benign we can be loving and protective toward the infant in the sexual partner and in our own children. Insofar as we are paranoid, whether through fear or envy, in our relations to the true self, we will not be able to love or even tolerate the infant in our partners and children, or patients. As we feel strong in our ability to protect the child in ourselves we will be able to protect and value the child in the spouse, the child of the marriage and the child in the patient.

* * *

In his paper on *Female Sexuality* (1931) Freud makes clear the main psychic difference between men and women: the little girl's change of object from the mother to the father. In sexual development two very different confusions may be said to arise: for men there is the incestuous confusion of cathecting a sexual object of the same gender as mother. For women there is the confusion of a split in cathexis in the inception of sexuality. Thus we may see in women an intense ambivalence toward the mother and in men an idealisation of women in a cult of the 'mystery of woman'.

I took Freud (1931) to suggest that the little girl shifts her cathexis from mother to father. Now it seems that it was a mistake to infer that a de-cathexis of mother would be intended. Obviously we all retain an intense cathexis of the mother irrespective of our gender. He must have intended a change of object by the little girl in the process of sexual orientation from the object of primary cathexis to the object of secondary cathexis.

Thus, sexualisation draws with it, and needs to do so, a component of primary maternal cathexis, hence the significance of infantile transference in adult relationships. My point is not so much that for women there is a split in cathexis which is confused, and necessarily so, but that the cathexis is confused for men too. Those who work with young children are used to the idea that the little boy also sexualises his cathexis of father, seeking to offer himself to him as a woman. It is so important to overcome envy to make an alliance with the father for the dissolution, or at least accommodation, of the Oedipus complex. A healthy polymorphous bisexuality, or homosexuality, is essential to development. It is precisely through a man's bisexuality that he can, in a feminine identification, cathect the father and thereby dissolve, or at least accommodate the Oedipus complex. From Meltzer (1979) we can infer that it is crucial for the successful analysis of homosexuality to distinguish this essential polymorphy from the perverse assumption of a homosexual orientation for destructive purposes.

I think this point needs emphasis: there is a homosexual component in each of us. It is essential to normal development. It is a cause of shame and anxiety in the course of normal development. It is essential that the practitioner be able to distinguish this kind of homosexuality from a homosexuality assumed for the purpose of perverse attacks on the internal parents and for the purpose of denying dependency.

In his chapter on the architectonics of pornography in *Sexual*

States of Mind, Meltzer (1979) writes of the precarious, 'knife edge', distinction between polymorphy and perversion, between pornography and art. Just as some art challenges our capacity to know the difference between art and pornography so homosexuality challenges our capacity to tell love from hate, perverse from polymorphous. Homosexuals may find the knife edge quality of homosexuality just as ambiguous as others do. They may feel shame about their homosexuality. Even if they do not suffer from the internal persecution which attends the homosexual symptoms of heterosexuals they too are bound to introject the persecutory projections which society directs at them from this widespread shame. I speculate that the shame of homosexuality is probably close in nature to the shame of masturbation. This comment may help in thinking about the psychotherapy of homosexuals but this is not the occasion to discuss it further.

In psychotherapy homosexuals may need to overcome their shame of homosexuality sufficiently to distinguish their perverse from their loving impulses. It is common in psychotherapy for destructive, envious, sadistic organisations to make us feel that no good can survive in us. The capacity to introject and maintain in the inner world a good object can have a particular application for homosexuals: that is fostering the belief in the capacity to love a partner of the same sex in a faithful enduring relationship, capable of carrying the dependency of the partners and the children of the partnership, be they concrete or metaphorical children. The psychotherapist, no matter to which sex he or she may be oriented, may need to have made a good analysis of both homosexual and persecutory components if this work is to be successful.

References

Balint, M. (1968) *The Basic Fault.* London: Tavistock.
Bion, W. R. (1962a) *Learning from Experience.* London: Karnac.
—— (1962b) *Learning from Experience.* London: Karnac, ch. 28, para. 9.
—— (1962c) *Learning from Experience.* London: Karnac, ch. 27, para. 10.
Blake, William (1977) Notebook poems and fragments, in *The Complete Poems.* London: Penguin.
Chasseguet-Smirgel, J. (1985) *Creativity and Perversion.* London: Free Association Books.
The Economist (1997) 'Birds do it, bees do it . . .' unattributed article reporting on an international conference of animal ethologists in Vienna. Issue of 30 August.

Fairbairn, W. R. D. (1952) *Psychoanalytic Studies of the Personality.* London: Routledge.

Freud, S. (1905) 'Three essays on the theory of sexuality', *Standard Edition* 7. London: Hogarth Press.

—— (1931) 'Female sexuality', *Standard Edition* 21. London: Hogarth Press.

Guntrip, H. (1968) *Schizoid Phenomena, Object Relations and the Self,* The International Psycho-analytical Library, 77. London: Hogarth Press.

Klein, M. (1946) 'Notes on some schizoid mechanisms', in *Envy and Gratitude and Other Works 1946–1963,* Delta Books. New York: Dell, 1977.

Kris, E. (1935) 'The psychology of caricature', *Psychoanalytic Explorations In Art.* New York: International Universities Press.

Laplanche, J. and Pontalis, J.-B. (1973) *The Language of Psychoanalysis.* London: Hogarth Press.

McDougall, J. (1978) *Plea for a Measure of Abnormality.* New York: International Universities Press.

Meltzer, D. (1979) *Sexual States of Mind.* Strath Tay: Clunie Press.

Meltzer D. and Harris Williams, M. (1988) *The Apprehension of Beauty.* Strath Tay: Clunie Press.

Rosenfeld, H. (1971) 'A clinical approach to the theory of life and death instincts: an investigation into the aggressive aspects of narcissism', in *Melanie Klein Today, vol. 1: Mainly Theory.* London: Routledge, 1988, pp. 248, 250.

—— (1987) 'Destructive narcissism and the death instinct', in *Impasse and Interpretation.* London: Routledge, 1990.

Chapter 10

The power of sex

Celia Harding

Sex and power are a potent combination indeed. We are bombarded by sexy images on advertisements implying that we will become irresistible if we choose this product. We are drawn into heated political debates about changing sexual norms – for example, lowering the age of homosexual consent or the content of children's sex education – as if civilisation itself is at stake. The media captivate our imaginations with sexual scandals in the corridors of power: even the mighty can be undone by sexual temptations. These social phenomena are reflected in people's personal sex lives. In the consulting room one frequently hears about sex in the context of power relations between intimates. Many patients' sexual problems are linked to their anxieties about being captivated by their partner's (ph/fantasised or projected) power, losing themselves in the process. These anxieties make sex problematic, at best, and terrifying at worst, rather than a profound and pleasurable experience that comes naturally.

In this chapter I explore what makes us so susceptible to the power of sexuality. I locate the roots of the connection between sex and power in infancy. I speculate that this connection reflects something (universal?) about human nature, originating in the intricate connections between body and mind (Freud 1915: 121f). The first experiences of physical and emotional intimacy are with mother. Her intimate involvement in every detail of her infant's bodily and emotional functioning registers in the infant's body and mind, powerfully influencing the infant's impressions about itself. In particular, children develop a sense of their (positive and/or negative) agency and personal empowerment through their impressions of their parents' responses to their bodily and emotional impulses. These early impressions are templates for experiences of sexuality in adulthood (Wrye and Welles 1994; Mann 1997).

The roots of sexuality in infancy and childhood

Pre-oedipal sexuality

Freud (1905) suggested that adult sexuality develops from infantile sexuality. He scandalised his audiences by suggesting that infants are born with sexual impulses that play a central role in organising their physical, emotional and cognitive development. This has been confirmed by child observation though of course we are referring to a proto-sexuality in children that is not at all the same as adult sexuality (Horne, Chapter 5).

The infant's first pleasures are oral: feeding, drooling and sucking and, with the cutting of teeth, biting and chewing too. Internal mental representations of the self and the world (originally the mother's breast and nipple and/or the bottle) take shape from the sensations coming from the mouth. Pleasurable sensations from caresses of the skin's surface, and from movement of the body and musculature, augment the infants' experience of themselves. When they reach the age of about two, caretakers begin to concentrate on their child's toilet training. The child's pleasures of holding on and letting go acquire new dimensions as they learn to master their sphincters. In the process they learn more about pleasing and displeasing their caretakers with their achievements and failures. Meanwhile, children become aware of increased pleasurable sensations from their genitals. Observers of children maintain that the more manifest preoccupation of boys with the penis is matched by the little girl's awareness of her outer and inner genitals (Kaplan 1991). Children increasingly form mental representations of their physical and emotional experiences and of their caretakers' responses to them.

According to Freud, the sexual drives aim for satisfactions in active and in passive forms. Young children's oral, anal and genital strivings are first directed towards mother in both active and passive forms. Satisfactions from 'being done to' during the relative helplessness of infancy and childhood become interchangeable with satisfactions from 'doing to' as children practise active versions of what has hitherto been 'done to' them on their toys and significant others (Solnit 1989: 338). In this way relationships develop, with each partner doing and being done to. Here is a root of agency and empowerment in the psyche, of approaching other people and the world and initiating relationships with them. As Laplanche and Pontalis put it 'if each type of sexual activity is viewed – as the evolution of psychoanalytic theory encourages us to do – in its relation with the type of object striven after, then the notion of instinctual aim will tend to give way to that of "object-relationship"' (Laplanche and Pontalis 1973: 23).

Mother plays a significant part in her child's infantile sexual development. Freud suggested that:

> [mother] not only nourishes [the infant] but also looks after it and thus arouses in it a number of other physical sensations, pleasurable and unpleasurable. By her care of the child's body she becomes the first seducer. In these two relations lies the root of a mother's importance, unique, without parallel, established for a whole lifetime as the prototype of all later love relations – for both sexes.
>
> (Freud 1940: 188)

Mother stimulates her infant's mouth, skin and anal and genital areas in the course of feeding, holding, playing, affection, and nappy changes. The intense intimacy implicit in these ministrations and interactions carries unconscious erotic meanings for mothers; and these meanings are, equally unconsciously, conveyed to the infant (Laplanche 1976). Infants are sensitively attuned to their mother's responsiveness to their impulses and feelings. The earliest experiences of reciprocated instinctual impulses are found in this relationship.

The infant's relationship with mother (and often father) is conducted through a physical intimacy unparalleled until the sexual relationship between adults. Wrye and Welles (1994) suggest that mother and baby interactions are organised around mother's management and exchange of her baby's bodily fluids. This intimate and intense bodily contact and involvement with each other mobilises, in them both, the whole range of erotic feelings, 'tender, sensual, and romantic to anal erotic, sadistic and masochistic' (1994: 35). Growing children register positive and/or negative feelings about intimacy based on mother's initiatives and responses to them during physical and emotional interactions. These impressions may be resurrected in adulthood when primal body fluids again become 'sensual conductors' of sexual intimacy: 'adult genital sexual contact through seminal and vaginal fluids recreates these earliest erotic connections between mother and infant' (Wrye and Welles 1994: 143).

Infant observation supports the hypothesis that physical intimacy between mother and infant anticipates the quality and shape of sexual intimacy between adults:

> The overt behaviours by which one recognises adult lovers in the phase of falling in love consist mainly of gazing into each other's eyes without talking; maintaining very close proximity, faces inches away and parts of the body always touching; alteration in vocal patterns; movements in synchrony; performing special gestures such as kissing, hugging, touching, and holding the other's face and hands. We see the same set of behaviours performed in infancy with the mother or primary caregiver.
>
> (Stern 1993: 180)

Oedipal contributions

As they move into Freud's phallic stage of development, children attend to their erotic impulses emanating from the genitals. They express these impulses in active and passive modes towards both parents in line with the bisexual nature of human psychosexuality (Freud 1905, 1924b). The phallic stage is intertwined with the Oedipus complex and part of this developmental process involves establishing a gendered position in relation to both parents (Freud 1923: 31–33). When active wishes are associated with masculinity and passive wishes with femininity new dimensions are added to active and passive modes of relating to objects of desire. Maguire (1995) gives a detailed account of the complexity of active and passive, masculine and feminine identifications, and their associations with power and weakness, in both male and female sexuality (see also Maguire, Chapter 6; Colman, Chapter 7).

The aspect of the Oedipus complex directly relevant to my theme is the 'primal scene', which Freud explored in his case-study of the Wolf Man (1918). This is the 'scene of sexual intercourse between the parents which the child observes, or infers on the basis of certain indications and phantasies. It is generally interpreted by the child as an act of violence on the part of the father' (Laplanche and Pontalis 1973: 335). McDougall defines the 'primal scene' more broadly: 'the child's total store of unconscious knowledge and personal mythology concerning human sexual relations, particularly that of his parents' (McDougall 1972: 372).

According to Freud (1908) children make sense of what they see and hear in terms of the mental representations they have formed from their infantile polymorphous sexuality. Sexual curiosity is aroused when children become aware of babies and start to wonder where they come from (Kaplan 1991: 50f). Even when parents give truthful explanations, children do not have first-hand knowledge of mature genitals with which to understand the 'facts of life'. They make sense of the information they are given on the basis of their own experience and reasoning.

Three-year-old boy: Mummy why have you got a big tummy?
Mother: Daddy's given me a baby.
Little boy: Daddy, did you give mummy a baby?
Father: Yes, I did.
Little boy: Daddy, I think mummy swallowed it.

Freud thought children did not connect parental sexual intercourse with babies. Nevertheless, children become aware of their parents' sexual activities as they make sense of what they see and hear when the parents are together. When children witness the primal scene their excited polymorphous sexual impulses are aroused. They understand what they see and hear in familiar terms such as the pleasures of eating and biting, and the pleasures of 'mastery' or control, developed in the context of anal and urethral retention and expulsion. Freud suggested that children commonly perceive their parents' sexual intercourse as an act of violence by father towards a resisting mother. He calls this the 'sadistic theory of coitus' which 'has in part divined the nature of the sexual act and the "sex battle" that precedes it' (1908: 220–1).

The primal scene inducts children into painful realities: the differences between the generations and the sexes (McDougall 1972; Kaplan 1991). Children's genital immaturity precludes them from giving or receiving adult sexual satisfactions with their parents. Besides, the parents already have a relationship from which the child is excluded. This is a painful, sometimes unbearable, reality to face: 'it is the parents' mutual desires that are dominant while the child, as an outsider, must endure his exclusion passively and helplessly' (Kaplan 1991: 62). Witnessing the primal scene sexually excites children. They manage their sexual frustrations and the trauma of recognising the differences between themselves and their parents, by incorporating these experiences into phantasies that will underlie sexual excitement in adulthood. In phantasy children can adopt an active or passive role as desired. Here are the roots of erotic ph/fantasies organised around a witness to a couple's sexual intercourse, aroused and frustrated by their exclusion from it. Here too is a source of erotic ph/fantasies organised around one partner dominating the other: one partner arousing the other against their will; one partner controlling the ebb and flow of the partner's sexual arousal; one partner resisting the other, the most extreme version being rape. Work with adults in psychotherapy suggests that making sense of the way their parents relate to one another is very important to children and unconsciously influences their sexual phantasies in adulthood.

In her novel, *The Chimney Sweeper's Boy*, Barbara Vine describes a sexual relationship which can be understood as based in an erotic, unconscious phantasy of the parental couple. Following her father's death, Sarah finds herself drawn inexorably into a compulsive sexual relationship with Adam. They meet only by arrangement of, and in the company of, a group of mutual friends. In public Sarah and Adam treat each other with overt contempt and hatred. Their verbal abuse comes to stand for 'foreplay' when, without any pre-arrangement, they leave their friends and meet for sex. Their communication is confined to what they want to do sexually to one another. Sarah is bewildered by her compulsive attraction to Adam and her sexual arousal as she anticipates each meeting. The reader however has privileged knowledge, understanding that Sarah is caught up in an unconscious phantasy parodying her parents' relationship. Her father refused to sleep with mother after their children were born and treated her cruelly, oscillating between verbal abuse and indifference. Unconsciously Sarah had eroticised the painful relationship that she saw but could not understand. The spell between Adam and Sarah was irreversibly broken when he insulted her father publicly as part of their ritualistic, sexually charged, abusive treatment of each other in public. Unwittingly Adam exposed the unconscious connection between Sarah's sexual excitement and her incestuous desires for her father. Her intense sexual excitement aroused by Adam's verbal abuse and cold detachment depended on keeping this erotically exciting phantasy of father unconscious, apart from her idealised, 'sexually innocent' conscious feelings for him. Once the connection was made her thraldom to Adam evaporated.

Early experiences of power and vulnerability, control and helplessness are integrated into the body–mind self. In their relationship with mother, children discover how their instinctual impulses and feelings are received, and how they may, or may not, satisfy their instinctual wishes. When parents are comfortable with their physical and emotional life, they will be predisposed to accept their child's developing instinctual life. They will feel at ease with, and responsive to, their children's active and passive approaches towards them, helping them to discover what they want, need, think and feel. In these favourable circumstances, children are given the opportunity to develop a secure sense of their identity. Child-responsive environments enable children to develop sophisticated and flexible repertoires of ways of relating to others and the world. Conversely, when parents are uncomfortable with themselves, they will feel uneasy with, or anxious about, their child's overtures towards them and the world. They may feel compelled to control and restrain their child's desires and self-expressions. Children are likely to feel inhibited about exploring and discovering themselves and their world, and their sense of self will be denuded, contrived on the basis of what they perceive as allowable (by the self and parents). When parents interfere excessively with their children's needs and wishes children find it difficult to form a secure sense of who they are. In an unresponsive environment, the child's active and passive approaches to the world and others are channelled into restricted forms of expression based on doing or being done to, bullying or bullied, complying or defying. The child's approaches to the world, whether active or passive, become increasingly dogmatic and inflexible in reaction to feeling helpless in the face of 'powerful' authority. Relationships come to be experienced only in terms of who will dominate and who will submit.

Ms B was an only child born to middle-aged parents. Looking back she realised that she was expected to fit into her parents' adult world and was discouraged from 'being her age': 'children should be seen and not heard'. She came to therapy because she could not decide what she wanted. She found herself copying other people's choices and finding they didn't suit her. She quickly realised that she didn't know who she was. She felt criticised in all her relationships and full of resentment that no one ever took her seriously or made a place for her. Conversely she would turn the tables and be scathingly critical of other people and reject them. She was uncomfortable with her feminine sexuality and tried to engage men with her considerable intellect but she felt driven to seduce them (usually authority figures) into a sexual liaison. Afterwards she felt abused and demeaned.

Welldon (1992) writes about extreme cases where mothers abuse their 'domestic power' over their babies. She shows that mothers have considerable power over their babies especially in the pre-oedipal stages. Faced with her baby's demands and her own deferred needs, mother may not have the internal resources to contain these demands and her feelings about them. In order to survive she may resort to perverting her power as a mother by requiring her child to serve her needs.

> I suggest that motherhood is sometimes chosen for unconscious perverse reasons. The woman would know that in achieving motherhood she is automatically achieving the role of master, in complete control of another being who has to submit himself or herself not only emotionally, but also biologically to the mother's demands, however inappropriate they may be. Indeed, as is generally accepted, some women who feel inadequate and insecure find a child becomes the only available source of emotional nourishment.
>
> (Welldon 1992: 81)

Adult sexuality bears the imprint of the way parents exercised their 'domestic power' in raising their children and the way those children experienced that power over them.

The adult's experience of sexuality

Intra-subjective dimensions of adult sexuality

Adult sexual fulfilment involves an ecstatic 'letting go', a powerful experience of surpassing the boundaries of the self with another person. Through this we can recapture something of the earliest infantile experiences of feeling at one with mother. Under favourable circumstances we can temporarily allow our feelings to overwhelm and submerge our sense of self, trusting that this is a transitory experience: the conscious self will come back together again and not be extinguished forever. However, people lacking a secure sense of their own identity will fear that they will cease to exist if they surrender themselves in ecstasy.

Adult sexual intimacy draws on infantile experiences of intimacy with mother before we had words and concepts to organise our experience and before we had a sense of having a separate identity from mother. This quality of pre-verbal immediacy and directness contributes to feeling defenceless in the throes of sexual arousal (Stern 1993: 180). The physical and emotional intimacy between lovers resonates beyond the usual sphere of conscious control, at pre-verbal levels of the psyche, in what McDougall calls the '*body's* memory' (1995: 157).

When the body responds at a reflex level, the conscious mind has limited influence over physical reactions. Regina Pally (1998), exploring what she calls a 'biological unconscious', uses fear as her example, but what she writes could apply equally to sex: both fear and sex involve brain and body changes over which the conscious mind has very limited control. These feelings 'may be stronger than our ability to inhibit them volitionally' (1998: 353). Many basic fear-reactions originate in infancy and once established are not amenable to modification through subsequent experience and rational thought. It seems to me that the same is likely to apply to psycho-somatic reactions associated with intimacy and sexuality. When strong positive or negative responses to physical intimacy are registered in the body-self, people have a limited capacity to control their responses.

Our sexual excitement is aroused most forcefully by phantasies derived from remnants of infantile sexuality. Freud (1940) described how the earliest experiences of sexual arousal – in sexual abuse, sexual explorations and experimentation with other children, inadvertent arousal in the course of child care, and the sights or sounds of adult sexual activity – mould sexual excitations into particular configurations and sexual phantasies. When these become too disturbing to the child's developing consciousness, they are relegated to the unconscious. Sometimes these experiences are overwhelming and cannot be processed psychically and the child may enact their traumatic experience in disturbed behaviours.

With sexual maturity, people become aware of what arouses their sexual desires. They may find themselves excited by things they regard as shameful and morally reprehensible: their 'treacherous body' is excited by, and longs for, things they find unacceptable. In these circumstances the emergence of the erotically exciting and wished for, forbidden and feared, feelings and fantasies are likely to be greeted with tremendous resistance: mental resistance to arousal struggles with mounting bodily desire.

Inter-subjective experiences of power and sex

When people are sexually aroused their usual inhibitions evaporate and they are drawn into an increasingly compelling momentum of desire towards climax and fulfilment. This insistent and highly focused quality of sexual desire can feel irresistible: the body seems to acquire a mind of its own. Because the sexual drive is so powerful, sex and power are understandably regarded as a dangerous combination. This danger is compounded when someone finds it difficult to tolerate the powerful nature of their sexual arousal and their partner's capacity to intensify their sexual excitement. They manage their anxiety by projecting the power of sexuality onto someone else whom they now see as controlling their sexual arousal and desire whilst they experience themselves as helpless.

This process of projection begins in infancy: the meanings infants give to their physical and emotional states reflect their confusion about what comes from inside and what comes from outside. We imagine, for example, that infants with colic attribute their pain to an outside source inflicting it on them. Even after young children learn to distinguish between inside and outside, the muddle between the two persists especially when trying to identify the source of something disturbing. When mothers interfere in their infants' experience of themselves, their capacity to distinguish between what is coming from inside and what is coming from outside is further impaired. Adults whose mothers interfered in their experience of themselves are likely to associate physical intimacy with someone doing something to them, arousing their desires against their will. In sexual relationships, they may experience their partner's power to arouse and intensify their sexual arousal and desire as the power to control and exploit them physically and emotionally. Their sense of helplessness in the throes of arousal is intensified by the pre-verbal nature of their wishes and fears and by the shame, disgust and guilt they may feel about their sexual desires. In psychotherapy we tend to find that the more patients experience their feelings as intolerable, the more they are inclined to attribute the cause of these feelings to someone outside themselves, beyond their control. This process of projection is reinforced when there is (or was in the past) an external reality to this perception.

Ms A suddenly announced that she wanted to reduce the frequency of her sessions. As we were exploring this wish she reported a dream in which her female therapist proposed marriage: she declined saying she was not 'like that'. Ms A was the youngest daughter of a single mother whom she experienced as wanting to keep her 'tied to her apron strings'. Feeling so controlled by mother enraged her but she also depended on mother for her survival. She resolved this dilemma by sexualising her aggressive feelings towards her mother. In the transference her fears and wishes about being taken over by mother, body and soul, were intensified by an erotic phantasy of being mother's sexual partner. She wanted to put a distance between herself and her therapist by decreasing her sessions as a way to manage these frightening unconscious wishes and fears that were threatening to surface.

An object relations perspective explains how the intra-subjective experience of powerful sexual desire easily slips into an inter-subjective experience where that sexual power is seen as imposed by someone else rather than originating from within.

Sexual partners have the power to arouse, and influence, the ebb and flow of each other's powerful sexual desires. Power phantasies – who holds it, how it is gained, how it is wielded, how it is negotiated – arise, in a very intense form, within the sexual relationship. Sexual fulfilment comes from surrendering to the physical sexual impetus excited by erotic phantasies. The imperative nature of sexual desire exposes people to experiences of being overpowered and overwhelmed. A person's capacity to trust in and surrender to physical intimacy derives from their experiences of depending on other people earlier in their lives. When a person's needs have been regularly met by people they have depended on – whether parents, caretakers, doctors, teachers – they are inclined to trust people in positions of power and authority. Conversely, when a person's needs have been exploited by the figures they depended on to meet their needs, they are inclined to suspect the motives of people perceived as powerful. They come to believe that if they allow themselves to be vulnerable and rely on someone for help they will be exploited, irrespective of whether the other person's actual intentions towards them are benign or malign.

In her novel *Without Consent*, Frances Fyfield (1996) illustrates an extreme example of someone who abuses his powerful position by exploiting vulnerable women. A doctor consulted for gynaecological advice selects women with sexual inhibitions and, arranging to see them privately, he rapes them without penetrating them with his genital (thereby safeguarding himself from a legal conviction of rape). The doctor seduces women with such skill that they succumb to the sexual desire and pleasure he arouses. 'He made the body lose control and take convulsive pleasure in itself, whatever the mind did' (Fyfield 1996: 207). The women are left humiliated and ashamed but feeling unable to prosecute because they had been sexually carried away even though they had not consented to sex.

This fictional example illustrates the multiple-layered nature of phantasy. First, it shows how strong pre-oedipal erotic components may drive sexual phantasy. In the story, the women are seduced into total surrender, a phantasy of merging with an other based in the early infant–mother relationship. Glasser (1979: 291) notes that people terrified of losing themselves in orgasm may instigate the merging they fear, by arousing it in an other. The doctor seduced the women, arousing and controlling their desires. His pleasure derived from the phantasy of making them want him against their will. Albeit in different ways, phantasies containing longings for, and fears of, infantile merger can be discerned behind the actions and experiences of the doctor and the women he raped.

Second, this story may be read as portraying sexual phantasies originating from the primal scene. In the doctor's behaviour we can glimpse a child subjected to the primal scene before he had the understanding to process what he had witnessed. He deals with his painful ignorance and genital immaturity, which precludes him from understanding adult sexuality, by phantasising that actually he has the secret of sexual fulfilment (McDougall 1972). In his phantasy it is he, not father, who can arouse mother's sexual desire so powerfully that, despite her shame and disgust, she begs him for more. In this phantasy the spurned son takes revenge: on his father by replacing him, and on his unfaithful mother (Freud 1910: 171) by arousing her desires to such a pitch that she is desperate for the sexual fulfilment only he can provide. He defends himself from his castration anxiety by not penetrating the women (representing mother) with his genital thereby deluding himself that he was no more committing incest than rape. We might further speculate that some of the women's erotic excitement and horror arose from phantasies of rape which may have played a part in their own primal scene theories and shaped their erotic phantasies (see Horne, Chapter 5).

Third, this story can be read as showing pre-oedipal phantasies overlaid with elements from primal scene phantasies. We can speculate that as a child, the doctor had an abusive relationship with his mother who controlled him out of existence (Welldon 1992). Feeling enraged and helpless in the face of mother's demands to meet her needs, he sexualised his aggressive feelings to protect both himself and his mother from his rage. He grew up looking, unconsciously, for opportunities to turn the tables in relationships exploiting the other to meet his own needs at their expense. The doctor discovers a way to control women at their most vulnerable through the 'sadistic theory of coitus' (Freud 1908): he prided himself on knowing precisely what women desire and how to arouse and control that desire. In phantasy he controlled 'mother' as she once controlled him (Royston, Chapter 2).

Fyfield illustrates an extreme version of sexual power where a range of sexual phantasies resulting in inhibitions and perverse practices obscures the line between consent and force, power and helplessness. The power of the sexual experience, and the need to surrender to it in sexual fulfilment, are sources of sexual excitement and resistance. Power, control and the attendant dangers are erotically charged. How this essential quality of human sexual experience is managed and negotiated illuminates a fundamental dynamic underlying human sexualities.

Those with a precarious identity are likely to fear the overwhelming nature of sexual experiences: the loss of physical and emotional control in sexual fulfilment threatens their identity. People may even be too frightened to become aware of their sexuality. One woman, unable to look at her body for long periods of her life, could not countenance the idea of touching herself sexually even after seven years of therapy. She took flight from situations that threatened to arouse forbidden and dangerous sexual excitement. Other people find their anxieties about losing their individual identity surface strongly when they marry: they experience the marital relationship as abdicating their separate identities fearing that they will be absorbed into each other if they get too close. Balfour et al. (1986) give a clear example:

> Mrs F. believed that she would drive her husband away if she revealed her true feelings and wishes, so she constantly tried to fit in with what he wanted. As she started to lose her sense of her self as separate from her husband, she refused to continue

their sexual relations, accusing him of always demanding sex on his terms. She felt that he had already taken away her independent mind and he would be taking her body too when they had intercourse. Subsequently she starved herself, enacting through her body her feeling that she had disappeared as a separate person by nearly fading away physically.

Those people fortunate enough to be relatively comfortable with their sexual desires can tolerate knowing that their desires originate from within, and can enjoy their sexual partner's capacity to heighten their arousal. However, even people who relish their sexual intimacy need to feel a secure and independent identity in other areas of their lives. The film *The Full Monty* portrays one character who became impotent after losing his job.

Partners in sexual intimacy are also made vulnerable by the closeness of love to hate. Kernberg (1995) explores the interrelation of loving and aggressive feelings in sexual relationships. The two currents of feeling continually vie for supremacy. An active sexual relationship requires a certain amount of aggression 'in the service of love': aggressive feelings are contained by love. Sexual intimates trust that their loving impulses will contain their hostility, so that the power they yield to, and exert over, one another emanates from predominantly loving motives. Partners may safely surrender control to one another to enhance their desires for, and pleasures in, each other when their union is loving. If hostile motives are dominant, each partner might abuse that control at the other's expense.

In health, the erotically exciting qualities of power, and its attendant dangers, are contained in sexual phantasies permeated with loving motives. Concern and respect for, and the desire to pleasure the sexual partner, set limits to the power which partners mutually and reciprocally give to one another. The active 'doing to' is not a destructive sadistic act and the passive 'being done to' is not a destructive masochistic act. Erotic excitement is enhanced through stimulation of all erotogenic areas of the body, flexibly and reciprocally, fulfilling the bisexual character of human sexuality. Kernberg in his inimitable and inclusive style summarises the search for pleasure in sex:

> [erotic desire is] a search for pleasure, always oriented to another person, an object to be penetrated or invaded or to be penetrated or invaded by. It is a longing for closeness, fusion and intermingling that implies both forcefully crossing a barrier and

becoming one with the chosen object. Conscious or unconscious sexual fantasies refer to invasion, penetration, or appropriation and include the relations between body protrusions and openings – penis, nipple, tongue, finger, feces on the penetrating or invasive site, and vagina, mouth, anus on the receptive or encompassing site. The erotic gratification promised by the rhythmic stimulation of these body parts decreases or vanishes when the sexual act does not serve the broader unconscious function of fusion with an object. 'Container' and 'contained' are not to be confused with masculine and feminine, active and passive; erotic desire includes fantasies of actively incorporating and passively being penetrated, together with actively penetrating and passively being incorporated. I have suggested that psychological bisexuality in the specific sexual interaction is universal for men and women.

(Kernberg 1995: 23)

When aggressive motives, rather than love and respect, drive the erotic and exciting qualities of power and danger, people exploit sexual desire to exert control and power over one another. This is the realm of sexual perversion where erotic excitement is motivated by hostility, hatred, and often revenge (Stoller 1985). Meltzer (1973) understands perversion less in terms of the content of the sexual activity and more in terms of the destructive motives behind it: sexuality driven by hostility is perverse because the sexual partners have turned making love into making hate. In particular, he argues that an unconscious phantasy of attacking the parents' sexual intercourse underlies perverse sex. The erotic qualities of power and control, resistance and submission become threatening when aggression is in the ascendant: the sexual encounter must be controlled to avoid destroying or being destroyed in the sexual encounter.

Sadism and masochism personify sexuality that has been requisitioned in the service of aggressive and destructive impulses rather than love (Freud, 1920; 1924a; 1930). In sado-masochism, the active and passive pleasures derived from the power of sexuality are perverted. The sexualised aggression that drives the sado-masochistic relationship frequently originates from early experiences with a mother (or parent figure) who used the child to gratify her own needs (Welldon 1992). Partners in a sado-masochistic relationship experience each other in phantasy as the mother who denied their needs leaving them with a legacy of hatred and destructiveness from their frustrated needs and a flimsy sense of self. The power of a sexual relationship feels threatening to people with a fragile identity. They long to merge and lose themselves in another person but they fear being absorbed and lost forever. They aggressively attack the other person because their survival feels threatened by their desires to merge with them. But if they destroy the other they will be left alone and isolated, which equally threatens their fragile identity. Glasser (1979) suggests that one solution to this 'core complex' dilemma is to sexualise aggression, controlling and keeping the other at a safe distance – not too close and not too far away – by relating sadistically to the other. Sadism and masochism epitomise an extreme variation of power exercised in a relationship where aggression is sexualised for the survival of both partners and the relationship. Making hate is disguised as making love.

Sexual encounters may be controlled by both parties through enacting a shared fantasy with agreed parameters. When a person's identity is very precarious, sexual fantasy has to be enacted and choreographed in a ritualised performance to provide 'reassurance' that loss of control remains securely under the direction of the self. 'If I control my own sexual excitement and loss of control, then I can reach orgasm *and* keep my identity intact.' By *contriving* a loss of control and surrender in fantasy people create an outlet for intolerable feelings through sexual practices, whilst circumventing the danger of losing their identity. Fears and hostile wishes may be mastered (temporarily) by expressing them in ritualised performances in which the traumatic situation is reversed and turned into sexual excitement.

Minette Walters (1995) illustrates a sexual relationship in which power and control are regulated through a sado-masochistic scenario in her novel *The Scold's Bridle*. Duncan is only able to achieve sexual arousal and satisfaction through a sado-masochistic ritual under his direction. His long-standing partner in this performance is Mathilda, a woman who was sexually and emotionally abused as a child. The 'scold's bridle' was inflicted on her as a cruel instrument of chastisement. As so often happens in real life, Mathilda converted her helplessness as a victim into the sadistic power of the perpetrator of abuse. She was therefore type-cast for the role Duncan required in his sexual scenario. By requesting Mathilda to place him in the scold's bridle and castigate him, Duncan used Mathilda as his means to obtain sexual arousal and relief. He arranged to be placed into a submissive, humiliated position, whilst Mathilda 'forced' him to lose control. Because he had choreographed the performance he felt reassured that he was actually in charge of his own excitement. The crisis came when Mathilda attempted to exert her power over Duncan beyond the parameters of their agreed sexual ritual and his actual helplessness in their relationship became apparent to him: he took desperate measures to protect himself by turning the tables on her. Here is an example of the power of sex driven by aggression not love.

Acknowledgements

I wish to thank my analyst and my patients for their insights into these matters. I am indebted to Josephine Klein for her guidance as this chapter progressed. Thanks are also due to Susan Budd, Michael Lamprell, Dorothy Lloyd-Owen and David Mann for their comments and suggestions. I am grateful to Frances Fyfield for her permission to use her characters to illustrate these ideas and to Yale University Press for their permission to quote O. Kernberg.

References

Balfour, F., Clulow, C. and Dearnley, B. (1986) 'Shared phantasy and therapeutic structure in brief marital therapy', *British Journal of Psychotherapy* 3(2): 133–43.
Freud, S. (1905) 'Three essays on the theory of sexuality', *Standard Edition* 7. London: Hogarth Press.
—— (1908) 'On the sexual theories of children', *Standard Edition* 9. London: Hogarth Press.
—— (1910) 'A special type of choice of object made by men', *Standard Edition* 11. London: Hogarth Press.
—— (1915) 'Instincts and their vicissitudes', *Standard Edition* 14. London: Hogarth Press.
—— (1918) 'From the history of an infantile neurosis', *Standard Edition* 18. London: Hogarth Press.
—— (1920) 'Beyond the pleasure principle', *Standard Edition* 18. London: Hogarth Press.
—— (1923) 'The ego and the id', *Standard Edition* 19, London: Hogarth Press.
—— (1924a) 'The economic problem of masochism', *Standard Edition* 19. London: Hogarth Press.
—— (1924b) 'The dissolution of the Oedipus complex', *Standard Edition* 19. London: Hogarth Press.

—— (1930) 'Civilisation and its discontents', *Standard Edition* 21. London: Hogarth Press.

—— (1940) 'An outline of psychoanalysis', *Standard Edition* 23, London: Hogarth Press.

Fyfield, F. (1996) *Without Consent*. London: Corgi Books, 1997.

Glasser, M. (1979) 'Some aspects of the role of aggression in the perversions', in I. Rosen (ed.), *Sexual Deviation*, 2nd edn. Oxford: Oxford University Press.

Kaplan, L. J. (1991) *Female Perversions*. London: Penguin, 1993.

Kernberg, O. F. (1995) *Love Relations: Normality and Pathology*. Newhaven and London: Yale University Press.

Laplanche, J. (1976) *Life and Death in Psychoanalysis*. ET. Baltimore and London: Johns Hopkins University Press, 1976.

Laplanche, J. and Pontalis, J.-B. (1973) *The Language of Psychoanalysis*. ET. London: Hogarth Press, 1973.

Maguire, M. (1995) *Men, Women, Passion, Power: Gender Issues in Psychotherapy*. London: Routledge.

Mann, D. (1997) *Psychotherapy: An Erotic Relationship. Transference and Countertransference Passions*. London: Routledge.

McDougall, J. (1972) 'Primal scene and sexual perversion', *International Journal of Psycho-Analysis* 53: 371–84.

—— (1995) *The Many Faces of Eros*. London: Free Association Press.

Meltzer, D. (1973) *Sexual States of Mind*. Perthshire: Clunie.

Pally, R. (1998) 'Emotional processing: the mind–body connection', *International Journal of Psycho-Analysis* 79: 349–62.

Solnit, A. J. (1989) 'Psychoanalytic perspectives in children one to three years of age', in S. I. Greenspan and G. H. Pollock (eds), *The Course of Life*, vol. 2: *Early Childhood*. Madison, CT: International Universities Press.

Stern, D. (1993) 'Acting versus remembering in transference love and infantile love', in E. S. Person, A. Hagelin and P. Fonagy (eds), *On Freud's 'Observations of Transference-Love'*. New Haven and London: Yale University Press.

Stoller, R. J. (1985) *Observing the Erotic Imagination*. New Haven and London: Yale University Press.

Walters, M. (1995) *The Scold's Bridle*, London: Pan Books.

Welldon, E. V. (1992) *Mother, Madonna, Whore: The Idealisation and Denigration of Motherhood*. New York and London: Guilford Press.

Wrye, H. K. and Welles, J. K. (1994) *The Narration of Desire: Erotic Transferences and Countertransferences*. Hillsdale, NJ and London: Analytic Press.

Index

40th Congress of the International Association (1997) 10
abandonment, fear of 105, 148, 149, 150, 151
Abelove, H. 21
Abraham, Karl 21–2, 162
Active Imagination 73
activity and passivity 104, 107, 171–2, 173, 176, 183
Adler, A. 71
adolescence: fantasies at 92, 99, 101; masturbation 99; and sexual development 22, 90, 99–101
adult sexuality: influence of pre-oedipal sexuality 172–3, 181; influence of the primal scene 174–5, 181–2; inter-subjective experiences of power and 179–86; intra-subjective dimensions of power and 177–9; in object relations theory 40, 41–2, 55, 63–4
agency, roots of 170, 171–2
aggression: in children 3–4, 39–41, 90, 107; in drive theory 1, 8–9; and fear of intimacy 7; female 107; and love 183; male 122; in object relations theory 3–4, 39–42; role in sexual development 90; sexualisation of 184, 185–6, *see also* destructiveness
Ahlberg, A. 97
Ahlberg, J. 97
alienation 45–6
ambivalence 92, 94, 161, 167

anal expulsion/retention 43, 44
anal phase 22, 43, 44, 91, 171
anal-sadistic phase 40
analyst-analysand relationship: erotic transference in 11–12; homosexual clients 153, 155, 158–9, 165, 168; and the internal couple 140–1, 142–52; as paradigm of mother-infant relationship 5, 9–10, 11–12, 58, 62–3; patients as babies 63–4; sexual transgression 11–12, 58, 69, 71–84; as state of being in love 78, 80; understanding sexual experience in the opposite sex 57–8, *see also* psychoanalysis; psychotherapy
Anglo-Saxon attitudes to sexuality 52–7, 52n, 61, 65
animal sexual behaviour 21, 60, 162
Anna Freud Centre, London 93
annihilation, fears of 105, 129–30, 166
anti-love 165
anti-Semitism 70–1
antilibidinal ego 164–5
anxiety: during puberty 100; parental containment 138, 140
authority, children's reaction to inappropriate 176
autoeroticism 88–9, 98, *see also* masturbation

babies, childhood theorising on 86, 91, 94, 174